Spiritual Rebellion: Mindfulness with *attitude*
© Ondy Willson 2023
First Edition, First Printing

This edition first published by Wellseeing Books in 2023
Wellseeing Books @ ondywillson.com publications
Edited by Kerry Laundon @ LinkdIn and Rachael Chilver
Illustrations by Megan Hindley @meg_hindley
Layout and design: Mie Hansson @miehansson

Twitter: @OndyWillson
Instagram: @ondywillson
Facebook: @WellseeingOndy
YouTube: Ondy Willson

For more information about Ondy's courses and training schedule, visit:
www.wellseeingconsultancy.co.uk
www.ondywillson.com

For Ondy's guided meditations, visit:
SoundCloud via her website, www.ondywillson.com
The Insight Timer app, available at the Google Play Store and the Apple App Store – search for 'Ondy Willson'
YouTube – for talks and guided meditations, search for 'Ondy Willson'

ISBN 978-1-3999-6223-0

ABOUT THE AUTHOR

Ondy Willson is an international teacher and facilitator of mindfulness and Buddhism, a writer and storyteller. She specialises in secular courses that draw from ancient wisdom and contemporary psychologies. Ondy worked as a Drama and English teacher in Northumberland before moving into a Buddhist Centre in the Lake District, where she lived and studied for thirteen years. She then settled into rural Cumbrian life with her family completing her teaching career as Head of Belief, Philosophy and Ethics in a large secondary school. Throughout her career, Ondy has woven together storytelling, writing and teaching Meditation and Buddhist Psychology to bring her central message of mental and emotional health and wellbeing to others. In 2003, she founded the Wellseeing Consultancy to offer training in mindfulness, ethics, and emotional intelligence to individuals, groups and the corporate and public sectors. She has trained people from diverse lifestyles such as lawyers, social workers, prison officers, teachers and school-children. Having created such successful courses, she promised her students that she would one day write the book to accompany the practices. This is that book.

ONDY WILLSON

SPIRITUAL REBELLION

MINDFULNESS WITH **ATTITUDE**

Contents

Chapter 3. Being Human 75

My story – my conditioning

Incessant thoughts and emotions

The wise inner self

The whole package

My story – my choices

Life as education

Chapter 4. It's All in the Mind 97

How to know our minds

Working with the subconscious mind

My story – life as a secondary school teacher

Part Two – Walking the Talk

Chapter 5. Understanding Thoughts and Emotions 125

The stories we tell ourselves

The mind/body connection

My story – so much pride

The role of others

The world of emotions

Chapter 6. Managing Thoughts and Emotions 147

Dealing with destructive emotions

The feel-good factor: The constructive antidotes

How to be emotionally intelligent

My story – my fabulous career

Chapter 7. Reasons to Be Good 175

Goodness feels good because goodness is home

Goodness brings inner peace and genuine happiness

Inner goodness leads to outer peace

Trust yourself to be good

My story – my role as a teacher of Buddhism

Chapter 8. How to Be Good

Practising mindfulness without moralising

My story – compassion in action

Understanding what we mean by love

Doing good work

Having good motivation

Ethical mindfulness

Chapter 9. Wellseeing through Mindful Eyes

The art of wellseeing – changing our attitudes

My story – ego-games

The spiritual view

Chapter 10. How to Be Wellseeing

Social intelligence

Learning optimism

Games we play

Toxic behaviour

Seeing with wisdom

My story – believing what you want to believe

Interdependence

Chapter 11. The Spiritual Warrior

Paradise found

My story – Shiva at the Ganges

The web of Tantra

My story – the natural high of Tantra

Mindfulness in the world

Chapter 12. Spiritual Warrior Training

The importance of community

My story – bodhisattva ideals

Personalising your practice

Supportive Buddhist concepts

Does religion help?

The place of Buddhist psychology

This book is dedicated to my mum, Gay Willson,
and to my loyal Russian and Ukrainian students.

o o o

It is certainly true that without others we are nothing.

Preface

o o o

I have two motives for writing this book and one is quite straightforward, so I'll start there. I have a strong link with students of Buddhism and mindfulness in Russia, and have spent a few weeks at a time with them each year enjoying almost goddess-like treatment. My Russian students are incredibly respectful of their teachers generally, so together with an intelligent young monk translator, we would hit the stage like the hottest comedy duo in Moscow, and have them smiling in anticipation before we even start. Due to their enthusiasm for how I teach, they asked me to write a book – one that would accompany them in their practice, for when they themselves teach, or as something they could show their parents. Of course, things change and now I am not sure when or if I will visit them again. Our meetings are currently online and include those Ukrainian students who are still able to join us.

Now, Russia has a complex history and is not renowned for its openness and acceptance of free speech. I am convinced they have recordings of me saying something droll about their government, and just like some of those audacious girls in Pussy Riot,[1] I will be dragged off to enter some prison nightmare. Now, I have been to Siberia, and it is beautiful and the people are charming, but we do have that grim institution in mind that I don't want to personally test. Even going up and down in tower block lifts is a challenge to me. The apartments have reinforced doors and many locks. Plus, the faint smell of melancholy.

---

1   Pussy Riot is a Russian feminist protest punk band. Three of its members were sentenced to imprisonment for their 'hooliganism motivated by religious hatred' in 2012.

I get some very suspicious glances when I smile at the neighbours when my senior students host me, as if they are saying, "What is there to smile about?" However, my personal experience with the Russians I know through my classes and courses is always very positive. My students are mainly young people desperate to change their country into a democracy. Some of the older generation tend towards caution – conditioned by their complex history.

So much of the youth are absolutely starving for philosophy and psychology to help them in their lives, and give them hope for the future. (Of course, I can only generalise as my encounters have been with such a specific audience.) So this book is dedicated to my students. I know they will read it, in English if they can, or once it is translated.

My second motive is a little more complex. In taking fingers to keyboard, I had to consider what I could offer that was fresh to those readers who can access mindfulness as easily and greedily as sugar on a doughnut. What can this book propose that is not offered elsewhere in the whole library of mindfulness books that now fill the multinational warehouses?

I am a woman endowed with ordinariness. It is my special gift. I have children and a grandchild, and have had to work hard to bring home an income to support my family. So I am much like everyone else. That I integrated a strong commitment to my spiritual development is not so ordinary, but it shows how spiritual practice can take place in ordinary lives and isn't as wacky as some people might think. Am I a religious freak? Probably. But is spirituality the entitlement of the religious? Can it only be practised in caves, deserts or forbidding monasteries? I practise my path in the kitchen, in bed, on the toilet and in the garden. My spiritual teachers are my children, my friends and those who don't like me very much. I am a Marmite kind of girl, and I know I can be intimidating to some and inspiring to others. With this self-knowledge and self-reflection, I knew that I could reach many people who feel conflicted in this materialistic world; inadequate; not worthy, or other impossibly discouraging attributes, because I am one of you. Spiritual practice is not above or beyond you. It is for everyone. So my second motive is to bring mindfulness to the masses, so that we might all become spiritually motivated.

Mindfulness with attitude

"Spirituality I take to be concerned with those qualities of the human spirit – such as love and compassion, patience, tolerance, forgiveness, contentment, a sense of responsibility, a sense of harmony – which brings happiness to both self and others [...] There is thus no reason why the individual should not develop them, even to a high degree, without recourse to any religious or metaphysical belief system. This is why I sometimes say that religion is something we can perhaps do without. What we cannot do without are these basic spiritual qualities."

The Dalai Lama

Ethics for the New Millennium

The unfortunate side effect of mindfulness is that sometimes those who practise it somehow manage to make those who don't practise it feel like lesser beings. Mindfulness practised with attitude is different. It is the awareness we bring into every aspect of our lives with the attitude of developing genuine spiritual qualities, defined in the Dalai Lama's quotation above. There will be no room for smug smiles.

Unless mindfulness practice accompanies a genuine understanding of its place in spiritual development, then it is in danger of becoming something we do that just helps us to do those things we have to do in our everyday lives.

Mindfulness is a fantastic tool for our wellbeing. Humanity faces mental and emotional challenges that have always been there, but perhaps are in sharper focus since modern-day life became more complex and demanding. Faced with so much information that it threatens to explode our brains, and charged with balancing so many different roles within our one single being, many of us simply 'exist' rather than fully live. Current mindfulness practice focuses on changing the quality of our lives through managing our thoughts and emotions so that we feel less stressed and more relaxed. Its original purpose, however, was not only to make our lives more enjoyable and manageable, but to go beyond conventional experiences of reality into a state of sublime spiritual awareness. Mindfulness can put materialism in its place. It can offer us a way of life that sees material stuff for what it really is and enables us to live more meaningfully. By making mindfulness a spiritual practice once more, we might loosen our stranglehold on life and become simply better people. Not fanatics and evangelists, but nicer, more contented human beings with grounded attitudes and spiritual aspirations. For the sake of our species and our planet we need to rebel against materialism and hedonism. We need a spiritual rebellion.

Spiritual rebellion

My subliminal motive in writing this book is to open the door, left closed for too long, to acknowledging the importance of our spiritual life. 'Spiritual' has become a dirty word; misunderstood; used to describe all sorts of superstitious ideas that many believe should consign themselves to history. But mindfulness is not an irrational belief. Instead, it paves the way to spiritual realisations; the ultimate goal being to achieve enlightenment.

Enlightenment is a state of mind achieved when a mundane view of the world is transformed into a state of pure awareness. The Buddha[2] described it as "removing the dust from our eyes". By *mundane*, I mean all the worldly concerns that get in the way of realising this blissful state. Think buying stuff, drowning sorrows, climbing ladders to 'success',

---

2   The Buddha is the name given to Siddhartha Gautama who was also known as Shakyamuni Buddha (referring to the name of his clan), or Gautama Buddha. He renounced worldly life and went in search of spiritual knowledge that led him to realise the nature of reality, commonly referred to as Nirvana – freedom – and liberation from the ego. 'Buddha' means 'enlightened one', and the Buddha went on to teach how to become enlightened. He became known as the historical Buddha who came to teach others how to be liberated from samsara – the world of suffering and the continual cycle of life, death and rebirth. Because many beings have practised this path, there are other 'buddhas'.

trying to control life, celebrity aspirations. Think materialism, hedonism, status, power and the desire for praise and admiration. Now, we don't have to give up fun stuff in order to move towards this blissful state, but being aware of its effects on our minds will help us find balance. Awareness pulls us back from being like dogs gagging for a titbit reward, and more like the intelligent and gifted species we are. We need mindfulness practice that incorporates this wisdom and sets us free from the limitations in which consumer society has put us.

In this book, I suggest that spirituality is a vital aspect of human development, and that to plonk mindfulness on the mental health and wellbeing shelf misses the point or, at best, just sees half the picture.

I hope this book will help you to think about life a bit differently – to consider the place of spirituality in your life, not necessarily through religion (I explore religion more in Chapter 12), but through the development of spiritual qualities, as defined by the Dalai Lama in the quote above, that can help us all be the extraordinary individuals we really are.

If we take a deeper look into ourselves, then we cannot avoid some of the questions that our meditation practice raises. Questions like:

- What is the purpose of my life? Why is life so hard?

- Mindfulness helps me to keep calm in normal life, but what if something terrible happens, like my child becomes sick and dies, or I suffer life-changing injuries, or my partner leaves me? How can it help me then?

- Mindfulness is a great wellbeing tool, so why do I still get depressed, fail in so many areas of my life, and continue to feel like I'm doing it all wrong?

Mindfulness as it is generally practised today doesn't address the big questions of "Why me? What have I done to deserve this? Why do some people live only a very short, painful life and others live to be one hundred? How come some guys get all the luck?" I hope that this book can help you to nurture your spirituality and go some way to answering the questions that nag us.

My story - before mindfulness

When I started delivering secular courses and sessions, mindfulness was not a word on many lips. Those of us who practised meditation knew mindfulness was a part of our practice, but a means to an end rather than the end itself. I called my work 'Inner Management' – a term I used to refer to how we can develop aspects of our inner selves. These courses covered three aspects of inner development that are common to all religions:

1. Life holds meaning
2. Goodness leads to happiness
3. There is more than this life

Within these three divisions we explored 1. meaning and purpose; 2. how being good brings peace of mind, and 3. the continuity of consciousness.

Unless we consider the third aspect of Inner Management, then we are still left with many holes, some of them dark and deep, in our understanding of 'why'. This is the role of our spirituality – to investigate the purpose of life and to therefore give it greater meaning than its short span. One could say that to be alive is to be spiritual, but unless we engage with spirituality, it can be like a seed on the floor of the rainforest, dormant, waiting a hundred years for a tree to fall before it can receive sunshine and water to grow.

My courses were born from my classes with the secondary school students I taught in Religious Studies. They were hungry for self-knowledge. Then later, taking the ideas to adults, we explored further and I was able to develop the Mindfulness Based Mind Training programme.

The spiritual rebel

The self is more complex than brain function. Practising mindfulness in order to develop a healthy brain is a noble spiritual practice in itself. So, no one has to feel that they have to sign up to a belief system. But we can all bring deeper meaning to our practice and find purpose in our lives, however short or long, however blessed by good fortune or not, by examining those mysterious aspects of ourselves that are defined by linguistic labels such as ego, soul, spirit, God, gods – you name it. By understanding that we may be in the process of developing an inner spiritual self that need not be defined by belief in the divine, but by a sense of our own self-awareness that is individually unique but totally interdependent with all humanity, is arguably the most important aspect of mindfulness training.

Being spiritual doesn't mean that we are weird, odd or delusional. We can reject accusations of being flaky. Being spiritual is everyone's right and can be everyone's goal, supported by science and religious wisdom, so avoiding the pitfalls that come with being uninformed or susceptible to fundamentalism. Being spiritual means opening our minds to embrace the whole world, not just some of it.

Become spiritual and be proud of it. That's the subtext of this book. Understand exactly what is meant by being spiritual, and we can form a view of ourselves and the world we live in that is whole and wholesome. In this way we can truly transform it, without noisy protests or flashy acts of anger, but simply by rejecting mundane obsessions to engage in the ultimate act of rebellion – that of the spiritual rebel.

Introduction

∘ ∘ ∘

This book is a manual for developing the self by applying mindful awareness to all aspects of our lives until it becomes as natural as breathing. It is aimed at anyone wishing to know more about mindfulness and how to feel empowered to practise it in everyday life, without feeling some sense of inadequacy. The book may add to your practice, may start it, or may deepen it as you start to consider that, as a species, it is justifiably essential to consider that we may have something about us that goes beyond the brain.

Modern-day mindfulness has strongly rooted itself in the results of scientific evaluation of its effects on the brain. This is good. It means that mindfulness doesn't fall prey to accusations of being New Age-y or weird, which has opened up the practice to millions of people who might have otherwise rejected it as too 'spiritual' or 'hippie'.

However, in my experience, it means that mindfulness has become most commonly associated with fixing brain malfunction and addressing temporal neuroses stemming from childhood trauma, and therefore neglecting certain universal truths about the human condition.

Self-reflection and meditation within mindfulness practice are key to leading us to becoming more than we could ever possibly imagine. And that doesn't mean in any conventional measure of success, but in the hidden meaning of our lives – what we give, what we learn and what we leave for others.

Mindfulness for real life

As a busy, full-time working woman, wife and mother, finding time to meditate was a luxury. If I found a few minutes and tried, I would fall asleep in the process and this would make me self-critical. However, my training in analytical meditation enabled me to think deeply about topics as they arose. While cooking and cleaning, I would sift through my day, looking at what was good and bad and, like the rest of the world, my bias was towards the negative, observing how my ego had been dented. However, I started to put issues right in my mind and helped myself have positive views of people rather than forming aversion to those who rubbed me up the wrong way. I began to see how sensitive my ego was, and how defensive. Through examining my conditioning – the moulding of my 'self' through the powerful influences of my upbringing and society – I tried to fathom how this negativity bias had become a default reaction. Before I fell asleep each night, I would again contemplate anything that had appeared important to me during the day, even from television. My relationships with my partner and children didn't escape my analysis. It's not unusual to get to a place in a long-term relationship where you question its viability. Sex can become a chore and communication limited. It's a tough road keeping the romance alive, and being mindful will be heavily challenged by feelings of being taken for granted and taking others for granted. (But perhaps I've opened up a can of climaxes!) Basically, any action, anywhere, can be utilised for spiritual progression. It's your mind, your choice, so do what works for you. In the kitchen, as we sponge the dishes and glasses, feel the warmth of the soapy suds and smell the freshness. Even when emptying the bowl of soap scum and wiping it clean, we can be totally present. We don't judge the fresh soapy suds or greasy scum, we just experience them for what they are. Not ruminating but sensing.

How about in bed? Letting our minds relax as our bodies sink into the depth of the mattress and pillow, feeling the cool sheets on our skin, and hearing the sound of a blind nodding against an open window.

Or in the bathroom: washing ourselves mindfully, water against skin and towels rubbing us dry. Brushing our teeth, making them smooth and fresh, and being aware of the taste of toothpaste and water in our mouths.

The garden offers us a whole plethora of opportunities for spiritual and mindful metaphors and idioms. Preparing the soil of our minds, and digging out the weeds of destructive emotions. Planting the flowers of constructive emotions, watering them through meditation and contemplation. Trees, roots and branches can be utilised for our reflection. Being present in nature without analysis is one of the most relaxing and sensual experiences. When we garden, we can too often see what needs doing rather than merely experiencing the beauty around us, even of those persistent 'weeds'.

Mindfulness in nature can also present us with challenges. One of the most powerful guided meditations that I experienced was being asked to consider that when we are enjoying our lovely gardens or our beautiful countryside, they are actually battlegrounds for sentient beings all just trying to survive. Insects whizz around our heads trying to get blood out of us. As we walk, we step on numerous beings just trying to get to food or safety. As the cat stalks the bird, as the bird snaps up the ladybird, as the ladybird sucks the greenfly... you get the picture. When we hear all the lovely birds singing in the dawn chorus, they are screaming out their territorial rights, desperately trying to attract a mate and warning other birds not to poach. There's no damn equanimity or peace of mind in the animal world, that's for sure. We look at the world as our toyshop and are rarely mindful of the different levels of dissatisfaction and suffering that are going on around us all the time. What we really want is to say, "Oh what a lovely day! I'm so happy." And pretend.

Transformation is wonderful, but so is realisation, and by that I mean recognising what is real, not an illusion.

The teachers in our lives

I am a practising Buddhist, and have been for over forty years. Mindfulness has Buddhist roots, so I come to the mindfulness table with full knowledge of its mentally nutritional components and make no apology for referring to the Buddhist teachings that further explain mindful practices.

Some mindfulness teachers like to push Buddhism under the rug and teach mindfulness only in relation to neuroscience and modern psychology. This is a bit sad, because without the deeper truths that underlie mindfulness, we're just skimming stones on the surface of an ocean.

Buddhists are famously opposed to conversion as they agree that you can only take horses to water, and not make them drink. Traditionally, a student would have to ask a teacher three times for teachings before they bestowed them. I always liked this attitude, as conversion is really about making people see the world the way you do because you think you are right, and so is very ego-centric.

There is a saying in Buddhism that if you're looking for a teacher and feel frustrated, don't worry, because when you're ready, the teacher will find you.

My children are my teachers. They are an example of what love can be and they challenge me to let them grow and fly. My friends are my teachers with their comparable lives, their ability to laugh and cry with me and to share their hopes and fears. Those who teach me most are the ones who don't agree with me, dislike me or give me a hard time. Every day I encounter them I have a choice – to get totally knotted up or to uncoil and let go.

Maybe this book will be one of your teachers, and pave the way to practising mindfulness with attitude.

What's in the book

Finding your way around this book should be easy. There is a natural progression from concepts to practices, plus some useful exercises, meditations and anecdotes from my life to encourage you to reflect on your life. My story is meant to be inspiring – in essence, "If she can do it, so can I."

Each part focuses on a particular aspect of mindfulness and spiritual development. Part One does the groundwork of preparing the soil of your mind and then Part Two does the actual gardening, focusing on the changes we are able to apply with mindfulness. The topics in Part Two fall broadly into four areas: thoughts and emotions; being 'good'; seeing well, or 'wellseeing'; and the spiritual culmination of all these endeavours. I conclude each chapter with some reflections on its contents and regularly consider, topic by topic, how to have both authentic mindfulness and spiritual integrity. These reflections are designed to unravel some common misunderstandings and attitudes in mindfulness practice today. I hope that the suggestions relating to spiritual integrity may also make you feel more comfortable around the concept of being spiritual. The meditations and exercises aim to make sense of each chapter and enable you to put into practice the ideas discussed. You can intersperse your reading with listening to the meditations, so have your phone nearby. If you prefer to read them, then you can find them transcribed on my website at www.ondywillson.com.

I also reference a variety of belief systems as well as neuroscience to balance the book. I don't draw distinctions between religions, but focus on what unites rather than separates us.

Part One: Talking the Walk

Here we look at what mindfulness is and what it isn't. Like yoga, mindfulness is in danger of losing sight of its original purpose and becoming something that we do to manage a stressful life. Yoga is a practice of poses and postures that train us, through becoming aware of the body, into knowing our own nature. Through the discipline of training our body, our minds are able to develop self-awareness, self-regulation and higher consciousness.

Similarly, mindfulness practice is like exercising a muscle; essentially, a practice done in meditation to discipline the mind to gain insight into our very mode of being. So you can see that the goal is the same as yoga, and the practices support one another. What we're in danger of doing is making both practices support our worldly lives – becoming fitter is always good, but being more beautiful, having longevity and being less stressed, so as to enjoy worldly life more, is contradictory to the original purpose. Instagram photos of bodacious babes in body-hugging clothing doing postures on rocks with waves crashing behind smacks of subliminal sexual messaging: "Because I do yoga, I am beautiful, and if you do yoga with me, you will be more beautiful and people will find you really sexy." Of course, being beautiful, having longevity and being fit is very nice, but if these are the motivations, then the benefits may only last a few years or at most as long as this life. Instead of chipping away at your ego and developing your 'self', practising yoga and mindfulness with worldly intentions may simply serve to increase your ego.

I define the pitfalls of mindfulness in order to clarify the short-sightedness of some contemporary approaches.

Part One goes further to look at what it really means to be human, and how we can more fully appreciate this precious life we have and utilise it to its greatest potential. It focuses on our inner world – about every aspect that is broiling away inside us that we rarely give time to, or indeed know how to consider. It will be a great way for you, dear reader, to reflect and really be able to become self-aware. The first step for this is recognising our ability to be objective about ourselves, and there are meditations and exercises in each chapter to support this reflection.

Considering what we understand to be 'the mind' is the major focus of Part One. It teases modern mindfulness manuals that focus on changing the brain. It challenges ideas about us simply being 'walking meat' and asks us to consider the different strands of being human, and how these strands point to something in ourselves that is other than the physical. It is an essential inward journey to give our lives meaning and purpose, and consider what we mean by spiritual development.

Part Two: Walking the Talk

This is where we discover how to apply mindfulness meditation to the way we think and feel; how to deal with all the dramas and crises that life throws at us, and transform them into positive outcomes. One could say that managing thoughts and emotions – our inner world – is the absolute foundation of mindfulness practice, and there are exercises and meditations that develop our ability to transform our minds, and so transform our lives.

The natural progression is then to look at our ethical choices. This is uncommon to much mindfulness practice, although I would argue that by managing thoughts and emotions, we encourage the natural tendency to be a good person. But we are experts in justification, and the ego plays many games to convince us that we are right. Looking at the concept of goodness is like taking a magnifying glass into our very hearts to check if we are being easy on ourselves and avoiding what is actually the right thing to do. Often, the right thing to do leads to difficult situations and life choices. It is always easier to fool ourselves in order to live an easy life. Understanding the natural law of cause and effect is key to this awakening, and I explore different tools to support some of the more difficult decisions we have to make in life.

Part Two also includes a section on developing our wisdom and compassion to such a degree that they can destroy tendencies like prejudices and judgements. We are introduced to concepts such as equanimity, an under-used word Buddhists use regularly that needs deeper consideration, and how barriers to this can fool us into dividing the world into strangers, enemies and friends. We look at our prejudices and our attitudes that inform whether we will be givers or takers in life – bringing warmth and light and adding to the richness of existence, or sucking up all that we can to support a more shallow side of ourselves. We also look at whether we can develop a healthier way of seeing: 'wellseeing' for wellbeing.

The last two chapters consider how all these aspects of our training lead us to be deeply and profoundly mindful in all aspects of our lives – to become spiritual warriors. Not only will our lives be enriched with awareness of self and others, but beyond our death, the imprint of our life will be a wholesome and nourishing addition to humanity. The negative view of humans destroying the natural world and generally being considered a greedy and selfish species will be valid no longer as we utilise the fullest potential of what we can achieve as human beings.

This world need not be a place for privileged and luckily conditioned humans to stand above those with lesser opportunities, but a more integrated place in which we can all learn life's lessons, regardless of what life dishes up, and in fact *because* of what life dishes up.

My story for your reflection

Woven into the thread of the book, I recount different episodes in my life that have taught me and had a profound effect on my journey. I tell them for your own reflection on the effects of living with spiritual awareness. My life so far has been extraordinary in its ordinariness! No fame or fortune; just men, children, grandchildren, career choices and homes, yet amongst that ordinariness is a central spiritual force that would throw me into making uncommon life decisions. Doing things that I believed in rather than to make money has been a driving force for me. I'm still here to prove that you don't have to renounce the world in order to be spiritual. Whatever our path, we all have to get through a great deal of suffering – whether that is physical, emotional or mental. The Austrian poet Rainer Maria Rilke said, "How much suffering there is to get through", as if suffering were just part of the human condition. I suggest that mindfulness can offer us a way to manage suffering, but also, if one is motivated enough, to utilise it as a vehicle out of suffering.

Part One

Talking the Walk

When we discover the truth that dwells in our innermost being, we find words of wisdom.

Chapter 1

Talking Mindfulness

o o o

> In 1980, I went on a course at a Buddhist Institute housed in a chilly Gothic mansion in the English countryside. It changed my life. After three weeks of sitting in front of a Tibetan Lama wrapped in a blanket (me, not him), I was convinced of the importance of spiritual development. I went back home, handed in my notice at the secondary school where I taught Drama, and sold my house. After three months tying up the bits of my life, I moved into the Institute – and so began my inner education.

How do you describe a way of seeing and being that transforms your life? It takes more than a brief definition to convey the immensity of the mind and its workings. It's like showing a child a Mercedes-Benz, giving them the keys and saying "Go! Drive!" Mindfulness is just one cog in that complex engine, but it's vital. My Buddhist studies gave me much more than mindfulness, but it is the practice that underpins everything. So here's a tiny taster before we even start on the starters.

Mindfulness means being present in the moment, fully open and aware, allowing experiences to happen and pass freely without assessing or judging them.

Is mindfulness just meditation? Is it intentional? Is it rational?

My attempt to prepare the ground of your mind is to firstly say what mindfulness isn't. I do this in order to do a deep clean of your mind, in case you have already engaged with mindfulness practice. It's a bit like a wash and polish programme for your car. It will still be your car, but it will be fresh and clean, with one of those perfumed air fresheners hanging in the windscreen. All the old sweet wrappers and empty coffee cups will have been swept away, and you'll drive with a revitalised sense of ownership and pride, seeing the world anew.

Mindfulness *isn't* a trend

Mindfulness has been in the public domain for some time. We hear it often enough, in the media, and even by those in arenas not usually associated with reflective practice, like football coaches and the armed forces. It's become fashionable. Who would have thought that? Certainly not me when I started to teach it formally back in the 2000s, and even earlier as a schoolteacher trying it out on curious teenagers.

In the 1980s and '90s, meditation was linked with spirituality, and no one was quite sure what that was. People who meditated were a bit weird. As one confused student asked me, "Is it true you live in a caravan up on't fell and worship the sun, Miss?" Working in an area generously littered with sheep and farmers, where religious practices ranged from mild Quakerism to evangelical Christianity, it was certainly fortuitous that I wasn't burnt at the stake at the time. Although I was declared by certain believers of the one true faith as an enemy to righteousness – a wolf in sheep's clothing, come (or perhaps sent) to convert the innocent.

Forty years later and mindfulness, as a label, is in danger of becoming passé, added to the list of wellbeing activities that improve stressful lives but are starting to feel sooo last year as we wait for the next new trend – hot mindfulness, or mindful sex, perhaps – to engage a restless and hungry public. But, being fashionable and current is all about NOW (and interestingly, so is mindfulness) – what we can do to immediately improve our lives and enhance our happiness (that always slightly unattainable and fragile quality) so that we fit in and are 'on trend', acceptable and worth knowing. This wish for an instant fix for our impatient and limited-attention tendencies – chasing the next new thing – is the actual antithesis of mindfulness.

Mindfulness can settle upon us like a mask: "I've heard about mindfulness and I'm going to try it because everyone else is and then I can say I'm mindful too." In this way, it becomes just another trend we do because we don't want to appear unfashionable. There are many masks we wear to appear to be something we're not. For example, we can smile when we're sad, wearing the mask of happiness to disguise our pain. Such masks are not bad, necessarily, because they are a form of self-protection, but they are not the real you and so will be difficult to sustain. If mindfulness is just a mask, then we won't truly engage with it, just bandy the word around as if we know what we're talking about – and even use it to feel superior. Then the practice is destined to result in disappointment and frustration and it will feel ineffective, so we wait for the next new trend. We are all looking for a quick and easy answer, but there isn't one. We want happiness and we want it now, but we don't want to persist if we don't get immediate results, especially when something new may be coming around the corner.

But relegating mindfulness to a cupboard, to be pulled out and experimented with when a crisis arises, is a waste. Life is short, and to get the real benefits we must continue to practise – not just when we hit a crisis, but because life IS a crisis.

If mindfulness was a means of communication, it wouldn't be a tweet or a text, or even an email – or whatever the new TikTok/Twitter communication is that's ready to stimulate the over-stimulated. It would be a letter, handwritten in ink on paper with a watermark; the novelist Charlotte Brontë's method of communication, written on a love seat by an open window that looks out onto large landscapes. Mindfulness requires sincerity, care and commitment in order to provide real rewards that aren't just for the present. In fact, being in the present isn't just for the present – it's for life, and it requires sustained effort. Within it is a stable world of wisdom that we can partake of whenever we get tired of whatever is about to spiral downwards in popularity. Be loyal to mindfulness and it will abide within you and serve you: no separations, no embarrassing fashions – just enduring mental support.

My story – reality versus the dream

Living in a Buddhist community wasn't quite the pastoral dream I had imagined. It seemed like all the misfits of the world were attracted to it. The Institute seemed to house a collection of people who were completely lost in the Western world and were attracted to this apparent House of Fools like riders in the storm are to a wayside inn full of light. Many had followed their Eastern gurus across the ocean back to the UK to rest themselves in this place of learning. But these were not your average students – these were intentional dropouts of the most serious kind. They saw through the Western dream their parents were sold and didn't want what they had bought. Many of them had joined the hippie trail to India and found some spiritual guidance, Christianity having become stale and hypocritical to them. Buddhism gave them answers to questions that had been burning inside them all their lives. Neither their schoolteachers nor parents had reached inside them like the Tibetan Lamas had, to pluck at their very hearts. This wasn't a trend or a lifestyle choice but a calling.

Mindfulness *isn't* a religion

If mindfulness was a religion, we would need to change the label. The label would be vital, connected to someone important or an ancient culture – a tradition that would give us status and confidence. We'd belong. We would proudly label ourselves as Mindfulian or Mindfulist, and there would be acknowledgement of what we belonged to.

However, labels separate us. We are boxed up, and then we box ourselves further into that label's requirements. What attracts us to a label can vary – we may be born to it, reborn to it, brainwashed by it – but the sense of belonging we experience when we identify with a label can give us purpose, hope and meaning. But religions always hold smaller boxes that we don't see at first.

All religions have moral structures at the heart of their belief systems that give them worth and stature. But we can corrupt these if we personalise them and imbue them with our own agendas, due to all kinds of life experiences that come our way. Values are skewed to feed and justify destructive emotions like hatred and anger, and we lay claim to the religion to justify our actions. Then the religions themselves identify with causes, cults and charismatic leaders claiming authority and entitlement.

Mindfulness has an advantage here. It has no fixed belief system, no moral authority (and therefore no guilt), no patriarchal structures and no places in which we must wear a mask of self-protection – hiding our real selves, becoming subservient or craving membership. Practising mindfulness does not require us to believe in anyone or anything, except in the power of the mind.

My story – life in a Buddhist community

The building housed about 80 people when I arrived: monks, nuns, teachers, Tibetan translators, Lamas and laypeople, including families. In order to live there, one had to show sincere interest in study and meditation and fulfil certain practical and financial criteria. The place was run by a few senior students of the Lamas, who felt it was their mission to help bring Buddhism to the West, and they had to learn pretty quickly how to run such a complex organisation. Some jobs were available, especially working on the never-ending building site, and these were remunerated in board and lodging, plus a small stipend. And I mean small. Some lived on benefits and spent their time in study and meditation, and some financed themselves or had jobs outside in the 'real world.' The squeaky new Buddhist charitable organisation had bought it very cheaply. The roof was full of holes, and you had to watch where you stepped. Central heating was not yet a feature on their projected list of improvements. Health and Safety was not applicable at that time either, especially in there. But husband number two and I were committed. After all, to do what we had done certainly took courage. He had been offered a job in the print shop – books by Tibetan Lamas were being rolled out with zeal.

I was told a job would come up for me. After all, I was just a wife.

In 1980, sexism was an established part of life generally, so I accepted the discrimination. That a good working-class girl like me felt mortified by the idea of claiming unemployment benefits was an understatement. The management team told me it was fine because my motivation was pure. I was taking money from the government, but I was helping to establish something that would bring benefit to the world. So while my man worked with his small stipend and free living expenses, I queued up at the local dole office. I don't think those early Buddhists were aware of the sexism. Arguably, the worst sexism is an unconscious bias, but the very teachings of the Buddha, I soon came to realise, were soaked in the superiority of men. They were better equipped to become enlightened. Our brains were the same, but evidently men were more rational, and women were too emotional. Plus, it was a dangerous world and risky for women to go off on their own and meditate (there was no acknowledgement that it was the men who were making it dangerous). This was the general explanation given. I think it gave many Buddhist women a sense of humility but I'm not sure it helped the men, many of whom already felt superior.

Mindfulness *isn't* just a leisure pursuit

Mindfulness is not a means of self-identification ("Look at me; I'm a mindfulness practitioner"). But the other end of this spectrum is to treat mindfulness as if it were merely another method for relaxation.

The disadvantage of mindfulness in a secular framework is that our motivation might be selfish. The best of religion gives us greater meaning and purpose – a sense that this is not all there is; that life's a mystery and one day, when we die, the purpose of our lives will be revealed. Religion gives us a larger framework – a tapestry on which to build depth and colour.

In my experience as a mindfulness teacher, many people are attracted to learning meditation when they hit a crisis. Mindfulness *is* a wonderful support system for depression and anxiety, but if we stop when we feel better then we lose the impetus to continue. And if we stop when our personal problems have been resolved, or feel less intense, like with stopping any practice, we have to start learning all over again if we want to return to it.

Mindfulness isn't a hobby, or a class that you sign up to for a few weeks. It isn't something whereby you can say, "Oh, I tried that, but I'm hopeless at meditation," or "I did mindfulness last year. I know all about it." To understand the importance of mindfulness practice, perseverance is the key. When we really 'get it' we find it impossible not to keep returning to it, because life keeps throwing problems and challenges at us and they never end: we need support. Our practice becomes as comforting as sinking into the sofa at the end of the day to turn on the TV – but instead of looking outwards we focus inwards.

Self-discipline is tough because with many things in life, such as our religion or career, we are in support groups: our peers, our workplace, our yoga group, our church or faith school. We need guides and support groups for mindfulness too, because it is a very rare and strong-willed human being who can tough it out alone on the spiritual path. Being alone with ourselves was really demanding during lockdown. We discovered the importance of others and our interdependence. The ones who cope with it best are those who are comfortable being alone with themselves. They are undoubtedly infused with strong self-esteem – that quality that often comes with reflective practice.

My story – the students

One of the most endearing features of life in the Institute was definitely the people I met. Although I had lived a small-scale hippie life before I went there, it was nothing compared to these 'inmates.' Our previous life in Northumberland was The Good Life meets living-off-grid hipster style. We were trendy teachers who grew a few pots of marijuana on the window-sill that passed for tomato plants when the farmer landlord came round. We grew vegetables in the garden, made home-brew, picked mushrooms from the fields and liked to get stoned on long Sunday walks along the famous Northumbrian Hadrian's Wall. We had a lot of friends, but they worked in relatively straight jobs, like us. These Buddhists were different.

I was eventually entrusted with the job of Tourism Manager. Nobody wanted the job. It meant you had to engage with the locals, who tended to be a tad conservative and yet were fascinated by the weirdos that had bought the old place. I had a budget and could employ some of our tribe to do things like serve teas, or be shopkeepers in the new café I was planning. I didn't know that these Buddhist newbies weren't like most people, who were able to hold down jobs and had stable home lives. Although they were charming, interesting and knowledgeable, they could be eccentric and turned off by Western values. When the café opened and there was a queue of curious locals waiting to enter, my new employees all disappeared. I found one later up a tree in the woodland. When I tracked down another, he turned and growled at me, like a wild animal. I didn't know until then that some of the people that had found shelter there were damaged – broken people who had found no place in the material world.

They had come to the right refuge. There was a massive heart beating for the lost there, and room for us all. Questioning and rejecting conventional life wasn't mad, but an intelligent response to the apparent greed at the heart of Western values. This was the perfect place to start a spiritual rebellion – the hippies had rebelled against the conservative values of the '50s and in my view should always be respected for enlightening the world about a different attitude to life. Theirs was a mission for peace, love and freedom, and Buddhism certainly fitted with their ideals. I see no need for the current use of the term 'hippie' to imply something flaky, because actually they paved the way for profound and meaningful change. Our studies and inner reflections gave us all opportunities for building the self-knowledge, self-esteem and confidence to live a life that was full of awareness. It was a place to heal and become whole.

Mindfulness *is* self-knowledge

So far in this chapter I have addressed some of today's general attitudes to mindfulness, with a focus on what mindfulness is *not*. Now I would like to discuss its aims and intentions. Let's look inside that engine and become DIY mind mechanics. What *is* mindfulness? Why is it a term? Where did it originate?

Mindfulness should be on everyone's curriculum. If it was, there'd be fewer narcissists, tyrants and wars, and less mental illness, suicide and general confusion. Yes, that's a big claim, but I stand by it. Understanding who we are, and why, and managing our thoughts and emotions must be the most important aspect of being human. But it is relegated to being an extra: something you do if you're unhappy. An evening class for the slightly discombobulated.

The challenge for mindfulness is that it is *not* a religion nor a fashionable wellbeing tool – there is no leader or distinct culture associated with it. It has existed for thousands of years, often without a label at all – understood by ancient civilisations who were just naturally aware and turned inwards without effort. It was then identified as a method for spiritual development, predominantly expounded and practised by the ascetics of India, who neglected their own physical comfort to attain spiritual realisations. Mindfulness later became incorporated into the Buddhist Steps to Enlightenment: the Noble Eightfold Path.[3] The Noble Eightfold Path includes ethical ways to live, and how to develop the mind in meditation.

One might argue that the attraction of modern mindfulness is that it exists as a distinct practice *outside* the confines of religious belief structures.

---

3   The Noble Eightfold Path is the fourth Noble Truth and one of the main teachings of the Buddha, consisting of eight right ways to live your life: right views, intentions, speech, action, livelihood, effort, mindfulness and concentration. The first Noble Truth is that life is dissatisfaction and suffering. The second is that the cause of this is our desire, and the third is that to end this suffering we need to end desire. The fourth is how to do this and encompasses the Noble Eightfold Path. More about these concepts are incorporated and woven into the content of this book without necessarily referring to them explicitly.

After all, as a species, we're tending towards ditching religion and embracing science. Now that mindfulness is scientifically proven to bring mental and emotional wellbeing, the battle of science versus belief appears to have been won. It was a turning point for meditation teachers everywhere. My bank balance certainly benefitted greatly from organisations who wanted their employees to relate better to others, and improve their focus and concentration. Thank goodness for all the research and fact-finding. Wired up Tibetan monks (who meditate a lot) were proven to be happy. We wanted some of that in the West.

Of course, we didn't want to shave our heads, wear robes or live frugally, but maybe if we just incorporated a bit of meditation into our lives, we could have it all.

The proven benefit of mindfulness is why it has become so popular in so many areas of wellbeing training. We meditate, we become more rational and our behaviour modifies. It is a practice that crosses the boundaries of all religions and none – anyone can do it and no one tells you what to do, when or where. The discipline comes from recognising the consequences of our mental, verbal and physical actions and taking responsibility for them. There are mindfulness teachers, but they are qualified by a whole variety of organisations that have arisen from the wellbeing revolution. There is no one bible where laws, rules and teachings are written, handed over only to the chosen ones and administered through visions and mystical apparitions. There is no spiritual leader, whose words are handed down the ages as the 'one and only truth'. Our development of mindfulness practices are the rewards in themselves and so we can enjoy our lives without becoming trapped, guilt-laden or obsessed – or blinded by faith.

There is so much freedom and beauty in this concept that it's hard to see how we might lose our way within it, but we are human, so we do.

Humans are sensory beings – basically animals with bigger brains – experiencing the tangible and knowable world through our external connection with it and spending our time trying to improve this external environment of what can be seen, heard, smelt, tasted and touched. Historically, humanity has strived to perfect the physical aspects of our lives to such a degree that we have been in danger of only valuing personal comfort and stimulation. Of course, we need the basics to survive – many of us are fortunate to have achieved that – so as with Maslow's Hierarchy of Needs,[4] a well-known theory for human development, we then move to improving and building upon those survival basics to achieve psychological fulfilment. But, unlike the pyramid Maslow uses as a symbol for our own personal mountain, we seem to baulk at the progression towards self-actualisation – becoming our ideal selves – and become side-tracked, trapped on the wheel of comfort upon comfort; the hedonistic treadmill that can never be satisfied, so our striving for happiness continues. But we're mistaken. External sources of pleasure are transient, ephemeral and not meant to last. There's no permanent contentment found on that wheel, hence all that running!

Mindfulness meditation opens us up to our inner world, where we can find that self-knowledge and really make progress as human beings. But some people find that far too challenging. If we look under the rug, what will we find? The older we get, the more we want to live in denial – emotions suppressed, ego-mask intact, lives slipping away with someone we're not sure we even like anymore… Why stir things up when we can pretend we are thumbs up A-OK? It would be like admitting that our lives had been in vain. And it's so easy to be distracted by pleasure and comfort. Another glass and we forget everything! We avoid what we don't want to see and, like horses in blinkers, trot around without awareness, in denial and led by our senses.

To make the most of mindfulness, we don't need scientific facts and figures. We need to believe in the adventure and let it take us beyond the confines of established ways of thinking so we can completely free ourselves to be our 'selves.'

---

4   Psychologist Abraham Maslow created a five-tier, pyramid-shaped model of human needs. At the base are our physiological needs for food and warmth, followed by the need for safety and security. Then comes the need for belonging/community and love, followed by self-esteem and finally self-actualisation, or being the best we can be. His theory stated that these needs were hierarchical in nature and one couldn't proceed towards self-actualisation without the others in place.

My story – Buddhist studies

Learning about your 'self' happened every day in the Institute. We had daily prayers, complete with rituals and mantras, but what I was hungry for wasn't the religious aspects of Buddhism, but the psychology. The Lamas had sent two Geshes, or teachers, to reside there. (In those days, the assignment must have felt like a short straw for them as they generally thought we Westerners were heathens. Well, if they thought it, they didn't show it.) 'Geshe' was the title given to a learned Tibetan teacher who had studied Buddhism for around 20 years, fulfilled retreat obligations (lots of meditation) and finally passed all their exams. It was the kind of course you could only fulfil at a monastery. A PhD is possibly closest to its status because this implies being a specialist in one's field of study, but the practical purpose wasn't to kick-start a great career and/or earn loads of money, but to become enlightened and help others attain enlightenment. They were appointed to help us.

Each morning and evening we would engage in learning about the mind. We would meditate and learn more esoteric practices, such as Tantra – the motorway route to enlightenment. In those early days, the teachings were fresh and juicy subjects for discussion. Our egos were ripped apart as we learned very quickly that we weren't who we thought we were. I guess you could say that, as a couple, my husband and I had arrived at the Institute for mixed reasons. There were many obstacles to achieving our ordinary goals – from buying a house in the country to getting the great overseas jobs we'd applied for. When we made this choice, all the obstacles fell away. This offered us a different way, but perhaps we thought it was going to be a bit like living in a commune – a free and easy lifestyle with the exotic brushstrokes of Eastern mysticism. Our hedonistic flights of fancy were soon crushed by enduring the relentless close-ups of looking at who we really were. We weren't on slow roast but in a pressure cooker – fast-tracked for reasons of which we were then unaware. Eventually, we came to realise that the Lamas saw that the survival of Tibetan

Buddhism would rest in the hands of these early 'Injies' (the name they gave to us predominantly English-speaking people).

Mindfulness *is* a spiritual practice

Mindfulness practice that leads us to living with awareness relies only on our own inner guidance. Our own psychology informs us. We plumb the depths of our own innate knowledge. We may get inspiration from many external sources, but we can always turn to our own inner source of wisdom. The rules and laws of moral guidance become a natural awareness of what brings us actual, true happiness and actual, true meaning. Such freedom! But also many opportunities for getting lost and influenced by others as we build trust in this inner source of guidance.

To use mindfulness practice to benefit ourselves can only lead to trendy, transitory wellness as we continue to judge others and feel the superiority we mistake for self-esteem. The view being, "If I meditate, I'm calmer. I can see through others because they're not practising mindfulness and I feel better about myself compared to them." The subtext here is "I'm a superior being", which dangerously leads us to feel we are *better than others*. So we use the practice to feed our egos instead of to enable us to understand everyone's common human psychology. We need to remember that we're all in this together, at every level, religious or not, experienced meditator or not. We are all desperate to feed on whatever it is we find in the bins of psychological survival.

In order for our mindfulness practice to really morph into living with awareness, we need to give it purpose and meaning. A Buddhist practises mindfulness to discipline the mind to achieve insight into the nature of reality (Wisdom with a capital W). This enables them to escape the confines of material life and go beyond this world of suffering to a state of bliss. A Christian may practise mindfulness to become a better person so that when they die, they go to heaven. They share their motivation in the belief that this life is just part of the journey.

So one of the first steps is to ask yourself *why* you want to practise mindfulness. For less stress? To manage difficult and challenging relationships? To deal with anxiety and help with depression? Or because your organisation thinks that those who practise mindfulness have better working relationships with their colleagues? Maybe you've been told you have to do it. These reasons are all noble and beneficial. There is nothing wrong with any of them, but they are all temporal reasons, and practising mindfulness for just these reasons is like driving that Mercedes-Benz for the school run. It contains so much more power than the purpose for which you are using it.

This book strives to constantly remind you how far mindfulness can take you in this life. Yes, it's a great vehicle for elevating the mundane experiences of everyday life, but look inside the engine! It has so much fuel – for self-actualisation, for enabling you to fill that forever-elusive potential you're meant to be realising. And perhaps beyond!

Whatever your belief system, if you utilise mindfulness wisely it will serve you not only in the practical everyday challenges of ordinary life, but also in developing the extraordinary inner journey of your 'self' – a source of dynamic spiritual energy in the universe.

My story – the teachers

Contact with the Geshes and visiting Lamas gave us incredible highs. They had a quality to them that I couldn't find in Western society. They were celibates, had a strange combination of both male and female energy and had a lightness of being, even if they were solid and fleshy. There was one Geshe I had a strong feeling for. He smiled so much, and wore Buddhist authority like the lightest mantle, yet could cut through your delusions as if with a sword. I had a particularly challenging psyche at that time. I was fine with the daily teachings, but when it came to in-depth study groups on some of the more profound philosophical points, I became confused. This Geshe was so kind. He told me that when my mind was happy, I would be able to learn more easily. It was such a simple statement, but so profound. I felt completely at home with the teachings I'd received, but my personal life was deeply flawed and I couldn't look at it. It was an obstacle to my spiritual development. Put simply, my meditations and spiritual practice couldn't progress until I had worked on my relationships – both with myself and others. When I recognised, through guidance, that I had some strong destructive attachments to conventional life, my spiritual development could begin.

Living mindful lives

I describe mindfulness meditation in all its glorious detail in the next chapter, but here I'd like to focus on how we can live mindful *lives*. This is our practice *outside* of meditation – 'off the cushion' as we might describe it. We practise mindfulness in meditation, and then out of meditation we bring that same quality of non-judgemental awareness into our lives. We start to experience life more holistically because we aren't continually labelling and judging what's happening. Mindfulness practice subdues and pacifies our egos, allowing us a much more open and tolerant way of life. To make a start with bringing mindfulness into your everyday life, try the following activities:

- Start with something in nature – a tree, a leaf, a weed. Pay it 'bare attention' by just observing it, like a scientist observes something under a microscope with interest and precision. If you find yourself thinking about it and giving it special qualities ("What a lovely flower. The colour is so intense!"), stop, take a few breaths and return to the object. Notice how it appears to your senses: how you see it, how it smells, its sound and touch.

- Try being mindful of your surroundings. Really experience them rather than walking through them absentmindedly, absorbed in internal chatter. Take your time. Look at the things that you generally take for granted – a fence, a park bench, a tree, the flowerbeds – with new eyes, noticing their details, perfect in their imperfection.

- When someone says something that upsets you, try taking a few breaths and mentally stepping back so that you can respond rather than react. A *reaction* is emotional; a *response* clarifies the communication and enables you to take things less personally – not in a cold, unfeeling way, but in a more interconnected way, with understanding and tolerance.

Reflections

○ If mindfulness becomes unfashionable, will you move on and drop it? Have you done this with other practices, like yoga?

○ Are you religious? How does mindfulness fit in with your belief system? Are there any contradictions?

○ Do you think your religion has got it right, and others have got things wrong? How does this affect how you feel about yourself in relation to others?

○ Do you agree that people can be religious but not spiritual? And if so, what exactly is the relationship between these labels?

○ Do you justify your behaviour all the time, or do you sometimes question it and find that maybe you have got some things wrong?

○ How do you feel about the idea of spiritual practice being principally the development of good qualities (as defined by the Dalai Lama, which I share in the Introduction to this book)?

Authentic mindfulness

○ Mindfulness can be incorporated into your belief system without contradictions.

○ Equality and tolerance are embedded into mindfulness practice. That means respect for all.

○ Mindfulness helps you to be objective about your ego and manage it without getting too upset. With practice, everyday mindfulness will become as natural as breathing.

Spiritual integrity

- ○ Your spiritual practice is your own business, but you need to ensure it's not flaky and like a moveable feast, otherwise your ego will be in charge and it'll easily influence you.

- ○ Build a really clear picture of how you would like to see your spiritual path progress. We have so many means for assessing skills and building qualifications, yet the most important aspect of ourselves is left to find its own way down a long meandering path that often ends in cul-de-sacs. If you want to progress spiritually, then you need clarity of purpose and intent.

- ○ You start with the heart. All mindful awareness comes from the place of feeling, not from the place of thinking. The only way to connect with your heart is to meditate. So get ready for open-heart spiritual surgery in the next chapter.

Chapter 2

How to Meditate

∘ ∘ ∘

If you know how to meditate, then you won't need this chapter. You can move on with my permission. But glance through it first, as it tends to be more detailed than your average beginner's guide and you may pick up some tips.

Introducing meditation

To understand where mindfulness and meditation align and where they differ, it might be helpful to put mindfulness on the shelf for the moment and focus on meditation, to avoid confusion. So, let's start with what meditation is.

Meditation is to turn inwards and become familiar with our minds.

Meditation literally means to 'turn inwards.' We become very quiet and very still; we lower or close our eyes and turn our attention to our minds and away from the outer world as if we were gazing with awe and wonder at a beautiful new-born baby. And then we start to attend to what we find. Of course, just like that baby, there'll be shit as well as sugar.

The Tibetan word for meditation is 'gompa', which literally translates to 'become familiar with'. It's the perfect description because you are meeting a new friend when you meditate for the first time – your own inner world – and getting to know it. And every subsequent time you meditate, you get to know it even more.

The goal of meditation is to observe our mental activity and manage it in order to:

- Understand how our minds operate
- Develop a loving and healthy relationship with who we are
- Make inner changes to the way we think – for the better
- Develop meaning and purpose through understanding the nature of existence

Very slowly, we discover that the path towards a genuine understanding of the human condition, and finding inner peace and happiness, lies within us – in our minds. This is a big awakening when we realise we have spent our whole lives trying to find happiness from anywhere but our minds! We could have saved a lot of time, effort and money. Why did nobody tell us?

Meditation enables us to deal with our thoughts and emotions so that we have more control over what we think and feel, and we can bin disturbing mental events. And you'll be pleased to know that they're environmentally friendly because they can even be recycled – transformed into more useful thoughts and even life lessons.

Every day, we're bombarded with sights, smells and sounds that stimulate our senses, thoughts and feelings. By familiarising ourselves with how all this stimulation affects our minds, we can begin to manage the outer world influences on our inner world with more awareness. Sensory experiences prompt likes and dislikes, and these can lead to disturbing emotions. By meditating regularly, we strengthen our insights and qualities, enabling us to manage these judgements and so avoid prejudices. This in turn restrains us from actions that might lead to difficult outcomes for ourselves and others. Our inner self will be encouraged to guide us in our life, rather than our more basic sensory desires, and so life becomes sweeter. It's really like recognising that your pet has a wild streak that needs taming!

Turning inwards to nurture the inner self is a common religious practice.

What we call the 'inner self' depends on our belief system – 'God within' points to our potential for becoming closer to God. Buddhists use the term 'buddha nature.' The word 'buddha' means 'enlightened' and is also synonymous with 'awakened' and 'liberated', pointing to our potential to tame the ego – a sloughing off of the self-centred obstacles to our higher nature. Quite similar really.

Nowadays, with the common Scientific Materialist view of there being just one life, with no afterlife or rebirth, the goal of meditation has been watered down to simply being a method for coping with this short span of years, to find peace and freedom from the frazzle of modern life. It's not necessarily a criticism, as not to meditate would be madness itself given that it offers us so much. But isn't it awe-inspiring to think that we can meditate to manage the ups and downs of everyday life *and* maybe take our improved selves into a next life, to eventually find 'paradise' or 'liberation' – a permanent freedom from dissatisfaction and suffering? It's such a hope-filled goal and gives us such meaning and purpose.

The Zen Master's quotation below powerfully captures the ultimate goal of meditation – to look within in order to find truth. It's a bit of a mouthful – but go with it. Let it take you beyond the page, out of the window and up into space. When you're ready, come back and find out how to take this inspiration from dreaming to reality.

"Meditation opens the mind of humankind to the greatest mystery that takes place daily and hourly; it widens the heart so that it may feel the eternity of time and infinity of space in every throb; it gives us a life within the world as if we were moving about in paradise; and all these spiritual deeds take place without any refuge into a doctrine, but by the simple and direct holding fast to the truth which dwells in our innermost beings."

Shunryu Suzuki
Zen Mind, Beginner's Mind

Reality meditation

There are a few other issues about meditation that it's helpful to clarify. So here we go with what it's not (in brief).

Meditation isn't:

- About emptying the mind – it's about *focusing* the mind
- An opportunity to space out and avoid looking after the kids
- Selfish – we need to help ourselves before we are equipped to help others
- For those who are scared of looking at what's on their mind
- About contemplating one's navel (I've never really understood that)
- For anyone suffering from a mental or physical illness that may not benefit from turning inwards (you need a degree of mental and physical strength, so if you are in a fragile or vulnerable state be sure to seek medical advice before you meditate)
- A reason to feel all saintly and superior

Meditation enables us to know ourselves more *honestly*. Because it calms and relaxes the mind, it increases our sense of wellbeing so we can be more gentle with ourselves. Instead of giving ourselves a mental slap with negative self-talk ("You're such an idiot!"), we can have a rational internal discussion instead. In this way, we learn to trust our inner self, just like we'd trust a kind aunt more than a strict parent (who is so attached to us and may be terrified we're going to mess up). Remember, our inner self is our best friend.

Using meditation to train our minds leads to greater self-knowledge and self-development because we discover our higher nature and strengthen that rather than the voice of our ego. As we meditate, we sit in tolerant acceptance of the internal chatter, much like we would with a small child who is finding their way in the world, letting everything be, while, in the words of Joseph Campbell,[5] we *"learn to rock with the waves"*.

Mindfulness meditation

Let's bring mindfulness back into focus now and get clarity about where it fits with meditation, before I gently lead you by the hand to your meditation seat.

In ancient India, mindfulness *was* meditation. The Sanskrit word for mindfulness actually translates to 'non-forgetfulness' or 'recollection'. In order to find greater truths, one needs mindfulness to keep the inner eye on the ball. Mindfulness helps us remember. It's like looking through a telescope and adjusting the lens to see that rare bird clearly – without all the other distracting fauna and flora.

We understand mindfulness now as a *type* of meditation. (There are other types, which I explain later in this chapter.)

Our contentment strongly depends on the state of our minds, and mindfulness meditation stabilises the mind by removing the clutter accumulated through sensory involvement. Through mindfulness meditation, we aim to pacify the mind by observing the body, feelings and mental states without conceptualising about our experiences ("I'm itchy – that hurts", "My skin is prickly – I don't like it", "I need a snack – I'm hungry", and so on). We can see what's actually happening and consider what we imagine to be happening, or what elaboration we add to the experience through our storytelling and the ego's need to substantiate and satisfy itself.

We pay 'bare attention' to the object of meditation (the body, the feelings, the thoughts). It's like standing naked in front of the mirror and seeing yourself as you really are, without judgement.

---

5   Joseph Campbell was an American professor of literature who worked in comparative mythology and comparative religion. His work covers many aspects of the inner human experience. The full quotation reads: "In meditating, meditate on your own divinity. The goal of life is to be a vehicle for something higher. Keep your eyes up there between the world of opposites watching your 'play' in the world. Let the world be as it is and learn to rock with the waves."

Our experience is then a direct presentation to the senses, with no decoration or disguise, and no prejudicial view.

We observe, but we don't identify with the thoughts that arise, which we allow to dissolve in our minds rather than solidifying them. The view is that our thoughts are not us.

They come and go, like tourists, but our awareness is home. There's no judgement, assessment or any kind of dramatic appraisal – we're just looking. As we sit, we experience greater levels of peace, awareness and insight into our reality as it actually is, not what we make it (with us on centre-stage, personalising everything we encounter), so we are able to allow mental and emotional commentaries to fall away. We can then take this attitude into our daily lives. That's when we're being mindful.

Perhaps you can understand why mindfulness meditation is simple but not easy. Who hasn't, at some point, stood in front of a mirror and at the very least focused on an imperfection (or, at the other end of the spectrum, felt self-loathing)? We will all be aware of how our mind creates our reality. Someone suffering from body dysmorphia, like anorexia, will look in the mirror and see an obese person, while someone else standing alongside them may see them as being painfully thin. The main error is to see the body as the self. It's not. It's just a vehicle.

In mindfulness meditation, we merely notice the 'object' of our attention. We can't be *completely* free from conceptualisation, but as the mind gets used to the practice, it becomes more skilled at allowing an experience to just be. By practising mindfulness meditation, we can make our thoughts less habitual, with a certain kind of self-discipline, using our breath as the gentle reminder to let go of thoughts. It's like gently pulling on the lead of a puppy that constantly wants to run off. Then we can pay more bare attention and get a clearer picture of exactly what is being presented to our senses to find *"the truth which dwells in our innermost beings"*.

This truth is that everything is impermanent in nature, and therefore unreliable in terms of providing us with happiness. By observing the ebb and flow of our experiences in meditation, we can begin to deal with life differently. Not identifying with our thoughts is immediately liberating.

Let them go. They are not you.

In Buddhist practice, mindfulness is a tool for developing profound levels of concentration and insight into the ultimate reality of human existence. It's like watching a 3D movie – when we put on those charming glasses, we're suddenly presented with a depth of reality we couldn't see before. You can do this too because there's no one stopping you except yourself.

We practise mindfulness *in* meditation (mindfulness meditation), and then *out* of meditation we can bring that same quality of non-judgemental awareness into our lives (being mindful). It's like opening a window to let in the fresh air.

Other meditation techniques

There are two main types of meditation used for different purposes: stabilising and analytical meditations. Mindfulness meditation stabilises the mind. It's always necessary to stabilise the mind to begin a meditation, but then you could move on to a different kind of meditation.

Analytical meditation

By thinking about concepts such as impermanence (the inevitability of change), or compassion (understanding interconnection and developing concern for others), we think in a focused way. We're not wandering about like we're on a country ramble; instead, we're deliberately setting our mind on a topic to check on our understanding. There is a goal. We use 'good psychology' to see if the way we think is contributing to our happiness and peace of mind, or whether it is stoking the fire of dissatisfaction and anxiety. Good psychology is psychology that works for us, makes rational good sense and increases our confidence and self-esteem. (Part Two of this book will go into the details of 'good psychology'.) The purpose of analytical meditation is to move from an ego-centred way of looking at problems – influenced by our conditioning, others' opinions and our materialistic concerns – to find the truth of our problems. It's not brainwashing, it's like an anti-virus.

It protects us from junk thoughts.

Internal analysis helps us to develop a more realistic view of ourselves, and the world around us. It checks our assumptions about what we think is happening and helps us reflect rationally on daily problems. We should never believe a concept because we're told to, or because others think it, but check from our own experience. Examining topics enables us to challenge our ideas and come to our own conclusions. We become our own teacher – or therapist (at no charge).

Analytical meditation takes the form of an internal debate and may also use visual imagery as we recall episodes from our lives. It is essentially an experiential study of the self. We're under the microscope.

During an analytical meditation, if we have an intuitive experience – like an inner light bulb being turned on, or a warm feeling of bliss – we can hold the feeling and drop the analysis. This experience is telling us we have realised a truth. Then, when the feeling fades, we can resume our investigation without attachment or excitement towards the experience. But later, allow yourself to feel happy because it is such an achievement! It is a small spiritual rebellion.

Visualisation techniques

Utilising our creative imagination, we can visualise anything that will support our meditation. This may be as simple as visualising clouds in the sky or waves rolling onto a beach as analogies for thoughts coming and going (stabilising meditation), or reviewing a remembered unpleasant incident to analyse how we might have behaved to change the outcome (analytical mediation).

Throughout the book I share meditations that are stabilising, analytical and use visualisation. You get the full monty.

Guided meditations – turn inwards, tune in and watch

A guided meditation is exactly what it says on the tin. Someone else guides you through the meditation, gently giving you instructions and space in which to meditate, to keep you on track. Sitting with someone or listening to someone guide you through a meditation is like having a good tour guide point out all the sights and then bring you back home. You're too interested to wander off.

You can access guided meditations on many different apps and websites. Almost everyone has access to podcasts these days. At the back of this book (in the section 'Appendix: List of Guided Audio Meditations'), I list all of the meditations referred to in this book and explain where you can find them as audio versions (indicated throughout this book by the symbol of a conch shell) and transcribed versions (in case you would like to read them first). From here on, maybe it's a good idea to keep your phone and the earpiece of your choice by your side.

So, now we know about the different meditation methods, let's look at the preliminaries.

The Preliminaries: preparing to meditate

Approach all meditations with these 'undressed attitudes':

- **No expectations.** To begin with, just give up any expectations of yourself. Take the pressure off.

- **No meditation.** This sounds contradictory, but it simply means not to make your meditation something special.

- **No result.** Again, accept the contradiction of not aiming for something. Wanting a certain result can set us up for failure.

When we put on clothes, to some extent we create an image, but these undressed attitudes are without adornment and open us up to an authentic way of being within the meditation. Traditionally, they are known as the Three Purities.

So just do it, and develop a good habit that will support you throughout your life, in good times and bad. Sometimes your meditation will fall into fluffy drowsiness or escalate into flights of fancy. Sometimes your meditation will feel blissful; sometimes it will be really difficult. Just rock with the waves, as the man says.

Building a solid foundation

Start with your body. You need to be comfortable yet alert.

You are not just a mind, floating in space, but you have a body that needs to support you, and physical attributes that can aid you. Think of your meditation like a pyramid.

At the base is ***relaxation***

(checking and correcting your posture, breathing and tension levels).

You build on that by ***stabilising*** the mind

(by following the breath or visualising sky or seascapes).

Your fuel is your heartfelt ***motivation***

(stating your intention).

Then, at the pinnacle, you develop ***watchfulness***

(sometimes known as *vigilance*).

LISTEN

How to Meditate: Beginner's Instruction meditation

As these instructions are the crucial foundation for all meditations, I describe the stages of this beginner's instruction meditation in full in the following sections.

Relaxation

You are at the base of the meditation pyramid: relaxation. This has three parts to it: posture, breathing and a body scan to release tensions.

Posture

You can meditate while lying down, standing, walking or sitting. You can choose to sit on a chair, but lotus (sitting cross-legged with each foot on top of the opposite thigh) or half-lotus (with only one foot on the opposite thigh) yoga positions are ideal for those who can.

The key is to be free from tension, and to be comfortable yet alert.

Feeling sleepy and woolly isn't meditation. So your body needs to be uncurled – you're not in the womb – and alert. You're not turning off, but tuning in to your inner TV.

Sitting and lying postures.

If you're sitting on a chair, the back needs to be straight with the shoulders down and the chin slightly tipped forward so the neck is straight. Uncross the feet and place them firmly on the floor. Ensure the height of your seat enables you to do this. If you're seated on a cushion, or kneeling, your legs will fold, and your hands will be on each knee, palms either downwards or upwards. Your hands need to be in a position where you can forget about them because they're so comfortable. You want to avoid finger fiddling.

If you prefer lying down then when you are flat on your back, you place your hands above your bottom to gently push the buttocks down while straightening and lengthening the spine. A mat will be more comfortable than a bare floor, and a small cushion may help to support the neck, depending on your age and strength. Then you take your arms out from behind your back and place them a little way from your sides with the hands palm upwards in an open and loose way. Nothing about the posture is tight or controlled.

You loosen your facial muscles so that the lips are softly touching, the jaw is relaxed and the tongue is resting loosely on the roof of your mouth. Your eyes can be closed or half-closed, gently gazing at a space about one metre ahead on the ground if you're sitting, or up at the ceiling if you're lying down. Keep a soft focus. Having your eyes open helps you stay alert for longer meditations, but you're not looking *at* anything.

Over time, you'll naturally develop a sense of the most comfortable meditation position for yourself. In the meantime, you may like to try this seven-point checklist to mentally remind yourself of your posture.

Check the position and comfort of your:

- Bottom
- Hands
- Backbone
- Mouth, jaw and tongue
- Head
- Eyes
- Shoulders

Then, focus on the breath:

Breathing

The next part of the relaxation stage is abdominal or deep breathing. Abdominal breathing can feel counterintuitive to begin with, but stick with it. When you breathe in, you balloon your stomach; and when you breathe out, the stomach distends, moving towards the spine. Shallow breathing from the chest just doesn't give you enough oxygen.

Try taking some deep abdominal breaths:

- Start with three deep abdominal breaths to oxygenate the brain and let go of obvious tension in the body. Inhale through the nostrils, exhaling softly through the mouth in a controlled and regular way and allowing the abdomen to fill and empty.

- Continue with natural, regular breathing in and out of the nostrils if possible, but still from the abdomen. It should feel effortless.

When you get used to relaxing and using the abdomen like this, you'll enjoy taking a few deep breaths whenever you need 'a breathing space' during your day.

Body scan

The third part of the relaxation stage is the body scan, which relaxes subtle tensions and corrects your posture. Your mind checks over your body like a medical scanner and it registers any tension, no matter how slight, if you fully focus. People love it; it's so relaxing that it can send you into deep relaxation (or even to sleep!).

A full body scan is a meditation in itself, and is also called *mindfulness of the body*. It usually lasts about 25 minutes. Thoughts subside as you rest your awareness on your body. The body scan releases the more subtle tensions you carry unconsciously simply by bringing them into your awareness.

 LISTEN

Full Body Scan/Mindfulness of the Body meditation

When you conduct a body scan meditation, you're like an inner scientist, travelling through your body with a mental microscope, super aware, very focused and objective – no liking or disliking – as you relax your body, releasing all tension as you go, before you move on to the next part of your body. The purpose is to be free from the distractions of the external world and focused on an object of concentration within your immediate experience, like the air in your nostrils or the rise and fall of the abdomen. You will feel what are called gross sensations – obvious ones, like itches and aches, or sensations of heat and cold – and then more subtle sensations, like feeling your heartbeat in every part of your body and the throb of blood as it passes through your veins, or the tension held in muscles you didn't previously know you had.

A sensation like an itch provides you with a good opportunity to practise objectivity. Observe the sensation, experiencing the subtle changes until it passes. Avoid reacting to it and scratching it. If you feel cold, observe that sensation deeply until you can let go of your judgements. This is true mindfulness of the body because you are stabilising, calming and focusing the mind *using* your body. Your body becomes the object of the meditation. Conceptual thoughts largely diminish and you can become aware of any tension felt in a body part. The body scan dissolves stress as you become aware of more and more layers of tension in the body and release them.

When you get used to the practice, the body scan can be a much shorter check-up for relaxation purposes before you move on to a different meditation – and as I mentioned, it's also an effective aid for getting to sleep! If you use it for this, then you lie flat on your back in bed and roll over onto your side as soon as you feel drowsy (and before you start snoring!). Many people fall asleep during my guided body scans as we do this lying down on yoga mats with cushions and blankets, often during a busy work-day. It's a great power nap!

Stabilisation

Following relaxation (posture, breathing, and quick or slow body scan), the second step of the meditation pyramid is stabilisation. To stabilise the mind you practise *mindfulness of the breath.* Following the gentle flow of your breath as it passes in and out of your body enables you to let go of thoughts, focus your attention and attain a more spacious mind. Stabilisation meditation can lead to a very pleasant and serene state of mind.

Mindfulness of the breath is the main method and the starting point, but visualisation techniques can also be brought in to stabilise the mind, like watching your thoughts as if they are clouds in the sky or waves rolling onto the shore.

Start every meditation with mindfulness of the breath. If you wish to extend your stabilisation into mindfulness meditation as a practice in itself, you can practise mindfulness of the breath for longer. It's as simple as that. Mindfulness of the breath would then increase your focused concentration.

 LISTEN

Mindful Breathing: ten minutes of clarity meditation
This meditation turns the preparation into the main event.

Another stabilisation method is to focus on the rise and fall of the belly as the air enters and leaves the body. Focusing on your abdominal breathing is useful if you have a very excited mind because it takes you away from your brain and into your body. It is still the breath that you are attending to.

"Just as in the last month of the hot season, when a mass of dust and dirt has swirled up, a great rain cloud, out of season, disperses it and quells it on the spot, so too concentration by mindfulness of breathing, when developed and cultivated, is peaceful and sublime. It is an ambrosial dwelling, and it disperses and quells on the spot unwholesome states whenever they arise."

The Buddha

Samyutta Nikaya, from a discourse of the Buddha

This quotation of the Buddha is an insight into the eternal relevance of stabilising our minds, despite its archaic turns of phrase. Notice that the Buddha refers to thoughts in general as 'unwholesome states.' This is a very delicate and complex point. You may notice that positive or constructive thoughts arise, but the practice of mindfulness meditation is to let go of *all* thoughts. You will be aware of their nature, but you do not distinguish. In this way, all thoughts are 'unwholesome' because they obstruct your ability to reach unwavering clarity and concentration.

During this stabilisation practice, you will find the spaciousness between your thoughts. Rest there. If this brings fear, then habituate yourself with spaciousness, enjoy the taste of it without chasing it. That's a challenge. How can you have an ice cream without wanting more? Enjoy it for what it is, but don't grasp onto the idea that it will bring you happiness – that's how. And now you're meditating on impermanence – the inevitability of change! And don't be afraid of spaciousness in your mind. Sometimes new practitioners are terrified that they might lose themselves if they stop thinking. It's okay. You're still there. It's like coming home – rest.

Motivation

Once the mind is relatively stable, you can set your motivation, which helps you commit to the practice and resist distraction. Motivation during the opening stages of every meditation is important because the mind easily wanders. "I am doing this meditation in order to develop concentration" might be a simple motivation.

Meditation isn't a worldly pursuit but a spiritual practice used to become not only calmer and more peaceful, but also more in tune with your innate goodness and the potential for development that lies within you. Therefore, another good motivation is to set yourself up with the aim of being a better person – though first you need to understand what you mean by a 'better person'. If you add 'for the benefit of other beings', then you decrease your chances of meditating for selfish reasons and increase certain qualities, such as loving-kindness. So your motivation may look like this:

"I'm going to meditate to increase my focus and concentration. When I'm able to do that, I'll be less confused by disturbing thoughts. This will lead me to being more rational and more kind to benefit myself and others."

Motivation is like any activity. It's much more likely to be beneficial if you're clear about why you're doing it. "I'm calling my friend because I think she's unhappy" is much more likely to result in a phone call than if there's no motivation. It's that simple.

When you set your motivation, you are opening yourself up to Shunryu Suzuki's *"truth which dwells in our innermost beings"* – which makes meditation a spiritual practice. If you are clear as to why you are meditating, then it sets the stage for the actual event. It's a mental prop.

Watchfulness

At the peak of the meditation pyramid is watchfulness. Relaxation, stabilisation and watchfulness are interconnected and support each other. Any time you notice a thought arising during your meditation practice, let it go and return to the breath. Watchfulness ensures you pull on that lead and rein in your undisciplined puppy-mind. Eventually, it will learn to walk alongside you and, one day, behind you. You'll be totally in control.

Don't indulge the mind by letting it get drowsy and sleepy, or by following thoughts because they're exciting or interesting. Drowsiness and excitement are the main enemies of meditation. If you get drowsy, half open your eyes to let in some light, and focus more intently on the sensation of the breath at the tip of your nostrils. Stay here and let the belly do its own thing. If you get excited and thoughts are rampaging around your mind, then that is the time to get away from the brain and bring your attention down into your body, feeling the passage of air passing through you. You could also return to the body scan as a method for calming the mind. Bringing your attention to the breath will enable you to *notice* the thoughts rather than avoid them. It's important to manage excitement and drowsiness rather than letting these inner hooligans take control.

If you're really struggling to still your mind, you can try using an external object of meditation, like a plant, a candle or an image, to enhance your concentration. When you're ready, you can then close your eyes and visualise what you have just seen. The attention to an object will help you keep focused.

Develop a state of mindful awareness where the observer mind is very vigilant, like the caring owner of that puppy, or a teacher saying your name whenever your concentration wanders, ensuring that you remain mindful of your breathing.

If you have things on your conscience or you are excited by stuff that's going on in your external world, then it is always more difficult to meditate as these are very distracting states of mind. If you behave ethically, your conscience is clear, and if you lead a relatively simple life then you won't crave too much pleasure, so then these attitudes will support your meditation because you will already be relatively calm.

Recap: Making your preparation

I start every meditation with the instruction 'make your preparation.' Basically, it means following all the advice outlined earlier. Here it is, summarised:

- Enter the meditation with the helpful attitude of the **Three Purities.**
- **Relax** the body by finding a comfortable posture and taking three abdominal breaths to refresh your body and mind.

- Check the body for tension with a body scan and then do a few rounds of abdominal breathing to **stabilise** the mind. Then follow the sensation of the breath entering and leaving your nostrils and let your thoughts go.

- Make your **motivation** for doing the meditation and then begin the meditation.

- With mindfulness meditation, you will then focus on developing **watchfulness.** If you are doing an analytical meditation or focusing on a visualisation technique then that will follow instead, although you still need to be vigilant that your visualisations and analysis don't turn into catastrophising dramas.

My story – meditation and me

When I learned to meditate I found it incredibly hard work. I'm very much a doer and it totally went against the grain for me. Sitting still and following the breath seemed counterintuitive to achieving anything! But I persisted and usually found myself either drifting off into flights of fancy about how I was going to become enlightened before anyone else and stun everyone there, or dozing off.

Living in the Institute was exciting and in itself a major distraction. The students came from all over the world to this unusual seat of learning, and we could indulge our social life, in between working on projects that would stabilise and expand this incredible place. Falling in love was a regular feature in everyone's lives, and the people were suitable objects of attachment – beautiful, youthful and exotic. I was not immune.

The 13 years I spent there taught me more about life and being human than anything I had learned in school or college, but I was a victim of strong desires like so many people, and wasn't ready for the discipline required for extensive formal meditation. This isn't to say that I didn't follow the teachings, but I balanced them with the pursuits of the young: parties, gatherings and intrigues. I wasn't alone. This was a mainly youthful lay community; as well as the monastic students, several families established themselves there and liaisons were formed.

One of the strong and powerful features of Tibetan Buddhist meditation is its emphasis on analytical meditation. We were taught to use visualisation methods to deeply contemplate topics that disputed our ordinary views of life. These are very detailed meditations with a systematic approach to learning. There were many topics: the preciousness of our human lives, and the rarity of its opportunities; the impermanent nature of existence, and how death can come at any time, thus increasing the importance of taking opportunities for spiritual development while we could. We also considered worldly concerns and their shortcomings. We looked at all the suffering in the world, in all the different realms of existence (Buddhism has a vast view of where and how we might be reborn), and we developed compassion through equanimity with a systematic step-by-step method. At the end of the meditations we would dissolve the learning into our hearts, and we always generated compassion for all beings, sitting with the realisations to which we had arrived. These were intended to change our minds, not in a superficial, intellectual way, but in a deep and profound way that would ultimately change our very actions. There was an array of meditations on the menu that accompanied each of the teachings, to bring them from intellectual pursuits to spiritual realisations.

There's a maxim in Buddhism concerning the levels of learning. This advice comes through a strong and ancient oral tradition, which is said to come directly from the Buddha himself. First, one hears the teachings, then one thinks about them and finally meditates on them. This takes the meaning into our hearts, as simply thinking is like watering the garden just on the surface, but never getting to the roots for growth. Of course, now we can access teachings from books and videos, but there's something about meeting a teacher, hearing them talk and making a connection with them that Buddhists would call a blessing. Simply put, it's like the fertiliser you sprinkle on a newly planted flower bed. It gives you extra nourishment.

This branch of Tibetan Buddhism belonged to the 'Gelug pa' tradition. It is the most dominant school of Tibetan Buddhism that focuses on study as a basis for spiritual progression, as exemplified by the Dalai Lama. The Dalai Lama advises us that meditation and prayer are not enough for spiritual progression, and it's through study we come to understand and are able to evaluate the teachings against our own experience. Mindfulness meditation was a preamble to relax and stabilise the mind before we launched into topics that messed with our egos and challenged everything we had ever thought, or never thought about in our lives, and what it is to be human.

When we finally left the Institute, after a schism that broke the hearts of many of us, it took me some time to recover. However, family life, teaching at school and re-entering a country community kept me busy and grounded. When I eventually felt ready to re-enter spiritual projects, I established a centre for spiritual learning to bring different spiritual practices, such as yoga, t'ai chi and Buddhist teachings, under one roof. My mind was soaked in Buddhist psychology by then, having totally aligned myself to the topics that had re-educated me. Actually, that sounds a bit like brainwashing, but it was never like that. I sat at the feet of these Tibetan Lamas because the conventional version of life that Western society offered didn't sit well with me. This had isolated me in social and work situations and confused me about who I was, and why I didn't fit in. The Institute and the people in it felt like home. I had come home. It was only much later that I realised it was not the place and the people but Tibetan Buddhism itself that had led me to finding my home. My authentic self.

My aim for the centre was to balance traditional Buddhist ways with meditations that were more suitable for the Western mind; suitable for 'ordinary' people that weren't religious at all.

Several teachers we invited stand out from those days. Alan Wallace[6] has an extraordinary mind and is now one of the foremost Western Buddhist teachers. His Buddhist education came from mixed traditions, and he was committed to sharing what he had learned with Westerners. We invited him several times, and his teachings on mindfulness finally permeated my distracted mind. He taught mindfulness meditation, unlike the analytical and visualisation meditations I'd been taught by the Tibetans. Finally, it seemed I was ready for a more stabilising style of meditation, and I began to actually enjoy it and want to sit and turn inwards.

Another great teacher was a Tibetan, Geshe Tashi Tsering.[7] He visited our group for 11 years, coming twice a year to expand and deepen our knowledge. He has a great understanding of the Western mind, and he soon realised how much we needed stabilising meditation. Mindfulness became more and more popular and we became better meditators for it. I owe my career in mindfulness training principally to these two amazing teachers who continue to nourish my mind.

I can honestly say that, despite all my immersion in the magnificent content of Tibetan Buddhist psychology and philosophy I received from the Lamas, it wasn't until I engaged with these teachers, so many years later, that I truly learned to stabilise my mind. However, the analytical meditations had softened and prepared me, as by then I was mentally cooked in Buddhist thought. I was like a stick of rock that revealed the word 'Buddhism' with every bite. These experiences informed the way I teach and continue to adapt the teachings to suit people who don't have my background. I was driven to share their wisdom with as many people as possible.

---

6   Professor B. Alan Wallace is an American scholar and practitioner of Buddhism. He was ordained as a Buddhist monk for 14 years and now lives in Santa Barbara, California, where he founded the Santa Barbara Institute for Consciousness Studies. He is renowned for bringing the meditational disciplines found within differing Buddhist disciplines together to provide clear meditation practices for Western Buddhists.

7   Geshe Tashi Tsering is currently abbot of Sera Mey Monastic University in India. From 1994 to 2018, he was the resident Tibetan Buddhist teacher at Jamyang Buddhist Centre, London.

Reflections

- ○ Are you crystal clear now on what mindfulness, mindfulness meditation and other types of meditation are and how to practise them? I hope so.
- ○ While practising mindfulness of the breath, consider the two voices in your head: the ego chattering away, and the whispering observer, quietly reining it in. This is your conscious connection with your subconscious 'inner self'.

Authentic mindfulness

- ○ Being mindful is an important part of spiritual practice. It destroys prejudices and judgements.
- ○ As well as practising mindfulness meditation, it is important to utilise analytical meditation if you are intent on developing your 'self'.
- ○ It's best to have a relaxed and flexible attitude to how you meditate, or it will feel like 'work' rather than enjoyment.

Spiritual integrity

- ○ Distractions are worldly pastimes and we need to recognise them for what they are. Enjoy your life, while recognising that our real purpose is to develop spiritual qualities.
- ○ The Three Purities are a useful guideline for living life generally. Expectations can lead to disappointment; concretising a project or activity is inflexible and being fixed on certain results can lead to frustration.

So now you know all about meditation, you can investigate 'the greatest mystery' of your life and 'widen your heart'. Once you have read the chapters that detail good psychology (see Part Two of this book) then you might revisit this chapter to understand the process in more depth. Enjoy the adventure.

Chapter 3

Being Human

○ ○ ○

Being born into this world as a human is a mysterious and extraordinary thing. It is possibly one of our most dangerous experiences as we emerge from the shelter and protection of our mother's womb into the unknown. It is choiceless and fraught with uncertainty. Who hasn't said at one time or another to their bemused parents, "Well, I didn't ask to be born!"

So, what constitutes a human being? What are the essential ingredients that, when put together, make up this marvellous mortal?

Bodies to die for

Our bodies are delicate yet perversely resilient: imperfect and subject to sickness, ageing and death like all other beings, yet perfectly equipped for survival. We are born with an innate sense of beauty and what is 'normal', and this tendency to judge what is pleasing or displeasing to the senses takes much of our energy. We spend a substantial amount of our money on making our bodies look good, feel good and remain youthful, as if the sole purpose of our life was to improve our appearance. However, the most important goal in our effort to maintain our bodies is not our appearance but our health and wellbeing. Having a human body gives us advantages over the animals, and recognising that the body is precious because of the opportunities it gives us for self-development, must be our greatest realisation.

To be born as a human who connects with spiritual teachings is arguably even more fortunate. In Buddhism it is called something special – *a* perfect or precious human life. Buddhist teachings say that it is unusual, like a flash of lightning on a dark, cloudy night, or, more quirkily, as likely as a blind turtle, who surfaces above the ocean only once every hundred years, managing to put its head through a golden ring floating somewhere on its surface. In other words, like winning the lottery. The reason for landing one of these impressive bodies is given as practising morality, generosity and having spiritual inclination in past lives. Of course, first of all one needs to work from the premise that we have had countless lives, which is common in many cultures – not only for Buddhists but also Hindus, Sikhs, some Christians and Native Americans, among others.

Being a human being is highly valued because it is only with our large, rational brains that we can make spiritual progress. Buddhists talk about many realms in which we might be reborn, including as an animal. The problem is that in these realms of existence there is said to be huge attachment: to food, sex, the past, pleasure, hatred (yes, we can be attached to hatred as a way of expressing ourselves) and many other distractions that centre on the comfort and pleasure of our most basic instincts… and those beautiful rational brains are missing.

Whatever you believe, it does seem quite extraordinary to be human. And to be a human who has the leisure to investigate why we are human, and what to do with it when we've got it, is even more remarkable. At some point, we all wonder: "Why am I me?"

Try the following exercise as an analytical meditation (see Chapter 2 for more information about analytical meditation) or perhaps as a reflective walk. You can also try this in a bar or café, quietly observing humanity play out.

 **LISTEN**

My Precious Human Life meditation

Sensory overload

We are sensory beings, just like animals, yet separated from the simplicity of survival instincts by a brain that has evolved into something much more complex than requiring food and a friendly pat. From the beginning, we are built to process our sensory experiences into an intricate system of dividing what we want from what we don't want, and then spend the rest of our lives dominated by the desire to satisfy these complex cravings and aversions.

When we're done with life, or life has done with us, we don't want to leave without a legacy – so making the most of it must be a priority. Of course, being able to enjoy life as sensory beings is truly a gift. The world with its wonders, nature's grandeur, and being an integral part of land, sea and sky, is awe-inspiring and humbling. But we now live with sensory bombardment, and our brains seem to operate like slot machines – a game of chance with a quick pay-out before we move on to the next thrill.

As we fill our minds with more and more stuff, it becomes increasingly difficult to slow the mind, be mindful and meditate, and let go of all the information and imagery we witness each day. So, ironically, it has become necessary for us to look to holistic activities like meditation and yoga for relaxation.

Mindfulness meditation is a good antidote to sensory bombardment – a method we can utilise to turn away from external stimulation and find calm and creativity within. Relentless stimulation causes our imaginations to race from thought to thought like the proverbial headless chickens, trying to find satisfaction. We literally create anxieties and worries related to this endless pursuit, so utilising mindfulness helps us find the calm space to replace these disturbing ways of thinking and so remove the stressors to find deep reservoirs of peace that can then support spiritual development.

Beautiful brains

Back to our brains – because they are the reason why humans are so truly amazing. They have so much power. They've developed a lot since we started walking upright about six million years ago, and they still have prehistoric tendencies to make us want to fight or flee, plus a super-softie survival tendency to take care of our offspring. What makes us so stand-up superb is the 'rational' brain that is the latest development in this particular model of *Homo sapiens*. It's this bit of the brain that separates us from the animals and that we can train to behave in a way that will bring us peace and contentment, rather than wasting it on superficial human pursuits like wealth and power.

The important thing to remember about the brain is that, no matter how wonderful it is, it's quite out of control – until we have engaged with it in a way that manages and moves it towards developing spiritual realisations. Our brain is like an orchestra without a conductor. It's going to make a cacophony of noise and be completely dependent on who is playing the loudest instrument at the time, until you, the maestro, take control.

Magnificent minds

The whole point of having a precious life is all to do with the brain and how we can alter its programming. We all have differing brain capacity in terms of intelligence, but our brains are flexible in their neuroplasticity so we can reprogramme them. But the *mind* is the boss. The mind is difficult to define and we confuse it with the brain, but Buddhism, mindfulness and, more recently, neuroscientific psychology work from the experiential premise that they are different. (I discuss this in much more detail in Chapter 4.)

Our awareness (which is like a mirror that reflects and comes to know objects) meets a mug of tea with our sight and touch awarenesses (i.e. eyes, hands and lips) and responds depending on our previous experience of that object.

Our sensory experiences are then processed by our mental

awareness/consciousness. It's how we identify and categorise objects. Our mental awareness is where our worries, anxieties, planning and processing take place. It's our mental awareness that informs the brain.

The following figure may help you get your head around this.

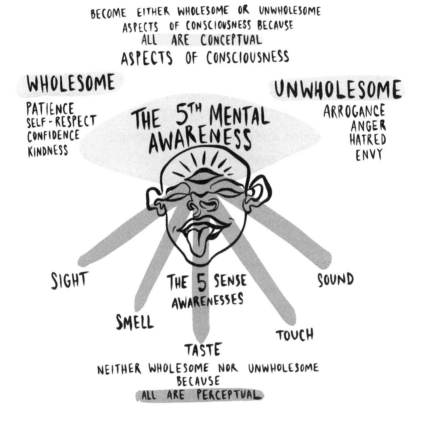

BECOME EITHER WHOLESOME OR UNWHOLESOME
ASPECTS OF CONSCIOUSNESS BECAUSE
ALL ARE CONCEPTUAL
ASPECTS OF CONSCIOUSNESS

WHOLESOME

PATIENCE
SELF-RESPECT
CONFIDENCE
KINDNESS

THE 5TH MENTAL AWARENESS

UNWHOLESOME

ARROGANCE
ANGER
HATRED
ENVY

SIGHT

THE 5 SENSE AWARENESSES

SOUND

SMELL

TASTE

TOUCH

NEITHER WHOLESOME NOR UNWHOLESOME
BECAUSE
ALL ARE PERCEPTUAL

A model of how the mind knows objects.

When we experience something through our senses, it is *perceptual*. This means that for a nano-second the sensation is pure experience. But it almost instantly becomes *conceptual* as our mental awareness starts to sort it out into 'nice' or 'not nice'. Do I like the taste of pickled onions or not? Do I like hearing someone shout at me or not? That's the work of the mental awareness.

So, the mental awareness then reacts. Pickled onions are perhaps a matter of, well, taste (genetics, culture, physiological stuff), but shouting is a different matter. Because then we're under attack, and frightened, so we put up the big red flag of warning because we feel threatened. Emotions then get involved, like interfering relatives, and if our mental awareness is untrained then we react to defend ourselves. Reactions arise automatically, so we get ready to fight or run. We are soon conditioned by a whole gamut of experiences that throw us around from pillar to post, or maybe from one person or experience to another, as we try to make sense of events. And without understanding this basic concept, we're in danger of being conditioned into irrational, emotional wrecks, who will falter at any drama and make crises out of them, when they could be avoided. And life sends us many dramas.

You see, the mental awareness has a choice – whether to go down the BIG REACTION route (which leads to disturbing emotions), or to be more rational and go down the REASONABLE RESPONSE route (which leads to calming emotions).

Animals have minds too, but they are limited by their brain capacity for analysis or making choices about how to live their lives. We know that some remarkable animals display emotions like empathy, and qualities such as courage, so we can't feel too superior. The main point here is that we do have superior intelligence and the ability to communicate intelligent thoughts due to our beautiful brains. All beings have minds, but only humans have amazing brains.

So, these are our basics. The underwear of our humanity. Now let's look at the clothing.

Continual conditioning

Conditioning is key to understanding ourselves. The Buddha called life 'conditioned existence' because we live our lives according to our conditioning, and we need to be aware of what is destructive within that conditioning in order to change it. Conditioning is more than being influenced. It is how we become what we are. The influences are so deep and so subtle that we think we are a certain way out of choice, but actually we are mainly just a result of our conditioning.

Our family, peer group, culture and religious beliefs all condition us to think and act in a certain way – and we can't depend on others having a positive influence on us. We all have experiences in our lives of bullying, hankering to fit in and wanting to be 'normal'. We think we're unique but, although that's true, we are clones really –forming an identity to fit in. Observe a group of teenagers: they don't look unique, although they wish to appear to be different to other age groups. They wear the same clothes, have the same hairstyles, desperate to be like each other, and all hold a phone like a mirror, reflecting themselves – in whatever social media app they're scrolling through – back to themselves.

For sure, we come with our own tendencies, but the rest is dependent on conditioning.

My story – my conditioning

I grew up in the 1960s. At that time (and it's not so different now) there was the concept of a route to happiness that everyone could achieve, having gone way beyond the Second World War to a society that had aspirations. Like many women of that time, my mother was a housewife, and was appraised by her ability to cook and keep the house clean. My dad was a travelling salesman, although he preferred to call himself a Sales Executive. I was quite intelligent and managed to get into a grammar school, although I was a dreamer by nature and destined never to achieve academically. Because I was a bit clever, my mum used to say I'd make a good doctor's wife. I didn't pay her much attention because I was going to be an actress, and you didn't need qualifications for that.

However, I was conditioned as a product of the culture at that time to fantasise about 'true love'. So I dreamed my way through secondary school and flirted a lot. Songs of the '60s were all about love. Not philanthropic love, but plain old sex and romance. Like most teenagers, I was desperate for an object for my fantasies and soon settled on a handsome boy who had the sexual expertise of someone twice his age. He fulfilled one part of my dream, but we weren't really a match. I didn't care; I was following the dream of there being one true love for everyone, like the songs said. We married, but within a few years discovered that it wasn't true love, and romance was not bringing happiness. We were conditioned. Conditioned by an ideal, put out there by a society that was intent on selling a dream – one true love, marriage for life, home, job, family, retirement, thank you and goodnight.

Personal tendencies

Our understanding of conditioning could suggest there's no such thing as character and personality, but that's not the case. So, why aren't I the same as my siblings, who had similar conditioning? What makes us each unique?

Tendencies are those things that individualise us. They form our character and personality. Genetically, we have certain tendencies, whether it's the tendency to lose our hair in middle age or gain weight after the menopause. As well as our physical tendencies, we may have a tendency to be either short-tempered or patient. Think of children who are quite different in character and may not reflect their parents' characteristics at all. We also carry imprints on our minds that come into this world with us – these too form our tendencies. This is easier to understand with an appreciation for reincarnation, as this is our *karma* – events imprinted on our minds from previous lives that are going to create a result at some point in this or future lives. They're like actors in the wings waiting to go on stage.

Karma requires us to expand our minds to the possibility that our individual lives are like sleeping, dreaming and awakening – but think dying (death of the body), intermediate existence (often called the bardo – the mind in a between-bodies state) and being reborn (the mind taking rebirth in another body). Alternatively, you might consider our lives as simply biological evolution, or perhaps gifts from God. But cause and effect is logical. What doesn't have a previous cause? It's a fascinating question to contemplate.

Compulsive habits

We are creatures of habit. Full stop. We make judgements and decisions based on past experiences and conditioning. These create mental and emotional habits and lead to a sense of us being a solid, self-existent person. We think, "This is me. This is who I am." And we don't want to change that, otherwise fear will set in, because we want to feel this sense of a fixed 'I'. It's like the seat on the sofa you always sit on; it bears your bum's imprint. It's your spot.

Our mental habits can be good or bad, but we can allow them to define us: "Well, that's just me, I am neurotic," or "You should know me by now, I'm a grumpy bastard." The important thing to know is that they are just this – habitual. We can change them. Just like someone who has a bad habit of biting his or her nails eventually stops – over time, and with encouragement.

If habits go unchecked, they become more and more difficult to break. Our habits let us off the hook so that we feel proud about being difficult or moody, as if others should let us get away with it. But, in the same way that a physical habit can be changed, we can also change the habitual ways we think, and this will enable us to be more kind, more patient and more beneficial to the human race. By changing your mental and emotional habits, you can take the bite off any implied failure, either by discovering that you can overcome your faults with effort or by simply recognising your ability to be your best self.

Enormous egos

Enter the ego. The 'I', 'me' and 'mine'. The *ego* is a crafty aspect of ourselves. This 'I' is focused on making everything fit its view of the world through the lens of its conditioning. It thinks it's the centre of the universe, always right, and always more important than anything else. In Buddhism, it's called *self-grasping* – grasping on to a sense of self as if it is solid and exists all by itself on this planet, justifying itself at every opportunity – I am 'me' through and through. We are also 'self-cherishing' – in other words, selfish: it's all about 'me', even though there's only one of me. The world has about eight billion human egos in it – all thinking they're right and that the world revolves around them. No wonder we live with confusion and uncertainty at the least, and war and greed at the extreme. It says something good about humans that most of us try to live side by side in harmony.

The ego identity is a mask that builds up over time and through experience to present the best defence system to others, to cope with adversity and to survive. The ego has a tendency to reinforce our habits and add bricks to our defensive walls. A baby has to learn to have a healthy sense of 'I' to flourish, but if its parents' egos have become unhealthy due to their own life experiences, then it is likely that the baby's ego will become damaged. Without education in personal development, it will soon fall foul of its conditioning and the healthy ego will become an unhealthy ego. And an unhealthy ego is a danger to itself and others.

Our inner education begins as soon as we can understand that conceptual thoughts are the result of our egotistic ways of thinking. They are not the ultimate truth, or even right; they are just ideas and stories based on our experience of sensory stimulation. Managing thoughts and emotions is damage control to the ego.

Incessant thoughts and emotions

Having thoughts that we don't conceptualise is a skill that mindfulness teaches us. This gets really interesting when we start to consider how many thoughts we have each day. The neuroscientists have counted them and there seems to be a general consensus that we have over 6,000 thoughts per day. We also have a negative bias that is repetitive. That means that when we say we're rubbish at something, we repeat that idea a lot. And these negative and repetitive thoughts are uninvited. If we smell something (perceptually), then we conceptualise it (decide it's nice or not). In much the same way, if we think something, we conceptualise it too (decide how we feel about it), but these thoughts are more dangerous because we think they reflect who we are; that they are a part of us. They're not. Thoughts come and go like smells and sounds – entering our field of experience via our mental awareness. But we can tell that sounds and smells are external so we don't think they're a part of us, even though we think our thoughts are. Of course we do, why wouldn't we? They're coming from inside of us.

So, let's talk about thoughts. Some of them are practical, and consciously created ("What shall we have for dinner tonight?"), while others are related to memories ("Mum would have loved that"). Other conscious thoughts that arise from our egos wish to strengthen the ego's identity, striving for that feeling of permanence ("Maybe I should get Botox"). The majority of our thoughts are connected to this poor old shaky ego that is constantly seeking to substantiate itself. So thoughts become worries or anxieties, and they frequently sabotage us so that we miss being at ease in the present moment ("What if I'm no good at this new job?" or "I wonder why Dad doesn't seem to love me the way he loves Ravi?").

The trick with compulsive thoughts is to see them as uninvited guests. They are triggered by many things and the longer we live and the more we plug into external stimulation, like social media, then the more our thoughts are stimulated. Even watching murder mysteries on TV may stimulate thoughts of violence and personal danger. And then we think we're bad for having weird thoughts. Or we feel terrified by all the things that could happen to us.

The accompanying emotions can feel like we're on a rollercoaster ride. They seem to manage us – pulling and pushing us into saying and doing things that we don't seem to have any control over. Recognising emotions for what they are and then sorting them out is our Big Job in life. Mindfulness is a wonderful tool for understanding and managing our thoughts and the accompanying emotions. If we can develop emotional intelligence, then we're doing a good job. Knowing what presses our buttons and recognising that we have a choice in whether to buy into our emotions, (letting them rampage through our relationships with ourselves and others), or guide them towards a more peaceful way of being, must be the real job description of a human being.

Whatever your philosophy, we must all agree that this is the premier goal of a human being and everything else should be relegated to the second division. Free the mind from its many influences and it will positively affect the quality of our lives. In other words, our internal freedom leads to our external freedom.

The mind can be a prison or a shelter.

The wise inner self

Imagine how your life would be if you could manage your thoughts and emotions – like toilet-training sweet puppies or kittens. Imagine your life with this calm inner peaceful awareness that lets troubling thoughts go as if they were as insignificant as junk emails – consigned to the spam folder and deleted. Gradually, over time, these thoughts would lose their power and disappear, as insubstantial as clouds in the sky, dissipating into nothingness. Imagine how this would improve focus and constructive thinking – how there would be more clarity and creativity.

This can be achieved with mindfulness practice and with awareness of the inner self that guides us. This inner self is perhaps more *us* than anything else because it keeps the poor old shaky ego in check and nurtures our extraordinary selves. It's possibly the best friend we will ever have, but its voice is quiet. It's a whisper and it's only activated by awareness. Without nurturing the inner self, it will be drowned out by the ego; shouted down, bullied and ridiculed. The ego-centred 'I' is terrified of this whispery self because, once awakened, it is the equivalent of the tortoise in Aesop's fable *The Tortoise and the Hare*. It is steady, determined, deliberate and patient, whereas the ego is the hare – all appearance and swagger, boastful and brash. And we know who wins in the end.

There are many ways of understanding what this voice is, but there is no one way to identify it. We could call it our conscience – like Pinocchio's moral friend, Jiminy Cricket, advising us what is right and wrong.

When we meditate, and awaken and recognise this quiet, calm voice, we have begun the best relationship we will ever have: with our inner self, or our inner guru, as my guru defined it. It will bring self-esteem, confidence and resilience rather than sabotaging us, and it will bring us everything we require to cope with whatever life flings at us. We will have minds like non-stick pans: the gunk won't stick because our goodness coats us.

In India and Nepal, people have a wonderful way of greeting each other. Instead of saying "Hello" they say "Namaste", which means "I greet the god within you", or "the sacred in me greets the sacred in you". It serves people well in that they recognise that every one of us has something of the divine – something that is our potential for being the best we can be. (As I have mentioned before, in Buddhism, we call this 'buddha nature'.)

Whichever belief or label we adhere to, we can start to understand what we really mean by being spiritual: it means to be guided by that voice that is taking us on an inner journey to self-development in its most positive form because it brings us inner peace – in other words, genuine happiness.

"If you follow your bliss, you put yourself on a kind of track that has been there all the while, waiting for you, and the life that you ought to be living is the one you are living. Wherever you are – if you are following your bliss, you are enjoying that refreshment, that life within you, all the time."

Joseph Campbell
The Power of Myth

This bliss is the voice of our inner self. It's invaluable and meaningful and will serve us better than anything else in our lives.

In meditation, we can give our inner self the label 'observer' because we recognise that there is an aspect of ourselves that is able to monitor and manage thoughts. It doesn't think; it's awareness itself.

The whole package

One of the primary practices to awaken and encourage this essential relationship with ourselves is to reflect on undoing the knotty ball we call 'me'. It's complex, with different aspects, in much the same way we might view a house, with its rooms, functions, cupboards, nooks and crannies, imperfections, walls, comfort zones, attic, boundaries, garden, and spaces underneath the floorboards. This 'me' is our house and we must use the inner self to unravel its mysteries.

The ego's craving for existence is the builder of the house:

Oh housebuilder! Now you are seen.
You shall not build a house again for me.
All your beams are broken,
the ridgepole is shattered.
The mind has become freed from conditioning:
the end of craving has been reached.

The Buddha's 'inspired utterance' recorded in the Dhammapada,
Verses 153-154

The inner self is the one who sees and unties the knots – the one who stops all the building of walls and partitions and attends to its misconceptions.

My story – my choices

I didn't get in to the drama school of my choice, and found myself attending one that clearly had different expectations of its students. The experience of drama school was not wholly positive. I didn't glow with the looks of a goddess, nor did I have a posh accent, so the parts I managed to get, although credible, were minimal. The director accepted my application because he said I reminded him of a former student. Well, it clearly wasn't Helen Mirren, although as far as I know she was the only famous one to come out of that school.

At the end of my time there I had a choice. And this is what is still interesting to me. Why did I choose to flee as far north as I could, rather than get an agent and stay in London, as so many of my peer group did?

I knew Northumberland from forays to visit my sister, who had a baby on the way and a husband who had followed his career as a special needs teacher there. I loved its wildness and huge skies. It was unlike the soft and voluptuous south. But to leave my dream behind?

I try to be as honest as I can about this choice, because there were so many strands to the final decision. City life made me physically ill; my sister was an emotional magnet; my home town (that I commuted to London from) was getting a bit tense, and I had experienced a frightening confrontation with a drug-fuelled gang of 'mods' (mods and rockers were the opponent gangs in youth culture during the '60s) who tried to break into my flat; my boyfriend and I wanted to get away from the small-town restrictions of everyone knowing everyone else; I wasn't getting on with my mum, who hated my boyfriend; I fell in love with a wild place. Isn't this multitude of strands always true when we do something? People say, "Why did you do that?" And you choose one answer… but it's never that simple.

In life, there are always literal reasons to point to but, in my experience, there is definitely a hidden purpose to our decisions. It is true that there is still a part of me that wonders if I was just scared. Would I have made it as an actress? Might I now be someone who enjoys recognition of their talents, opportunities and fame? My mum would sometimes point to an actress on TV and say, "That could have been you, Ond." Which is funny because, at the time, she didn't engage, encourage or comment much at all on my acting ambitions. Maybe she didn't want me to fail. After all, her own expectations of life were very limited to marriage and family, and there was a '50s attitude lingering in her that to think 'beyond your station' was arrogant.

Later, when I finally arrived at the Institute, I marvelled at the fact that I had found it. I rejoiced that I wasn't a struggling actress in London. From a spider's web of contacts, I had met someone who had been on a retreat, and that word 'retreat' had fascinated me. At the time, I thought my friends and colleagues would be fascinated too, and when I told them about this extraordinary, exotic place, I was surprised to find that there was little interest. They certainly weren't attracted to changing their sun-filled holiday plans for a course in a cold, echoing building with no home comforts. But I was.

And here's another interesting thing. My boyfriend, who was now husband number two, felt the same. So we helped each other up that step to something higher. That's what it felt like. Lots of doors were closing in my face; lots of cosmic events were pulling me to make unthinkable choices because I was meant to be at that place. Perhaps being drawn to Buddhism was the implicit purpose of our relationship, because we didn't last more than a year together there.

We had experienced a lot of obstacles to buying our dream cottage, furthering our careers and trying to find what was best for us, but all the obstacles, failures and frustrations just melted into nothingness when I was in that place with all those amazing people because I felt as if I was at the centre of the universe. This is where I was meant to be – the place I had thought was always somewhere else. Before, nothing could have been further from my mind. Me? Religious? Are you kidding? It felt like we were being guided here and the obstacles to 'normal' life were for a reason.

We moved to the Institute a few months later, arriving in our little red Mini followed by a huge removal van full of furniture. We had given up secure jobs, a place on the housing ladder and a friendship group of culture vultures, as opposed to the religious hippies who eyed us warily.

Arriving there was a BIG challenge to our egos. There were temporary rooms and a caravan before the small profit from the sale of our house paid for a basic barn conversion. Some of the hippie community didn't really warm to us – we were quite different and we had no experience of all the alternative ways of living that we had to get used to: vegetarianism; no alcohol; don't pick the flowers, it hurts them; it doesn't matter where you live because you should be renouncing attachments... it was pretty hard-core. Many of them had bonded in India and Nepal and had formed friendship groups that were hard to penetrate. Plus the place itself was freezing and uninviting. Sometimes I did wonder, "What the hell have I done?" – although I would never admit that to my mother, who was mortified by my move.

But I was driven. The daily teachings and meditation sessions seemed so extraordinary, and were absolutely mind-blowing, yet shared such obvious common sense. (Yes, it didn't take me long to absorb the hippie-speak.) It all made for a life fully lived, even if it was a lifestyle that had never been on my radar. The Tibetan Lamas were from a planet I had never visited, and I fell in love with them all in a way that transcended any kind of love I had ever known. They made it okay for us to challenge the ego and their compassion was limitless. It was really their example that kept me there and they became my role models. So we had forsaken security and material benefits, but the rewards were immeasurable. And if I hadn't listened to my inner voice there was absolutely no rational reason to do what I did. As far as everyone else was concerned, we were crazy and had been lost to a cult.

My ego had to battle with many misconceptions there – so much pride and anger surfaced during the three-week course before we made our choice. Several times, I was about to quit and return to the comforts and 'normality' of home.

Everyone seemed to know more than me, and attitudes like sarcasm and gossip were relegated to the hell of negativity. I was out of my depth – my whole adult life had been devoted to cynicism and I often used spiky humour to look down on the vast majority of humanity. My sense of humour was rooted in trying to find self-esteem. Having to look at these emotions and ways of thinking afresh, control them and let them go meant I was virtually losing my personality. It was frightening.

Life as education

"Children must be taught how to think, not what to think."

Margaret Mead

Coming of Age in Samoa

Human beings are special creatures who have the capacity for enormous development when we enter this strange theatre we call life. Yet, remarkably, we're not trained to get the best from our lives through understanding what makes us tick and how to navigate through the incredible amount of stuff we're going to encounter before we die. We're not given scripts, like actors, to practise our lines and our moves – it's just a little push from behind and we're off. No rehearsals possible.

One of the important messages in this book is that even if formal meditation doesn't always fit the requirement, without it as a tool in your life you're poorly equipped for solving problems. What meditation gives us cannot be over-emphasised, and if we were all taught it from an early age, this planet would be a healthier and more peaceful place to live. Imagine being encouraged to find your inner self and listen to it as a youngster?

Giving us the tools to manage being human is sadly ignored in our educational institutions. Society has developed systems, but they are rarely overhauled. Subjects that feed our intellectual brains take priority, but the topic of being human and how to get the best from our selves is barely given lip service. No wonder we suffer from more mental illness now – it is such a vast and changing landscape that we crawl through that we need an introspective toolkit to cut through all the obstacles to mental wellbeing. Poor mental health is this century's greatest health issue and, arguably, the biggest threat to the human species.

Reflections

- Spend some time reflecting on your own body. Is it serving you well?

- Consider the 'ingredients' listed in this chapter of what it means to be human – our bodies, senses, emotions, minds and consciences – and assess if you have what you need to develop your inner self.

- Try to keep an open mind about the distinction between the brain and the mind. If it is creating confusion for you, just consider the possibilities of spiritual development.

- Give yourself time for reflection away from sensory stimuli like social media. Does being alone with yourself give you peace of mind or does it create fear?

- Think about your own conditioning. Can you identify ways of thinking, or attitudes you have that came from others that shaped you?

- Consider everything you value about yourself. Really focus on your qualities, and also the opportunities that have come your way. You might even consider how some seemingly negative situations led you to better circumstances, or how much you learned from them. Think about your potential. This can be done in an analytical meditation but is easily relocated to a long reflective walk, alone or with a like-minded friend.

Authentic mindfulness

- We're special, but not that special. Everyone has the same potential.
- A true practitioner will utilise mindfulness for self-awareness as well as for relaxation.
- Humility gives us strong self-esteem. We don't have to boast to be big.
- If you find yourself judging someone, thank them internally. That person is enabling you to develop your practice by revealing your prejudices and critical voice.

Spiritual integrity

- Bring the topic of spirituality out of the closet. Discuss it with friends and family and be open to their ideas.
- Spirituality is an art form. Practise it like you would painting, writing or singing.
- There's a big difference between spiritual materialism and genuine spirituality.
- Enjoy the freedom that finding your spiritual self gives you.
- Explore religions. Avoid thinking that there is just one true religion. They are all there for different types of people to engage in. There are many ways up the mountain. Nothing's worse than an evangelist preaching at you, unless you are the evangelist preaching at someone else. That is MUCH worse.
- Being human means we have limitless power, and if we can source it and refine this power we can draw on it for life.

Chapter 4

It's All in the Mind

○ ○ ○

"A man is but the product of his thoughts. What he thinks, he becomes."

Mahatma Gandhi

An Autobiography: The Story of My Experiments with Truth

Understanding what we mean by 'mind' is essential if we want to work with it. We can't take for granted that we are all talking about the same thing because the mind has subtly different connotations depending on different points of view and attitudes. Being mindful is usually interpreted as being 'aware', but what does that actually mean?

If we're going to work on the mind, be mindful, look inwards, then we need to know what we're looking at... or for.

In Chapter 3, we dipped our toes into the puddle of mental awareness – an *aspect* of the mind. How about jumping into the *ocean* of the mind now?

The nature of the mind

The mind has three *qualities* as described by the Buddha himself, and they are:

- Luminosity
- Clarity
- Knowing

The description of the mind by the Buddha and other great meditators is straight out of meditation experience. No scientific evidence nor religious belief is attached to these direct, personal experiences, just an explanation of what one encounters when profound stages of meditation have been realised. You can put the brain under the microscope, but not the mind – meditators are the qualified scientists of the mind.

Through training their minds and meditating, yogi(ni)s discover the nature of the mind for themselves because it occurs through personal experience. There are plenty of detailed accounts of the insight gained during meditation in meditation manuals and texts, and if we follow the guidance, we can also experience different states of consciousness. As with any skill, we need training, but because this skill is an inner process, we are the only witness to our achievements.

Let's take the attributes of mind in more detail, one at a time.

Luminosity

Here, we are talking about the intrinsic nature of the mind – the usual synonym is a mirror (without the frame). It reflects objects. Yes, it's pretty hard to get a hold of this quality – we like to see things and touch them, to experience them through our senses, rather than have them be an ethereal, insubstantial concept – but the mind is not physical, material matter within us. It is pure energy that is internal animation. You can't *see* this energy, but with reflective exercises and meditation, you can *experience* its power.

Clarity

When we hold something with our mind that is unhindered by any thought, there is total clarity of experience. The object is reflected back to us without conceptual colouring. It doesn't need labelling or identification – it just is. When the mind meets an object without the barriers presented by our egos, we call this experience *non-dualistic* ('no object or subject'). There is no me and a glass of water, there is just unity of experience; in other words, an absence of conceptualisation about the glass. This clarity is a quality of mind that is accessed when the ego is destroyed to reveal just pure, untainted, ungarnished experience.

Knowing

We are able to know an object by meeting it. The mind has the potential to know everything. When our minds are not obscured by sensory stimulation and mental distractions, we can experience natural clarity and its potential for insight. When we're free of ego-based judgements, conditioning and projections, we can see things as they truly are.

The scope of the mind

Now this gets really fun when we consider the other defining aspects of the mind, which are known as its *scope*. The scope of the mind is:

- Beginningless
- Endless
- Indestructible

In other words, the mind is *limitless*. Rebirth is a part of the Eastern culture from which Buddhism emerged, and the Buddha himself did not contradict this. When he attained enlightenment after prolonged meditation, he described being able to look back so far into previous lives that he proclaimed the mind as beginningless. Hence the goal in Buddhist mindfulness of developing our 'buddha' (awakened) nature rather than the more secular approach of developing a healthier self for the purpose of this short lifetime. We practise secular mindfulness to improve this life, but Buddhist mindfulness is for all our future lives as well – until we've totally cleaned up our act and become enlightened 'buddhas' (awakened or purified ones). You get the picture. It's the same practice, but the motivation is different – and that makes a big difference.

A crucial aspect of this discussion is to contemplate that when the mind is purified it does not end. It is still energy, and science will agree here that you cannot destroy energy. But it can be transformed – and that is of course what we are doing in our mind training. When it is transformed we become buddhas - enlightened energy.

Not knowing the qualities and scope of the mind is like being gifted a computer in the 19th century. Yet, this is the situation for most human beings right now. We remain unaware of the power and possibilities that we all possess right here, right now, inside of us, at no cost - except effort. It would be a tragedy to waste this human potential.

The following Nature of the Mind meditation is the basis for experiencing the extent, power and potential of the mind. It opens us up to the consideration that mind is not matter and therefore not the brain.

LISTEN

The Nature of the Mind meditation

"The nature of the mind, which is all-knowing, aware of everything, empty and radiant, is established to be the manifestly radiant and self-originating pristine cognition, present from the beginning, just like the sky."

Padmasambhava

The Tibetan Book of the Dead

Try to relax into the practice so it becomes just another aspect of being human, like the need for physical fitness. What kind of mind we have to work on depends on the mind we have already created due to the natural law of cause and effect - our *karma* (explained more in Chapter 3). In theory, we have all the time in the world, literally. But if we leave it for another day, like our dirty washing, then naturally our problems build up.

So, the message is: don't waste your precious, perfect human life.

The many names for the mind

Laying aside our bodily selves on the Grim Reaper's butcher's slab, let's consider what of our selves survives after death – and the shared terminology we (and many major religions) might use to describe the mind. The differences may be subtle, and perhaps merely semantics, but it's important to think about the differences in meaning to clarify our own views.

Consciousness

The word 'consciousness' is a synonym for 'mind' – a non-physical energetic aspect of a sentient being that is evolving through countless lives towards enlightenment. Consciousness uses the brain to develop domination over the ego and ultimately destroy it. (Don't confuse the term 'consciousness' with '*mental* consciousness' – or 'mental awareness' – introduced in Chapter 3, which is just *one* aspect of the mind.)

Buddhists often call the mind *consciousness* because it's so precise. With death, the body dies, but the mind, or consciousness, goes on into a future existence. This is not the essence of a person, nor anything permanent, as the law of impermanence applies to all things. We are but a continuity of consciousness – a mental continuum, evolving and changing moment by moment. Essence implies something permanent, which our ego would love to believe. ("Hooray! I'm 'me' forever!")

When my daughter was trying to teach me about my new phone, she explained about sim cards and phones being interdependent yet different. Sharing our predilection for Buddhist philosophy, she said, "The mobile phone is the body, and when the battery dies, the phone is just like a dead body when the heart stops beating. The sim card is like your consciousness. You can take it out of the old phone and put it into a new phone, where it will continue to collect data." Of course, technology is impermanent too, and now data is stored in 'clouds' – a bit like being in that intermediate state (the bardo). It does not die with the physical object.

The Buddha taught that everything is in a constant state of change.

Nothing about us stays the same, including our consciousness, hence the Buddha's definition of one of the Three Marks of Existence (or Three Universal Truths) as 'no soul'. In other words, our mind is not fixed as we understand the soul to be, but fluid and capable of evolution. (I explore the Three Marks of Existence further in Chapter 6.) Our consciousness came into our present body with the imprints it created in previous lives and, when we die, the consciousness at the time of death will move on to another life. The being that is reborn will not be the same as us – it will merely carry the evolving consciousness.

This interpretation aligns with mindfulness practice in that we recognise that we can change our minds and radically transform into the people we wish to be – even in this life. One of our fears is that we might lose ourselves if we transform the mind, but if we understand that we're more like a river than a stagnant pond, transforming our mind immediately changes into a positive attribute. There will remain some aspects of personality and genetic tendencies in this life, but they will be lost at death so we can let go of the 'eternal me' stories we tell ourselves. They may seem comforting, but they inhibit our development.

Soul

Christians, Jews, Muslims and Hindus all believe in an external God the creator, and they call the part of us that is not flesh and blood, the *soul*. They believe that the soul continues its journey until it unites with God. The soul has permanent features that forever represent who we are.

Because it doesn't advocate an external creator or God, Buddhism sometimes faces the question as to whether it is a religion or not. The Dalai Lama himself says that Buddhism is more a science of the mind, and religious practices are cultural add-ons that developed after the Buddha passed on to give us community support and physical rituals.

So, major religions disagree with Buddhism about the immaterial aspect of ourselves, as *consciousness* implies a different quality to *soul*.

Spirit

Some ancient civilisations, such as Native Americans and Aboriginals, have their own ideas about what continues after death. This is usually referred to as the *spirit* or *essence* of a person.

When people talk about spirit, it can mean that we have a certain quality that is 'spirited' – a liveliness and vigour about us. Spirit is usually understood to be a life force that animates us, like the 'chi' in t'ai chi. (Interestingly, 'life force' is one of the translations of 'mind' in ancient Buddhist scriptures.) According to recorded sightings and direct experiences from various sources, this spirit may manifest after death as a ghost (often called a spirit). This spirit may appear in different guises; for example, someone who dies aged 90 may appear to a relative in an earlier, more youthful physical phase of their life. Some people believe that the spirit may manifest in different forms, such as an animal or bird.

These are a sample of some experiences I have heard:

- "I'm sure it was the spirit of my mum when I saw that blackbird tapping at my window."
- "I can feel the presence of Grandad's spirit in the garden."
- "I have a spirit guide who helps me."

Buddhism agrees to some extent but goes further. At death, consciousness may manifest as a spirit, sometimes called a hungry ghost, if there is still a strong attachment to this physical reality – literally hungering for existence. Depending on the level of disturbance on the consciousness, it will remain until it can release itself from its past life. It is generally not understood as being a pleasant rebirth, but one that hungers to still exist as it was before. Until it can release its attachment to its past life, the consciousness can't move on to its next form.

I'm hoping that this short discussion on these spiritual aspects of the mind can help us be open and clear about what we believe in as we consider the common sense of the life after death theory. If we consider all the alternatives, we might then, as informed, intelligent beings, make our choices and live accordingly with a set of values and practices that can help take us where we want to be during our lives, at the end of our lives, and after.

How to know our minds

Uncertainty prevents us from committing to anything in life, and so developing a strong sense of *why* we practise something may bring us better results. We can all benefit from mindfulness practice because, regardless of our beliefs, it helps us change and develop our brains. These methods help us know our minds in the same way as the great meditators described them.

Meditation

Meditation is a tool we can use to find spaciousness between our thoughts and recognise how our thoughts and emotions, which are triggered by external events, run rampant through our minds.

It's only when we come into a relationship with our mind that we can really know it. If we just read about it and think about it, then it is like finding a mouth-watering recipe and never cooking it. Without meditation, we are external beings and will continue to be led by the nose towards more and more confusion. We need to become inner beings, guided by the awareness that mindfulness practice gifts us. Turn inwards, away from distractions, and we will find our material to work on.

Managing our thoughts and emotions

If we understand that our thoughts and emotions make sticky imprints all over the lovely mirror of our mind, then the first thing to do is to focus on the ones that cause us problems – our *destructive* thoughts and emotions. Constructive thoughts and emotions can stay, because they reflect our spiritual qualities. Mindfulness enables us to not only find spaciousness and clarity, but also to discover these spiritual traits.

"I will not let anyone walk through my mind with their dirty feet."

Commonly ascribed to Mahatma Gandhi

The nature of the mind is clear, luminous and knowing, so we can understand that destructive thoughts and emotions are just like stains that can be washed out. It sounds simple. Bung them in the washing machine at 60 degrees (okay, maybe 90) and get rid of them. But we need to remind ourselves that the mind is beginningless, so the reason the mirror is pretty filthy is because we have *done* a lot of stuff and *thought* a lot of stuff in this life (let alone past lives), and these are still polluting us, perhaps invisibly like a virus, but there nonetheless. We don't come into the world with a new mirror, but one that is already used. After all, our egos own it – and we know what a bunch of rapscallions they are.

No wonder the practice of working with thoughts and emotions is so hard. We need a laundrette of cleaning equipment. We need to know how to manage our thoughts and emotions. We need to know how to clean up our act. If we want the reward of a great cleaning product, then we need go no further than our observer mind that is refined through mindfulness meditation. Becoming aware of our thoughts and emotions, and so managing them from that healthy distance of rational observation, is like the magic blue whitener that transforms old grey tee-shirts into sparkling new tops.

The inner self

When we are in one of those rare states of non-conceptualisation – not projecting, storytelling or judging our experiences – then we experience a more pure, enlightened version of ourselves, and our potential for becoming fully awake (our 'buddha nature'). This may be defined as our unconscious intuitive mind, but in Buddhist and mindfulness psychology it is more likely to be described as *the inner self*, which suggests that aspect of ourselves that is uncontaminated.

But our inner self has a more tangible quality in that it is a point of contact – a meeting place of the ego and something higher or more than our ego. As previously mentioned, its voice is quiet and often expressed not as words but as images in dreams and reflections. Accessing this deeper and more profound expression of our inner reality is a method used widely by psychoanalysts and therapists for healing trauma and loss. This 'Self', as Swiss psychoanalyst Carl Jung describes it, might be described in other ways, such as the Higher Self, God within, intuition or 'buddha nature'. Jung – and his teacher, Austrian neurologist and psychoanalyst Sigmund Freud – interpreted dreams to help people deal with neuroses, and encouraged guided visualisation techniques for healing.

Things that get in the way of knowing our minds

The common term for everything that stands in the way of our personal development is *obstacles*. These barriers to self-awareness aren't permanent fixtures or insurmountable, but temporary states of mind that get in the way of our insights and understanding. They're caused by our conditioning, our tendencies and our karma (previous actions). These stains on our consciousness are hard to shift, but with the power of that super cleaning product, mindfulness, we can deal with them and flush them away like the dirt they are.

Defilements and delusions

We confuse our thoughts and feelings with who we are, rather than understanding that they are actually messing with our minds, like mischievous chimps. Due to this recognition that there's nothing about our thoughts and emotions that actually define us, and they are not based in any solid reality, they are also called *defilements* or *delusions* in Buddhist practice because they taint our minds. They are just personal projections. Working with our thoughts and emotions is the basis of mindfulness practice, both for short- and long-term benefits. Realising that we are not our thoughts can often be one of the most amazing discoveries for meditation beginners – like a light-bulb moment, or the door to a prison cell suddenly opening. Genuine freedom.

Ego

Our egos are a big nuisance, as they constantly interrupt our practice. They're like advertising on social media – always thinking they know what we want, but actually just continually trying to fill a void within us.

The ego is terrified of everything:

- Death (not existing, and losing those we love)
- Others who disagree with us (challenging our ideas about everything)
- Impermanence (there's nothing to hold onto because everything's always changing)

Our poor egos are big babies, needing reassurance but looking in the wrong places for external things that don't last… so then they're on the move again, constantly reaching forward for some kind of satisfaction and contentment. Our egos look for a way to solidify the self – which is impossible, because there is no solid self. It's like holding a baby in our arms and not wanting it to grow up.

This feeling of the earth continually shifting underneath us *is* terrifying unless we have access to the kind of wisdom that can get to grips with the ego – finally wrestling it to the ground to hug away its fears. Wisdom is our navigation app as we traverse our emotional earthquakes.

Sensory distractions

Our *mental awareness* (consciousness), as opposed to our *sense awareness*, is what is being distracted. Our senses stimulate the mental awareness, so the ability of the mind to be clear and knowing is hindered. Without the thoughts and accompanying emotions, the purity of smelling a rose, tasting chocolate cake or looking at a view would be unmolested by the annoying interruptions of our projections about them. As sensory beings, we need mindfulness to take care that we are not held captive by these projections.

Chapter 3 clarifies the differences between our mental awareness and our sense awareness.

Permanence

We grasp at permanence – of ourselves and everything we encounter – by sticking Post-it notes onto our lovely mirrors. We are discerning with physical stuff – we wouldn't say, "Oh, I see dog poo, so it must be part of me; I'll put that in my bag" – yet we are wildly undiscerning when it comes to the mental stuff in our lives. We say daft things like, "'Til death do us part," unnecessarily tying ourselves to a relationship for an entire lifetime. We set ourselves up for failure and then feel guilty if things fall apart. We should take care with the vows we make. It's much more sensible to say, "'Til we change our minds."

The idea of the death of our selves is the most frightening thing we have to deal with. Death of a loved one can be equally devastating. We are so attached to the idea that there is something about us that should last forever, and so desperate to ensure that everything and everyone else we are attached to also lasts forever, that we cause ourselves immense pain. We pretend that death doesn't really affect us. We tell ourselves that we won't die for many years to come so why think about it, and that sickness and old age happen to other people. We also grasp onto the idea that we won't physically change, and that our relationships will always be of the same quality. Frankly, we are fools, blinded by our frightened egos. If only we could see that there is no death of our *minds*, then we could relax our hold on... well, everything, and pay more attention to what is happening now.

Understanding impermanence, one of the Three Marks of Existence, helps us in so many life situations – to go with the flow and to let things go, instead of holding on tightly to what is no longer viable or possible.

We would be wise to change the way we manage death. Living and dying through the dreadful worldwide pandemic of 2020 taught us that not being prepared for death – thinking that it cannot happen to us –

is a sadly flawed philosophy. Better to think about it and learn about what happens at death and afterwards. Death is not the enemy, it is nature. We take nothing with us except our minds, so we had better take care of them. Preparing for death is a common Buddhist practice that isn't meant to be morbid; it means considering the inevitable and being prepared to face it with courage rather than fear.

Meditating on impermanence and death isn't designed by the Buddha to torture us about impending tragedies; instead, it's a reminder to make the most of our lives, aligning with the meditation on your precious human life (explored in Chapter 3) to reinforce the message, "Get on with it."

Certain analytical meditations have been devised to gently move us away from the idea that worldly life can fill the void in us, and to consider a more realistic, and holistic, approach on how to live. The following meditation may be helpful when you feel ready to try this.

 ## LISTEN

Impermanence and Death meditation

From head to heart – focusing on feelings

We know the brain sits nice and heavy in the head: when we're considering anything, we point to our heads as if to say, "I know." Another place we point to is in the centre of our chests, at heart level. This tends to be where we might say, "I feel for you." Lots of imagery shows this central place in our bodies to represent the heart. It's not the physical heart (which is a bit further to the left) but our spiritual centre.

"It is with the heart that one sees rightly; what is essential is invisible to the eye."

Antoine de Saint-Exupéry

The Little Prince

In meditation practice and all religious reflective practices, we move the focus of our awareness down to this heart level. It does take practice, because in our everyday lives, everything is focused on what's going on inside our heads. It is a mistake, therefore, to fuse the brain with the mind because it will interrupt the journey from our heads to our hearts.

Mindfulness meditation focuses on direct inner and outer experience – our sensations, breath, feelings and thoughts – in order to increase our awareness of the nature of change and our ever-changing self, plus to release us from subjectifying our experience: "I am not my thoughts." Mindfulness takes us away from obsessing over our thoughts and towards a more holistic experience.

The four applications (or foundations) of mindfulness meditation practices as originally taught by the Buddha enable us to achieve this new focus, moving away from the brain into awareness of our direct human experience, both in our meditations and 'off the cushion'.

Mindfulness is applied to:

- The Body
- Feelings
- Mind
- Phenomena

I explored mindfulness of the breath/body (physical sensations) in Chapter 2. Now it is time to have a go at mindfulness of feelings, which investigates our partialities. Feelings precede emotions, and they subtly lead to our judgements about everything.

Before you try the meditation that follows, think about what we mean by feelings and why we do the practice.

Consider these points:

- The different feelings of pleasure, pain and indifference that we experience in our day-to-day life
- All the decisions we make in life are prompted by our feelings
- Feelings help us to survive, flourish and prosper
- No matter what we achieve, our feelings continue to drive us to

hunger for something more

- We label our feelings as good or bad, which continues to drive our longing for only good feelings
- All emotions are subtly preceded by feelings of pleasure, pain or indifference
- Feelings are subjective and fuel our desires rather than exhaust them

Now, try the meditation.

 LISTEN

Mindfulness of Feelings meditation

We also apply mindfulness to the mind and to phenomena. I share a 'Nature of the Mind' meditation earlier in this chapter that explores how we apply mindfulness to the mind, so the next area to consider is phenomena.

Mindfulness of phenomena is the trickiest of the four applications to get to grips with. It is concerned with sensations that present to our awareness, such as smell, taste, touch, sight and sound, as well as colours and shapes. Mindfulness of phenomena is designed as a doorway to interconnectedness with everything we experience – that nothing is separate and that we can abide with (rather than collide with) our 'reality'. The elements are within us and outside of us, and the universe is a collection of elements as shared experience. This awareness of interdependence informs our progression on the path of meditation towards realising the ultimate nature of reality – non-duality, the absence of a separate self.

 LISTEN

Mindfulness of Phenomena meditation

Meditations on these four human experiences (the body, feelings, mind and phenomena) vary in degree from simple observation to finer and more defined investigation. Check out the recommended reading list if you want more detail and a more Buddhist approach (yes, it can get very analytical).

Find yourself a yogi(ni) and they will tell you their experiences of the mind. Our inner self – that awareness or observer character who watches what goes on in the brain and deals with all that weird, busy stuff that clutters up and masks our true selves – allows the great spaciousness of our true home to reveal itself within us.

Two thousand years ago, spiritual seekers in India practised mindfulness in order to train their brains to just shut up and become aware of a bigger picture. Until the brain chatter stopped, they couldn't see that bigger picture. Mindfulness then took them to concentration – a quality that isn't just for focusing on the job in hand, but takes one to a non-dualistic appreciation of reality, without judgements; when there's no more, "This is nice, and that's not. I like her, but I don't like him." It's as if the blinkers are taken off and suddenly we *are* fields and sky and WOW! It's all wonderful. A great awakening. That's when losing the stress of the day becomes losing stress for life.

Understanding chakras

Chakras are energy points within the body and aligned with the spine. They connect with organs and other internal bodily elements. By working with chakras, you can unblock your energy and restore your health and vitality.

Chakras are an important aspect of this discussion of the mind, as they are also non-material energy and yet clearly a vital aspect of our wellbeing. Meditators use visualised imagery of these chakras that correlate to colour and the elements. By visualising them with our creative imaginations we can transform any disturbing emotions that affect our physical and mental health, and rebalance the inner elements of fire, water, wind and earth that lie within our physical body and manifest as heat, liquid, air and flesh. It's like alchemy.

Strengthening the inner self

Turning inwards through meditation immediately introduces our external self to our inner self. It's not a formal introduction; it's more like when you're introduced to someone who isn't initially attracted to you. They're polite, but they aren't really seeing or hearing a word you say because they're too busy ogling your friend.

Until you meditate, your external self is like that person – not interested. The ego is out there, living it up, high on sensory stimulation and ego games. It's not listening to anyone who wants to spoil its fun. Then, one day, you face some kind of crisis and connect with wellbeing practices. Meditation is something you're not sure about, it seems so dull, and then – BOOM – you find your inner self. It was there all along, just patiently waiting for you to notice it. Not glitzy but genuine. The attraction ignites.

So many people I have worked with describe their first experience of meditation as amazing: "It's so peaceful and calm in there." They then expect the same experience every time they meditate. But it's like falling in love – the beginning of a romance is heavenly; then, after a while, just ordinary. The ego, addicted to high stimulation, is always disappointed when extraordinary becomes ordinary. But, like genuine love, the familiarity with your mind will lead to much deeper rewards.

Remember, meditation means becoming familiar with your mind: getting to know the ego, listening to your inner voice and strengthening your observational mind.

Fall in love with your inner self, make love to it and ask it to marry you. Make vows to it in order to protect the marriage, and stay faithful. With every outer experience is an inner mirror image waiting to be felt. Do not underestimate the power within. It is the most fruitful and reliable relationship you will ever have.

Working with the subconscious mind

Different types of meditation use visualisation practices to increase our potential for understanding our subconscious self. The subconscious usually reveals itself through dreams, so it is really useful to learn how to read the symbolism of our dreams – if we can remember them. Symbols speak to us in the same way that words do, but symbols arise rather than being selected, so they're more likely to reveal all that deep stuff that's going on inside us. The words 'arise' and 'deep' offer clues – symbols come from our heart centre as opposed to our brains.

Reading our dreams is a kind of mind science in itself. A strong image in our dreams is often interpreted as an aspect of ourselves. One woman I know was distraught that she dreamt of killing a delightful baby and felt disgusted by her actions. When I asked what the baby might represent, we discussed a new project she had been considering starting but it was too much for her now. Her subconscious was killing her baby. It wasn't that she was a potential murderer, just someone sadly recognising that she couldn't nurture a new project anymore.

Meditators utilise visualisation practices to generate beneficial imagery to counter negative thought patterns and behaviours. Jungian psychology visualisation methods join hands here with Tibetan Buddhist and Hindu techniques of visualising deities to awaken hidden qualities within ourselves.

Our dreams and fantasies play an important role in self-understanding and self-development, but they are often dismissed as irrelevant and just 'brain silt' washed up on the shores of our conscious minds. This is an unfortunate mistake, as working with the subconscious mind helps us know ourselves better.

As well as reading our dreams, we can read our meditations.

"Meditation is not for the faint-hearted nor for those who routinely avoid the whispered longings of their own hearts."

Jon Kabat-Zinn

(on the sign at the entrance to his meditation centre)

Whispered longings sounds like the name of a suggestive chocolate bar, but once we can get past the romantic sound of it, we need to think about the message. We need courage to meditate because we're going to become aware of what's really going on beyond our ego mask, deep within. Perhaps that's why some people dismiss it as hocus-pocus – because they're scared of finding out who they really are. Or perhaps they're worried that they'll discover they've wasted their lives on superficial nonsense.

Visualisation techniques (also known as guided imagery) are used widely in healing therapies today. The process allows instant access to the deep, hidden issues of fear, anger, identity, power struggles and defensiveness that prevent us from being authentic. There is a very neat explanation from American psychotherapists Charles and Patti Leviton, from a 2004 article in the journal *Annals of the American Psychotherapy Association*:

"Pictures are the universal language of the mind. These pictures provide a connecting link between the conscious and unconscious minds. Psychologist Jeanne Achterberg, PhD, often describes this process of imagery as being 'the midwife that births feelings from the unconscious to the conscious mind.'"

So perhaps we can now move our concept of mind into our bodies… down a bit, down, towards the middle, STOP!

"When the heart has acquired stillness it will perceive the heights and depths of knowledge; and the ear of the still intellect will be made to hear marvellous things from God."

Hesychius the Priest[8]

---

8   Hesychius the Priest was a monk of Saint Catherine's Monastery on Mount Sinai, and an ascetic practitioner and author. He is known as 'Our Holy Father.'

My story – life as a secondary school teacher

My path as a teacher intertwined with my spiritual path. Having trained as a teacher for secondary education in the subjects of Drama and English, a progressive Religious Studies department in the school where I taught during my time at the Institute became very interested in my involvement with Buddhism. Eventually, I segued into that department and enjoyed some of the most fascinating and educational parts of my working life (other than my Buddhist studies). Because I had to teach it, I had to learn it. And I soon developed a personal fascination with other religions. I eventually became Head of Belief, Philosophy and Ethics there and, with my brilliant department, taught unconventional subjects, such as Paganism. We even invited the only Pagan Chaplain from a university to speak. The lunchtime event attracted so many students that the hall was filled and they had to stand by the open doors. The lady didn't disappoint and arrived all in black leather. The students asked her questions like, "Can you fly?" ("No") and "Do you worship the sun?" ("Yes." Well, she did proclaim to be a White Witch: it seemed reasonable to me.)

As well as inviting controversial speakers, we explored Native American beliefs and made dreamcatchers and medicine bags. We created Zen sand gardens using forks to make patterns. A class of unmotivated and bored lads would often give me trouble, but I was particularly impressed at their capacity for absorption in these pursuits until I discovered that during the break that preceded the lesson, they would get stoned and turn up ready to space out, rather than focus inwards. Although not quite the kind of concentration I was looking for, at least they linked the soft spaciousness of being stoned with reflective techniques (so it wasn't a complete waste of time). It certainly made my job a lot easier, and I'm sure they look back on those lessons as peaceful and restful times. In my role as Religious Studies teacher, the topic of death was of great interest to teenagers. It seemed that the cultural aspects of shrines, churches and temples were rather yawn-worthy, but once I opened up the discussion about "Is this all there is?" then some very interesting theories emerged. Here are a few of my students' theories:

- This is all there is. We live and then we die.

- When we die we go to heaven. This is a place where all your dead family and friends are and you play football and party most of the time. No one gets sick.

- There is a hell, but not forever. That's just mean. Eventually, you burn up your sins and can go to heaven.

- We reincarnate. We come back as birds and bees and all sorts, and then when we're human we stay human forever.

We would discuss near-death experiences. I introduced them to the work of Ian Stevenson, an American doctor and psychiatrist who investigated those who remembered past lives, and Raymond Moody, another American doctor and psychologist, who recorded the accounts of those who had near-death experiences while suffering cardiac arrests under his care. A typical description of a near-death experience:

> "I got a warm feeling and I was in a tunnel. At the end of that tunnel was a bright, warm, white, vibrating light. It was beautiful. It gave me a feeling of peace and confidence. I floated towards it. The warm feeling became stronger and stronger. I felt at home, loved, nearly ecstatic."
>
> **Pim van Lommel**
> *Consciousness Beyond Life: The Science of the Near-Death Experience*

We also reflected on statements made by contemplatives about their spiritual experiences:

> "I was up in the mountains and awoke early, when the morning was still dark. I sat so very quietly day after day,

and then the most wonderful and terrible experience came. I disappeared. All that I am was washed away. I didn't know its name at first, and you can't give it names, even nirvana, because it's before names. And such bliss. I knew it was no longer my own heart and body, it was the world's."

Jack Kornfield

After the Ecstasy, the Laundry: How the Heart Grows Wise on the Spiritual Path

Neuroscience hadn't yet engaged with meditation in the 1980s and '90s but when the students experienced it for themselves, they loved it, and related to it as a spiritual experience – opening the door on something profound and other-worldly. I recognised then that our education system was ignoring a great hole in our children: to deny them the opportunities to be experiential beings of their most inner selves was to deny them bread itself. They were getting cake, chocolate and cola, but these were just creating a temporary buzz and more desire. What they weren't getting was nourishment of their own spirits, and acknowledgement and appreciation for their worth, regardless of their talents, IQs and skills. Unless the whole school community signed up to this, they might only ever get this encouragement in one lesson a week. But spirituality had to keep quiet, not attract attention, or there would be ridicule.

A secular approach to mindfulness education that focuses on our earthly life is missing a more important exploration of life and death, and what lies beyond death – in the same way, the education we give our children is too weighted towards getting a job in the material world. It's not that this approach is wrong, but for many of us it is hollow – something crucial is missing from our understanding of what it is to be mortal. If you teach a class about ancient religion then it's only natural that your students' eyes will cloud over. If you tell them you're going to discuss their ideas about why we're born and what happens after death, you'll be going into extra time.

Reflections

- Which ideas and beliefs about the mind sit comfortably with you?
- How do you feel about the holistic approach that the mind and body are interdependent?
- Consider your view on the purpose and meaning of life. Is understanding what the mind is an important feature of this reflection for you, or irrelevant?
- Which meditation was the most powerful for you? How important is it for you to experience the meditation rather than just read about the subject?

Authentic mindfulness

- If you remember your dreams, see if you can interpret their meaning to understand what's really going on in your mind. Remember, everything is an aspect of yourself.
- Try to incorporate all four applications of mindfulness – the body, feelings, mind and phenomena – into your meditation practice.
- Consider if practising mindfulness for just this life is short-sighted.
- Identify your biggest obstacle to knowing your mind and work with that first.

Spiritual integrity

- Recognising the interdependence of us all is a key spiritual practice.
- If you reject religion, be logical about your beliefs. Being airy-fairy will not get you anywhere. You'll have no true guidance.
- Thinking you're a spiritual person is correct. Thinking that

you're more spiritual than others is dangerous.

We all long for personal and relevant discussion about the purpose and meaning of our lives. The mental health of all people rightly need it if they are to be stable members of any society. Mindfulness can fill the hole, especially if we broaden its horizons so that our minds might also become as spacious and open as the sky. Understanding the nature of the mind is a crucial step to considering the extent to which mindfulness can give our lives meaning and purpose.

Part Two

Walking the Talk

When we walk with wisdom, sometimes we may trip and fall. Just get up, and keep on walking. Wisdom is always there to guide us.

Chapter 5

Understanding Thoughts and Emotions

○ ○ ○

"I yam what I yam."

Popeye the Sailor Man[9]

We have this wonderful opportunity, as people in a state of constant distraction, to work with our emotions when we understand how they arise. Traditionally, serious meditators use mindfulness meditation to virtually bypass the emotions – they are simply aware of them as phenomena appearing and disappearing, like clouds in the sky. Most of us will manage to meditate for an average of 20 minutes a day (if that), so taking that objectivity, or awareness, into our everyday lives is going to be our most applied skill – our most important gizmo. Forget the latest iPhone or Fitbit – the emotional intelligence developed through being mindful will enable our communications to be high quality and genuine, and our wellbeing will rocket. Trust me.

Let's remind ourselves that the practice of mindfulness involves two skills:

- Mindfulness meditation itself
- Being mindful in our day-to-day lives (by taking the objectivity that we learn and experience in meditation into our lives)

The learning required here is to retain a rational and objective view of everything – particularly what is going on in our own minds. Understand-

---

9   Popeye the Sailor Man was the main character of a popular cartoon that I watched as a child in the 1950s. His well-known saying "I yam what I yam an' tha's all I yam" – implying that he couldn't be anything else – captured my questioning mind.

ing that *our thoughts are not us* is step number one. What a relief! All that weird, negative broiling going on in our heads is just brain chatter, fuelled by a nervous ego that can't quite make sense of what is expected of it. And it's happening to everyone. EVERYONE! Even the Dalai Lama says that his emotions are present, but they're more like ripples on the surface of the ocean than the tidal waves you and I might experience.

The ultimate aim of a serious *Buddhist* meditator is enlightenment, so all emotions, destructive or otherwise, are viewed as obstacles to insight into the true nature of reality. But for most of us, utilising constructive emotions as antidotes to destructive ones is our key practice. The Tibetans don't have a word for emotion. They call them 'defilements' or 'delusions'… so you can see where they're coming from.

Developing a healthy relationship with your ego is hugely helpful. I have found it useful to give my ego a name because it helps me dissociate from all the nonsense the ego comes up with. I call mine Nora, which was inspired by the wonderful children's book *Noisy Nora* by Rosemary Wells – about a mouse called Nora who likes to make a lot of noise – which I would read to my children when they were young and still under my spell. I found myself identifying with Nora! So, whenever I realise I am being controlled by some egotistical aspect of myself due to fear or anxiety, I address myself in the way that Nora's mother addresses her, with a soft, reproachful look and tender admonishment to quieten down. This encourages me to be aware of what's unfolding in my mind without feeling like a bad person.

It's useful to give the ego a name because it enables us to stand back from this aspect of ourselves – treating it, if you like, as our own dear child. It's an extra trick in the bag to help us navigate our lives.

Fear triggers our more destructive thoughts and emotions. These might arise due to a primal instinct like survival, or due to conditioned experiences (seeking approval, fulfilling a role, achieving a goal), but essentially all destructive emotions are fear-based. Just as Noisy Nora is motivated by wanting attention because she's scared she's being overlooked, our thoughts and emotions can hold the key to understanding ourselves – which is what this chapter is all about. Chapter 6 then goes on to explore *how* we can manage our thoughts and emotions.

The stories we tell ourselves

In Chapter 3, I shared a diagram showing how the mind knows objects. Once we have been stimulated through our senses, the mental consciousness starts to grab hold of that information, and… well, it starts to make up stories.

One example scenario often arises in a working environment, but it could easily be transferred to a personal situation. Imagine you're walking down a corridor and you see (with your sight sense) and hear indistinctly (with your ear sense) two colleagues laughing and chatting. As you approach, they see and hear you too and then stop laughing and chatting and look away as if nothing was happening. As a result, you start to *feel* insecure and *think* that they may have been talking about you (the perceptual becomes conceptual), or sharing a secret they won't tell you. A number of emotions arise. As well as insecurity, there may be jealousy, paranoia, anger and sadness. You are jumping to conclusions because your ego has been pricked: just by a tiny pin, but the emotional fall-out may last for days. Through the stimulation of your senses, your mental consciousness – dominated by the ego – has reacted. You don't know what was happening between those two colleagues, but you made it all about you. It's like the mental consciousness is a puppet and the ego is the puppet master.

In each and every one of us there is a marvellous storyteller getting totally caught up in our stories, seeking out the worst possible scenarios in order to arrive at solutions that can protect us from all eventualities. In our minds, Little Red Riding Hood will get eaten by the wolf, Sleeping Beauty will never awaken from her slumber, and Roald Dahl's book-loving hero Matilda will be damaged for life with a personality disorder.

Believing in our own stories is a form of self-sabotage that can cause us a lot of problems. We need to be kind to ourselves and understand *why* we self-sabotage. Life is uncertain and we just don't know what will happen to us next, and so it's understandable that we are fearful, seek control and prepare for the worst.

But what mindfulness teaches us is that we need to ditch this attitude, along with our prehistoric DNA that needed us to be fearful to survive. Human beings are capable of subduing the mind that is driven by fear. And when we do this, we can actually enjoy life more, and undoubtedly be more creative, happy, motivated and philosophical beings.

Dumping this fearful attitude does not mean we will be putting ourselves in danger. Running from an assailant or fleeing a forest fire is still important for our safety and survival. We don't want to say, "Hey, come and get me, I'm okay with that because I practise mindfulness!" Having an aspect of our minds that is rational *and* mindful increases our chances of not only escaping from a real physical threat but also accessing our ability to assess a situation with intelligent reasoning, as well as softening the emotional and mental after-effects of our experiences.

Without mindful awareness of our emotions, we are stuffed. Riding that rollercoaster of ups and downs, we grab onto the ups and are unprepared for the downs – and we exaggerate the experience of both. When we are victims of the vast range of our emotions, then every day is a fairground ride without safety belts. Mindfulness is Health and Safety to minimise emotional accidents.

Hamsters on wheels

Humans seek pleasure because pleasure accompanies positive emotions. This search for only positive emotions we can liken to our search for happiness. We think it's very much about our bodies ("Mmm, eating chocolate tastes so good!"), but actually it is about the accompanying emotions ("Mmm… nice, nice, nice"). But even if sensory pleasure does make us happy, we know it's only temporary because as soon as the external sensory stimulation stops (the bar of chocolate is now just a silver foil wrapper), the pleasure stops.

Consider this frequent scenario from my everyday life.

When I've finished writing, I go for a walk. I watch a bit of TV and make dinner. After dinner, I settle down to watch a drama or film – something entertaining. My mind is in the habit of wanting to increase my sense of pleasure by getting something nice to eat or drink, so it brings up the image of what I've got in the cupboard or fridge. There's half a bottle of white wine. Maybe some chocolate or crisps and dip. I sit there, not really needing anything, but my mind is filled with desire. I'm watching the film, but my attention keeps getting diverted to the snacks and wine. I fight with it, because I'm putting on weight and don't really need it. Dinner was enough. But my willpower is so weak, and there's no one there to distract me, so I pause the film and indulge.

I do feel more content. I've rewarded myself. Why not? I work hard and deserve it. This is Nora's voice. This indulgence has become a habit and I know it's going to appear whenever I get into that end-of-day state of mind.

Now, the desire is always there and it's not just an evening visitor, but it's not really noticeable. During the day, I'm quite restrained. However, when I enter this evening scenario I am aware of how strong my desire is. My mindfully aware mind knows all this and sees it happening. But rarely does my inner self win. The desire is so strong within me and Nora is so noisy that I still act as if pleasure is happiness.

Now you might think, "So what? Don't deny yourself a bit of pleasure!" But giving in to desire creates endless desire, a process known as the *hedonic treadmill.* We are never satisfied, so we constantly seek more and more pleasure, under the illusion it is making us happy – when the reality is that seeking pleasure is simply fuelling our desire for more. If we can understand that *not* buying into desire means that we can *increase* our contentment, then we have more motivation to step off the treadmill.

In a world filled with desirable objects (chocolate, clothes, handbags), we are under a lot of pressure to succumb to the lure of pleasure. But this is not just about spending money on 'things we don't really need' – anyone can find themselves on the hedonic treadmill. It's not about your level of wealth, but your level of contentment. Whether your desire is for a second home or a can of lager, the craving remains the same.

The mind/body connection

In my training, when we're discussing disturbing emotions, someone will always say, "I'm not really a jealous person", and look at me with incomprehension as if they've never experienced it. What they mean is that nothing has ever happened to make them particularly jealous. But it's there, like a big green monster in the shadows of the mind, and if we are faced with something that might induce jealousy (such as discovering that our partner is having an affair), then that's when it comes out to grab us by the throat. And it can be subtle. More like a tickle in the back of the throat than a stranglehold. It is there every time we compare ourselves to someone who challenges our ego (because our ego finds them threatening). It is there in the playground, where the bully rules, secretly driven by insecurity. In every unpleasurable situation, our emotions can literally get the better of us. Anger, fear, jealousy and hatred can not only destroy our happiness but also make the beautiful ugly, and the healthy unhealthy. If we hang on to anger, then eventually that could manifest as a physical illness. Hence the mind–body connection. Some years back that would have been seen as new-agey-speak, but these days it has become credible with the advance of science. Studies that link wellness to mindfulness and research into the mind–body connection have refuted past scientific assertions that there is no link between our minds and bodies. In this way, science has caught up with traditional Eastern wisdom, which has long made this connection.

My story – so much pride

I've been working on my mind now for over 40 years, so it is a much more pliable beast than it once was. If I put myself into a beginner's shoes, I recall my own obstacles to mastering my mind. For me, honestly, I think the first step in recognising the nature of my ego was to overcome pride. I had a very argumentative tendency to 'take on' anyone who did not agree with me. I suppose, with hindsight, that this was an aspect of a defensive attitude I had built due to the family dynamics in which I was raised, as well as my own fiery tendencies. It was very important for me to be right. It was also vital that I knew best and knew first, and so 'I knew that' and 'I know' became part of my patter. Pride is a very tricky emotion. And compassion is its antidote.

During my first three-week course at the Institute, the intensity of listening to teachings and meditating on them day after day led to vivid dreams for many of us, which were part of processing the profound concepts we were being introduced to. Tibetan Buddhism is rich in imagery, so naturally the interpretation of dreams and visions was part of helping us understand our minds. (In this way, it is very similar in nature to Jung's use of symbolism to understand the psyche.) In those very early stages I had a mixed reaction to my experiences there. I was irritated by some of the students who wandered around as if they were in ecstasy: my subtext being, "Why wasn't I deliriously happy?" But I was stunned and inspired by the teachings that focused on compassion. The Lamas had me in the palm of their hands, but my contemporaries sometimes pricked my patience. At the time, I could not have assessed my emotions, but looking back I can see that I was experiencing feelings of isolation, frustration and deep anger that left a darkness in my heart. I wanted to be mainstream and accepted, but my tendencies to feel different and not quite understood were leading to resentment and jealousy. Then one night I had the most vivid dream. I was vomiting, bright orange endless sick that turned into an ocean. I was like Alice in Wonderland, my mouth a spout and the rest of me dangerously negotiating strange objects such as umbrellas, pigs and a girl I once worked with at a library, who liked to party and had flaming red hair. I awoke from the dream and was frankly appalled, thinking, "Well, that's it, there's no hope for me. I am a crazy, bad person."

I had 'karma yoga' to do that day, which meant working for the community, and mine was weeding in the large market garden. A woman was working alongside me. She was more experienced than I and very warm and friendly, so I felt able to 'confess' to her my dream. I suddenly felt able to tell her about my negative feelings as well as recounting the dream. This was already quite a step for me to take, and instead of being appalled, she announced how wonderful it was. She analysed that it was a dream of purification, meaning that I had massively purified my mind. Then she asked me how I felt, and actually I felt light and of course open enough to be vulnerable with her. I had overcome my pride. Of course, there would be plenty more opportunities to take this further, and there still are, but this experience was crucial. Admitting we might have got something wrong and being willing to change our minds is a great quality. The Buddhist antidote to pride being compassion, I think that day I had compassion for myself when I acknowledged I needed help.

'Purification' is a common term in Tibetan Buddhism and describes a variety of actions and practices that help us 'clean up' our minds to make room for qualities and contemplative skills. Dreaming of vomiting, excreting, coughing up symbols of our own inner darkness (like rats or toads – apologies to those who adore these creatures) are all seen as healthy psychological manifestations of our consciousnesses being cleansed by a positive attribute we have nurtured.

The role of others

"Hell is other people."

Jean-Paul Sartre

No Exit[10]

The world is filled with people we need to get on with, but who are very different to us. We could choose to only connect with our good friends – but even they drive us crazy sometimes. We could even change our opinions all the time to fit in with others, but that rarely ends well, as a

---

10   This Jean-Paul Sartre quote, from his play No Exit, is often misunderstood. It is a reference to Sartre's ideas about how we see ourselves from the perspective of another consciousness that causes us confusion and struggle with who we are.

lovely little fable about a man, a boy and a donkey explains better than I can (the earliest version is attributed to the 13th-century Arab writer Ibn Said, though later versions are attributed to Aesop). A man and his son are taking a donkey to market, a journey that is overshadowed by others' opinions of how they are travelling – with some criticising either father or son for riding the donkey, while others criticise them for not riding the donkey. Foolishly, the man tries to please everyone, which leads to increasingly ridiculous behaviour that ultimately ends in tragedy, with the death of the poor donkey. The moral being that if you try to please everyone, you will inevitably please no one.

The man feared disapproval, so he felt inhibited by the unwholesome feeling of self-consciousness brought on by wanting the approval of others.

If we all lived just to please others then we would be subject to a whole host of unwholesome feelings. Not being ourselves is a heavy coat to wear and does not lead to peace and contentment. But if we understand how our ego works and how we are conditioned, and also acknowledge that little percentage of our own character and personality that came into the world with us, then we can become aware of what triggers us to feel unwholesome emotions and learn to check them so that we can experience more wholesome emotions. This is *authenticity* and is not subject to others' influence.

The world of emotions

Consider what a map of your emotional world might look like. Your emotions may be represented by a lot of countries; some inhabiting large continents, others a whole load of lesser islands, yet size doesn't matter – our emotions are equally significant in terms of the inner conflicts they cause us.

Here are some familiar emotions and feelings, arranged as continents:

- **Anger:** Irritation, hatred, intolerance, loathing, rage
- **Sadness:** Grief, sorrow, cheerlessness, gloom, melancholy, self-pity, loneliness, dejection, despair, depression, unhappi-

ness, torment, nostalgia

- **Fear:** Anxiety, apprehension, nervousness, concern, consternation, misgiving, wariness, qualm, edginess, dread, fright, terror, phobia, panic, worry, timidity, paranoia
- **Enjoyment:** Happiness, joy, relief, contentment, bliss, delight, amusement, pride, sensual pleasure, thrill, rapture, gratification, satisfaction, euphoria, whimsy, ecstasy, mania, peace, lust
- **Love:** Acceptance, friendliness, trust, kindness, affinity, devotion, adoration, infatuation, compassion, yearning, patience, empathy, forgiveness, equanimity
- **Surprise:** Shock, amazement, astonishment, wonder, awe
- **Disgust:** Contempt, disdain, scorn, abhorrence, aversion, distaste, revulsion
- **Shame:** Guilt, embarrassment, chagrin, remorse, humiliation, regret, mortification, contrition, shyness

And let's not forget:

Jealousy, hope, faith, courage, certainty, doubt, complacency, arrogance, pride, sloth, torpor, boredom⊠

We can see there are degrees of an emotion, and ways of expressing that emotion that can be 'in your face' or concealed (but nevertheless present). Let's take our old friend anger as an example – the range of emotions associated with anger makes us aware that what we usually understand by anger is not quite accurate. When people say, "I never get angry," they mean that they don't shout and lose their temper – but they may not realise that being irritated is an aspect of anger, as is being impatient, resentful, exasperated, indignant, vexatious, acrimonious, annoyed, irritable, hostile or hateful, which of course can lead to the more violent displays of outrage, fury, wrath and vengefulness.

So, it's not accurate to say, "I never get angry." Perhaps you can swallow your anger but, underneath, you carry a deep resentment that, if not acknowledged and expressed, will one day turn into something physically harmful or explode like a volcano into an eruption of harmful speech. Think of that quiet, pleasant man who ends up killing his wife (neighbour: "Ooh, he was a lovely chap. Always helpful and so polite") who regularly features in television murder mysteries!

The choices we make

Let's return to the diagram in Chapter 3 (that shows how our minds know objects). This time, we're focusing on the emotions aspect.

A model of how the mind knows objects, focusing on how they lead to emotions.

I use the word 'wholesome' to describe emotions that we understand to be linked with a calm and peaceful mind. You might say, "How boring!" because it's nice to feel the adrenaline rush of fear followed by relief, or to be able to express one's anger freely in a cathartic manner. But let's investigate this view that wholesome equals boring by putting fear under the microscope. If you deliberately set yourself a dangerous challenge, such as rock climbing, and you're aware that the risk may bring reward (or not), then fair enough: that's your mountain (metaphorical and literal) and your thrill to seek. But if the fear is unasked for, such as the presence of someone walking behind you in the dark, then you can see that this isn't about adrenaline, or thrills – this is more about feeling a lack of control.

Fear itself is a safety lock. It keeps us alive. Fear is clearly an unpleasant feeling, but we can't say it's destructive unless it stops us doing things that would actually benefit us. If a child fears going to school because they have experienced bullying or peer group rejection, and the parents are overprotective and let the child stay at home, then the fear is being indulged, creating a stronger dislike of school that could lead to paranoia or anxiety. But if fear stops us from making a reckless decision that would put our lives in danger, like that same child saying no to taking drugs, then we can clearly see the survival button being activated. Fear's place in the list of emotions depends largely on the context. Living in an irrational state of fear and anxiety is *destructive*. Having a rational fear of dangerous situations is *constructive*. Fear arises in all sentient beings to ensure the survival of the species, so it is only destructive when it controls us. Fear needs training, like that puppy.

Unwholesome emotions are those that cause us confusion and upset – and, indeed, cause others the same if we point our fingers at them as being the reason for our upset. We spread all this confusion and upset to others – which is an important consideration, because as interdependent beings we know that, from our point of view, most upsets seem to be caused by other people. We point our fingers and blame others for our problems, which lays the foundations for divisiveness.

Having understood the fundamentals of the mind (in Chapter 4), we can see that *any* emotion disturbs it. Our challenge is to change unwholesome emotions to wholesome ones and then, building on those positive states of mind, eventually reach a stage in our development of mind that is without any emotion. Any emotion experienced is a temporary event. This is not a blank, detached way of being, but one imbued with profound levels of wisdom and compassion – ultimately, we are developing an enlightened mind. Why not aim for the moon?

The enlightened mind has two qualities: compassion and wisdom. These aren't defined as emotional states because they are permanent attributes of an enlightened mind – they are realisations rather than ego-driven reactions. And there is no attachment or aversion involved. This is not ordinary compassion… this is M&S compassion!

This destination seems far, far away, but there are many highlights and interesting excursions on the journey. Working towards an enlightened mind is our only choice, really.

Emotions – good or bad?

It's helpful to consider whether emotions are wholesome, unwholesome, both or neither. Some people say that emotions can be both wholesome and unwholesome, or think that it's good to express emotions such as anger. But the simplest way to define the quality of an emotion is to consider how we feel when we are experiencing it.

For example:

- "When I am angry, I feel hot, my stomach churns and I am extremely frustrated." Nice – or not?
- "When I am sad, I feel dark, depressed and tearful." Nice – or not?

It is perhaps easy to agree that we don't want to feel anger (it certainly doesn't sound pleasant), but what about sadness? It doesn't feel good either, but does that mean we shouldn't feel grief or empathy? Surely these feelings are part of being human?

With mindfulness supporting us, we can feel sadness but also become aware if it starts to turn into depression and gets stuck there (and so never moves on to acceptance). In Swiss-American psychiatrist Elisabeth Kübler-Ross's five stages of grief, she helpfully describes the common stages that grieving people experience on their road to moving on (denial, anger, bargaining, depression and acceptance). Mindfulness enables us to be aware of where we are and to seek the help and guidance we need from others in order for this progress to happen. It is a companion on the journey.

When we're dealing with emotions, it is important to recognise how they make us feel. The healing process for repressed emotions relies on this awareness and is part of the mind-body connection theory discussed earlier. *Somatic markers* are feelings in the body associated with emotions, and these feelings are what psychotherapists focus on when helping people come to terms with deeply felt traumas. Understanding that emotions can cause us illness if they're not expressed or worked with makes more sense when we recognise what they can do to us physically. Consider some of these common expressions: "I felt it in my gut"; "She broke my heart"; "I couldn't breathe"; "I couldn't look at it."

Familiarising ourselves with our emotions really helps us to see them for what they are, rather than seeing them as aspects of our selves. Because our emotions arise so automatically and we feel them so strongly, we need every trick we can muster to manage them because they feel so inseparable from who we are.

Where do thoughts and emotions come from?

If you're now going to the other extreme and coming to the realisation "I am an angry person!", then that too is unhelpful and untrue because even if we are quick to anger, we are not *always* angry. If I was an angry person, anger would be in my mind *all* the time. I'd have a heart attack very quickly! When we say, "I am an angry person!", we mean that we get annoyed really easily; we are in a fragile state of wellbeing because we have a strong tendency towards anger. However, because we have the tendency to get angry *quickly*, we are more likely to get angry *regularly*. So, how do our more disturbing emotions arise? Where do they come from?

Here's an explanation that takes the continuum of the mind as its basis. Buddhist psychology states that there are three necessary causes and conditions for a disturbing emotion to arise:

- The seed is present

- An object is present
- We give the object inappropriate attention

Let's consider each of these in turn – as well as what we can do at each stage.

1. The seed is present

Seeds are imprints from past actions that exist in our minds as a potentiality or predisposition. So if we believe "I am an angry person!" then we might think: "I've been angry before, so I'll be angry again"; "I'm in the habit of getting angry." It's an objective view of our reality.

For example, when we become angry, the experience leaves an imprint on our mind – a mark on the mirror – and this has the potential to ripen as anger again at a later time when the causes and conditions come together. It's like coming into a situation with someone who presses your anger button: the conditions are perfect for a blow-up. But the cause is *not other people* – those who press your buttons – but *the anger that is present in your mind*. Others may be contributory factors but not the actual cause – perhaps you're late to work because of a whole load of unavoidable reasons, and your line manager hauls you into the office to have a go at you for being late. This attacks your ego so you get angry, but you can't express your anger because your job is at stake. So, you simmer feverishly all day. When you get home, someone says something innocent to you, and the lid blows off and you boil over because you have the seed (or tendency) for anger on your mind. Everything else just contributes to the problem. The straw that breaks the camel's back is just one fraction of the bale you're carrying.

Seeds are always there, but we are not aware of them as having the potential to generate an emotional response – and yet they can cause our disturbing emotions to take hold of our minds. They're literally like flower seeds – or weeds – in the ground of our evolving minds. They need water and nourishment to grow. These seeds ripen into disturbing emotions when the appropriate conditions come together – such as when someone says something that implies a criticism – and BOOM!

The anger arises.

However, if we can destroy or weaken the seed of anger, our anger wouldn't arise – or if it did, it would be less likely to harm ourselves or others. We would have managed our anger.

Without these seeds, no matter what we encounter, a disturbing emotion would not arise. Your line manager could be as narky as they liked, but you'd be impervious, like wearing a waterproof mac in the rain. You'd be like Andie MacDowell in the film *Four Weddings and a Funeral*, hair soaking wet yet asking, "Is it raining?"

We can weaken these seeds by applying an antidote emotion – a positive emotion that has the effect of counteracting the nasty one, acting like a stain remover (though it doesn't entirely work until the ego is destroyed, but we are weakening the tendency). For example, cultivating loving-kindness can weaken the seed of anger (I talk about cultivating loving-kindness and other tricks in Chapter 6).

Think about which particular disturbing emotions most often arise in your mind and what kinds of antidotes would help weaken the seeds of those disturbing emotions by having a go at the Wheel of Destructive Emotions exercise in Chapter 6.

If we can be aware of the seed, then with steady, continued practice, no matter what the circumstances, we can maintain a healthy, mindful state. Disturbing emotions will not arise so frequently, and we can manage them better when they do.

2. An object is present

Destructive emotions can't arise unless they meet an *object* – anything that makes us upset, such as a certain person or the recycling bin tipping over in the wind – that stimulates these emotions. When we encounter certain objects that upset us, we can easily generate aversion towards them because we have projected aversion onto these objects already. For example, perhaps you don't like your neighbour. Whenever you see or hear them, your anger is stimulated and a dark feeling arises within you. Impatience is triggered at first sight.

The more objects we encounter, the more our disturbing emotions have a chance to strengthen and repeat themselves. So we become easily angered, which causes us even more problems. When we are angry, the rational mind is asleep and we can hurt ourselves (and others) in the moment of agitation.

There are plenty of objects we can point to that have a tendency to arouse our temper. But the damage spreads outwards when the objects are people. This is why we may encounter a lot of emotional problems if we have to be in the same place as a lot of people we don't really connect with, such as a school, a particular class you dread, a workplace or group of people you have to have meetings with, or someone who is causing pain and suffering to others (and who you perceive to be the devil incarnate).

Until we develop stable minds through being mindful and practising mindfulness meditation so that we are not disturbed by the objects we encounter, it may help to physically remove ourselves from these objects to lessen the likelihood of our delusions manifesting, running riot and causing big splodgy stains on our minds. This is a simple method that can be very helpful. Of course, there are times when this may not be possible (it's hard to avoid your partner), but recognising that you are likely to get upset because you have an awareness of your emotional predispositions can help you to be prepared. Arm yourself with antidote emotions – and other tricks such as breathing techniques and practising patience – and you can minimise the damage. (I look more at the antidotes in Chapter 6.)

3. We give the object inappropriate attention

A mind that dwells on an object (a person or thing) and grasps at it as a source of happiness will exaggerate its apparent qualities. As a result, the qualities that we ascribe to that object begin to appear very solid and permanent. When they fail to deliver to our expectations, our egos go into shock and disbelief. Equally, if we dwell on an object with aversion, we may exaggerate its apparent negatives, which fuels our unwholesome emotions and puffs up our egos. We're giving the object way too much attention – it becomes obsessive, and we find it difficult to remove the object from our minds.

Grasping at objects leads to exaggerating or imputing qualities that aren't there, resulting in strong aversion or desire. Just consider how obsessed we get when we fall in love: the mind embraces the object, making the person beautiful and a perfect object for our attachment. The phrase 'rose-tinted spectacles' comes to mind when we are dealing with attachments. The attachment is an illusion, because we all know that when we fall out of love with the same person, all we can see are their faults! This is a great example of how our mind gives attributes to an object that barely has anything to do with the object. (Replace 'object' with 'your ex' and you soon get the picture.)

Equally, we can become attached to an idea, and if that idea is threatened then aversion also arises. Take driving your car. It can be a very enjoyable experience. You feel in control as you sit behind your steering wheel, with everything in its right place: food wrappers on the floor, belongings scattered on the seat next to you, children strapped brutally into their car seats. What's not to like? Then you hit a queue, and someone zips in front of you. Nothing drastic has happened – you're not being hijacked, it's just that someone's a bit impatient for reasons you don't know and... whooooah there, Noisy Nora! Your ego is inflamed. Your attachment to being in control over your possessions and your life is being threatened by another vehicle. For some reason, having glass windows between you and the other driver enables you to express yourself in a way that you would not normally contemplate. You use a certain finger to show your displeasure. They honk their horn and wave their arms around. War is declared... because you are six feet behind them now in the queue. If you are guilty of this (and I suspect, along with me, that you are), then how do you have the right to criticise countries that declare war on each other? Just saying.

Using antidote emotions in a situation like this can be powerful (an approach that people who I've trained have found life-changing). Patience, empathy and compassion replace road rage as we consider what fuels the other driver – it helps us imagine their story. Perhaps they are late for a hospital appointment, funeral or their child's school performance. Using antidote emotions is so simple yet so profound. These methods are also discussed further in Chapter 6.

Disturbing emotions may flourish and abound to such an extent that they come to define you. ("He's such an angry man.") Free yourself from the illusion that external objects can make you unhappy (or bring you happiness) and recognise your addiction to pointing that finger.

Why should I change?

> "I say let the world go to hell, but I should always have my tea."

> *Fyodor Dostoevsky*
>
> *Notes from Underground*

If we consider the results of being angry or selfish, we can whittle away at this thorny stick and find that practising and developing our good selves actually results in increased self-esteem and the ability to be open-hearted. We don't become less, we become more. We attract others and therefore experience better relationships.

This is a cause for genuine happiness so why wouldn't we want to change?

Putting aside selfishness does not mean that we should put ourselves last. The concept of 'compassion fatigue', which I have witnessed in many people trying to put themselves last in the line-up of importance, shows us that if we do neglect ourselves, we can become damaged.

There is an idea that some people are naturally compassionate, and some aren't; some are attracted to the caring professions, and some aren't. But, unlike the view that compassion cannot be taught and developed – that I have heard some people in the healthcare professions share – mindfulness teaches us that it can. Of course, some are already halfway there, but their compassion may often discriminate – choosing who they will be compassionate towards – while others just need to awaken their compassion.

Buddhist teachings tell us that we are inherently good and that the 'bad' in us is just like stains on the mind. We can polish them away. Of course, some stains are harder to remove than others, but they can all be removed with practice. Practising mindfulness is like a free form of stain guard with a guarantee.

True compassion recognises that everyone and every creature is worthy of our love and understanding. All people suffer in ways we don't always see. It's easy to be compassionate to some people and difficult to be compassionate towards others because we judge some to be more worthy of our compassion. But we don't have to like everyone to feel compassion for them.

Hardened criminals may come from backgrounds that have conditioned them to be violent, and so we can see that in some ways they did not stand a chance of becoming balanced, well-rounded citizens. It is virtually impossible for such people to know that there is a way of life that is free from disturbing thoughts and emotions. Finding the way in to some people's minds requires great skill.

So, why wouldn't you want to change? Unless you're a masochist or hell-bent on punishing yourself, refusing to change would be like biting off your nose to spite your face (as the saying goes). This isn't an occasion to behave like a hormonal teenager and be contrary. The only person who will suffer is you, but it is the perfect opportunity for spiritual rebellion.

Having said this, I do know of many people whose egos are so stubborn that they literally set themselves up against the world. I like to be different too. I was always looking for an unusual fashion trend to start, or avant-garde music to champion. My image was cool but my ego was jumpy. It's a terrible time for self-esteem when you're a teenager. If someone had enlightened me, I would have swapped that 'cool chick' mask for the wonders of self-knowledge as quickly as sticky toffee pudding leaves the dessert bowl and finds its way down my throat... or would I? I guess we have to be ready and willing to change, and I doubt that my stubborn ego, which thought I was special and different, would have been ready back then. Now, I look like every other old lady, but inside I'm as flexible as a fairy.

Stubbornness is a very challenging emotion. Not wanting to change our point of view, way of life or opinion can keep us in a lonely place. It's like self-inflicted mental solitary confinement. We may turn out to be right sometimes, so it can be a helpful attribute. However, we are more likely to describe that as persistence or determination. People tend to be proud of their stubbornness, as if they are the only ones who know what is right (or perhaps they are scared of being wrong).

Stubbornness is a characteristic that requires a lot of discussion between the ego and the inner self, to determine whether we're ultimately being self-defeating or whether we'll achieve something great by sticking to our guns – which means not abandoning our position when the enemy is coming at us. I guess the enemy here might be anyone who is trying to get past our ego, but equally it could mean peer or societal pressure. If we know something from the position of our inner self then stubbornness can be a great virtue, but if we're clinging and grasping onto an idea to prove ourselves right, then we're just being dogmatic.

Reflections

- o   Do you have a tendency to identify with your thoughts and emotions and think that they are 'you'?
- o   Have you been in a situation similar to the example workplace scenario shared earlier in this chapter? Did it resonate with you?
- o   Consider how certain 'objects' (people, places, things) that you have encountered easily stimulate disturbing emotions in you.
- o   Consider from your own experience the people or things for which you have attachment or aversion. Do they really have all the positive or negative qualities that your attachment or aversion thinks they have?
- o   When does your desire overrule reason? Which wins?

In the next chapter I look at *how* to change – it's a very practical guide to working with your thoughts and emotions. It's like moving from your permanent address to your holiday home, with the idea that you might take up residence there if you like it.

Chapter 6

Managing Thoughts and Emotions

○ ○ ○

"Thoughts are like tourists; they come and they go. Your mind is the permanent resident."

Lama Thubten Yeshe

Mahamudra: How to Discover Our True Nature, edited by Robina Courtin

In Cheryl Strayed's autobiographical book *Wild*, she describes how she came to a place of loving self-acceptance through taking on the challenge of physical endurance. It's a gripping account of someone who chose to step into a dangerous, untamed world to overcome her personal demons.

Mindfulness practice is the mental equivalent of Cheryl's journey. But it is an inner quest. There are still metaphorical mountains to climb and deserts to survive, but we can face these challenges with gentle awareness. We don't require Cheryl's stamina or appetite for such a brave expedition, but we do need her courage.

The exercises and practices in this chapter will be your friends on the trail to help you on your way. Don't feel pressured that somehow you have to control your thoughts and emotions. You're just looking. Test out the interior design to self-awareness and consider if managing your thoughts and emotions might bring you more comfort and lead to you feeling more at home with yourself. (Note: I use different labelling pairs, all are synonymous: wholesome/unwholesome, constructive/destructive, positive/negative and pacifying/disturbing. Use what works for you. I think it's healthy to diversify a bit and not get stuck in a box.)

Dealing with destructive emotions

We looked at the primary causes for the rising and falling of our emotions in Chapter 5, so now we need to be aware of the secondary influences, internal and external, to become clearer on what supports our mental strength and what weakens it.

The principal cause of our problems is our own unknowing. Buddhists call this *ignorance*, but that can sound harsh. We're not stupid, we just haven't been taught. We've been told to be good, but not *how* to be good. We've been told to stop shouting, but not *how* to stop feeling so frustrated and angry that we can only shout at the moon. However, there are choices we can make that can offer us support – like the stabilising wheels on your first bike. Though we may be grown-ups now, we still need to build confidence.

External influences

The first step is to look around us. Is our environment and the people we know helping or hindering us in our spiritual development?

1. False friends

Peer group pressure and the influence of the majority mean we can quickly dump our moral convictions when the road gets bumpy. We have all been influenced by others to do things we didn't really want to do. What we want, more than anything, is to 'fit in' and we don't trust ourselves to make the right choices. This naturally leads to perhaps doing or saying things that we may later regret. This is when we become *inauthentic*: it's not really us, but our fear-driven ego that is desperate to fit in, so the inauthentic act sits uncomfortably with us... as if we have something stuck in our throat.

We can't blame our friends for our own weaknesses. They can influence us, but they are not the cause of our unwholesome emotions. And we all have the potential to be the bully as well as to be led by one, so being clear about this will help us distinguish between those who we can affect, and those who can affect us.

Until we develop more stable minds, we can keep those friends who have a 'bad' influence on us close to our hearts (by generating compassion for them), but at a physical distance. We need to be clear on who our 'good' friends are and cultivate them. If we have to be around powerful leaders who are taking us down a path we don't want to tread, we need to seek support and guidance from those we trust. This is not cowardice – this is common sense.

We need to have faith in our own convictions – this requires courage. We can step back and check in with our inner self to see whether what we are being asked to say or do sits comfortably with us, and have the courage to say "No", and more importantly, to change our mind.

2. Media

'Fake news', misleading information, conspiracy theories, gossip-led social media – all of these can either consciously or unconsciously influence us. This includes books, newspapers, TV and advertisements as well, but it's social media – such as our Facebook and Twitter feeds – that has the power to cause so much confusion and misunderstanding.

We have to be very careful in our relationship with social media to know who (or what) to follow and to believe. Media that encourages us to be *unethical* (to cause harm to others) or that stimulates our low self-esteem issues can lead to a distracted and confused mind that is ripe for disturbing emotions. Hurling verbal abuse in the form of a written tweet is too common and so unnecessary. There are examples of celebrities suffering deep levels of depression, even leading to suicide attempts, because they let 'trolls' control their lives. These anonymous stalkers are extremely damaged people who have no other way to express their jealousy and hatred except to bring down someone they envy via malicious banter. Know them for what they are, and if you keep compassion for them in your hearts then they will not disturb your mind so much.

It's easy to look at how others are affected by the media, but it's more useful to be honest with ourselves about our own contributions to misleading and harmful gossip, and the complicated outcomes that can arise if we engage in these activities. Ultimately, due to the law of cause and effect, we are lining trouble up for ourselves later. You know... what goes around comes around.

To help us step back from its negative influence, it may be wise to limit our time on social media. Practise putting that phone on silent and not picking it up. Take care to check whether what we're reading is true or false. Most journalism has at least a seed of truth, but everything written has political and personal bias. There is not one truth; instead, the personal projections of others influence us regularly through the media. Plus, how useful is it to fill our heads with information that is mainly destructive to our peace of mind?

Compassion is the most powerful emotion we can exercise when reading Twitter feeds that are full of hate. Compassion pours water on anger and puts out any fire that the online trolls wish to ignite. Not caring too much about what others think about us is a characteristic of good self-esteem. It's good to be informed, but we need to check that we aren't being manipulated.

Internal influences

Our thoughts, dominant emotions, habits, tendencies and karma all contribute to influence us, so there's a lot to manage. Being aware of how they affect us is the first step to managing destructive emotions.

3. Habits

Why do we develop unwholesome emotions without even trying? Why do we have to put such effort into developing wholesome minds? The answer is simple: because we are very familiar with negative thoughts and behaviours, which allows them to repeat over and over in our minds and become habitual. They defend our egos through inner dialogue, persuading us that we are right and others wrong.

Owing to our familiarity with habitual ways of thinking, it requires a lot of effort to subdue the ego and let go of unwholesome emotions. We effortlessly develop judgements, so becoming aware of these habits can help us check up on ourselves and gently, compassionately and with humour bring us closer home to our inner self.

Let's not feel bad about ourselves; instead, treat that inner critic with loving-kindness. Practising mindfulness enables us to quieten down the ego and recognise our tendencies and habits, which will make working with our emotions much easier. Our wonderful friend, the inner self, will support us in finding more intelligent and constructive ways of behaving. That is an incredible and admirable step on the road to emotional intelligence.

A habit doesn't go away by itself; in fact, it grows over time. The only way we can reverse this process is by training our minds in the constructive antidotes and becoming familiar with constructive tendencies – which is something I explain in more detail later in this chapter.

It's so important to understand that this is all about changing 'bad' habits into 'good' habits. It's not about us as people! Eventually, we can reach a point where a positive state of mind comes more naturally than a negative one.

The destructive power of low self-esteem

If we look at how these three influences (false friends, media and habits) impact people, we can see the destructive power of low self-esteem. Low self-esteem leads us to wish to be like others, so we look to the media for guidance, and from this guidance we form our habits.

Recognising low self-esteem can be tricky. Take a look at these characteristics of low self-esteem. They are attitudes and ways of seeing that fill us with self-limitations:

- **Guilt:** A paralysing form of self-torture; seeing one's imperfections and past actions as permanent features.

- **Scepticism/being judgemental and overcritical/cynical:** An unrealistic expectation of the self and others, with the reasoning that, "If it's not perfect, then it's worthless." Scepticism and cynicism are sometimes called 'crystallised forms of anger' that focus on faults and doubts. Cynicism is one of the main obstacles to compassion.

- **Perfectionism:** An unrealistic expectation of perfection – "People should be perfect" – that identifies someone with a past negative action as if this is who they will always be.

- **Limited world-view:** A focus on limits rather than on potential and possibilities for growth and improvement – "I could never do this, I can only do that." Limitations are actually a type of laziness as they don't create the energy for change.

- **Self-shame:** Keeping secrets about oneself, with thoughts such as, "I am disgusting, strange, weird, stupid, ugly." This creates a negative spiral – "Others never talk about it, so I must be really weird" – based on the delusion, "I should be perfect, because others are."

- **Pride:** If one is genuinely self-confident, there is no need for pride. To cover up their own insecurity, people act as if they are better than others, but only because they lack genuine self-confidence.

- **Improper humility:** The quality of regarding oneself as less than others. Humility is a positive quality as it counteracts pride and is 'other-centred' and often driven by active compassion for others. Lack of self-confidence, however, is often self-centred (feeling sorry for oneself) and paralyses us from taking positive actions. In fact, this kind of false humility is categorised under pride. Like limitations, it focuses on our faults.

- **Idolising people:** Overestimating others is based on – or will easily lead to – underestimating ourselves and wishing to be someone else, rather than valuing ourselves.

- **Fear:** Fear leaves people unwilling to make mistakes, be abnormal, not be liked, change, be hurt or take responsibility.

Fear closes the heart and mind off from the outside, leaving us lonely and frozen. Fear is responsible for underachievement and leads to people overlooking opportunities.

- **Pretending to be someone we're not:** If we are self-confident, we don't need to pretend to be something we're not. We are good enough – in fact, we're everything we can be.

- **Negative world-view:** The world is often a mirror of what we think of ourselves; a negative world-image and negative self-image can be two sides of the same coin and reflect an expectation of an unrealistic, perfect world. If we focus on all the problems there are in the world, rather than how we can contribute to improving the world, then our world-view will depress and de-energise ourselves and others.

- **Laziness:** The quality of being attached to temporary pleasure and comfort. Laziness acts as an excuse for underachieving and wasting our time on meaningless activities.

- **Depression:** The feeling that we have nothing to offer; we see ourselves as a problem and as worthless to others due to our low self-esteem. This can also lead to self-pity and closed-heartedness. Depression is immobilising and debilitating.

- **Lack of trust in others:** When we do not open our hearts to others, it is hard for them to open their hearts to us. In that way, we never discover that others struggle with the same problems we do. Real communication and connection prove there is nothing to be ashamed of to begin with – we are all humans, and we are all seeking happiness.

Mindfulness helps us become aware when thoughts crop up that reflect our low expectations of ourselves and others. We are so much more than this.

The Six Steps to Emotional Hell

To check in with you that you really understand how a typical ego-controlled reaction leads to unwholesome emotions, here are my Six Steps to Emotional Hell (in this case, following an argument). These steps apply to any life crises and daily dramas.

There is an argument over who cleans the house.

Step One: We have the imprint on our minds already and the tendency, or habit, to express a reactive emotion. We're human! Perhaps we are already anticipating that our partner has not done their share of the housework.

Step Two: We feel the emotion physically, as well as mentally. Due to not understanding how our egos work, nor how others are thinking, we may be very confused about the emotion, which leads to unpleasurable feelings like heat or cold in our faces and bodies, gurgly tummies, or galloping heartbeats. Needless to say, our egos will be running round our heads and trying to escape through our ears. ("Why didn't they vacuum? Are they aware that it's their turn? Are they being lazy and taking me for granted?").

Step Three: Because we're desperate to be right, we harbour misconceptions about the object of our problem (a person or thing) – in other words, we point the finger outwards (our partner is being selfish).

Step Four: Either attachment or aversion arises (or both). For example, "I am angry with my partner for giving me a hard time and putting me in this awkward position. My standards of cleanliness are higher than theirs, and I am right. I am attached to my home being clean and tidy to my standards."

Step Five: We say or do something unkind, possibly worse, which leaves another stain on our mind and makes the situation deteriorate further. (We accuse them of being lazy and dirty, and use other derogatory comments that go much further to alienate the person from us and exacerbate the problem.)

Step Six: We have cre*ated the cause to be awful* and we feel awful again and again and again. We help ourselves feel better by calling our friends to put our point of view across and get their support. We moan and gossip, trying to make the other person look wrong. We might also drink and smoke in the backyard where the kids can't see us, eat disgusting amounts of pizza or chocolate, or starve ourselves because we feel so sick and so on.

Understanding that our fear-driven egos cause us to always feel the need to defend ourselves is a way of understanding that this is actually low self-esteem at work. The healthy ego has accurate self-esteem – not pumped up superiority, but self-knowledge and self-love.

I think it's important not to think we're bad people when dealing with unwholesome emotions, but to feel that we are indeed mentally ill – but fixable. To help us develop a healthy ego with accurate self-esteem, we need to deal with unwholesome emotions by calling on the constructive antidotes. You can think of these as being a team of nurses, lovingly helping us to get better after the discovery of a serious illness. We can heal. We will flourish.

The feel-good factor: The constructive antidotes

Constructive antidotes are great multi-taskers, good at putting out the flames of many an emotion – which is good, because there aren't as many of them as there are destructive emotions.

Knowing which antidote to summon often involves applying whatever comes to mind first and trusting your intuition – and perhaps even combining them all.

Here are the main constructive antidotes:

- **Compassion:** Not wishing others to suffer.
- **Empathy:** Feeling with others and identifying with their pain and unhappiness (avoid sympathy, because that tends to take a superior position, and all these antidotes involve recognising our commonality).
- **Equanimity:** Avoiding having attachment to some people and aversion to others, while wanting everyone to thrive equally.
- **Feeling happy for others:** Rejoicing at others' good fortune.

- **Forgiveness:** Letting go of past grievances and understanding others' humanity (in that we all make mistakes).
- **Gratitude:** Recognising what others have done, and do, for you.
- **Loving-kindness:** Recognising that we are all in this together, extending heartfelt good wishes towards others, and wanting others to be happy.
- **Patience:** Being able to withstand difficulties without resorting to destructive actions, and extending our understanding of others' situations.
- **Tolerance:** Being able to accept differences and being open-minded.
- **Understanding:** Being able to welcome others' views and ways of being.

Jealousy and envy are common emotions that we can all relate to, so let's consider an example of how to utilise the constructive antidotes against them with 'feeling happy for others' as the antidote.

You look out of the window and see that your neighbour has bought a new car. It's very shiny. She looks delighted and, as far as you're concerned, smug. (To generate a destructive emotion in yourself, you apply a negative emotion to the neighbour, although in reality you are unlikely to have any idea what she's feeling: it's a mere projection of yours that she's feeling smug.)

You really are deeply affected by this acquisition and so you go over in your head all the reasons why it isn't fair. You mentally point the finger at your neighbour, identifying previous times when she seemed to be doing well, and you weren't. Your feeling of envy turns green with jealousy towards this woman. You work out in your mind a way in which you can spoil her pleasure and justify it with the idea that she needs to be taught a lesson because she doesn't deserve this reward. Later that evening, when it is dark, you take your dog for a walk and key her new car. You think to yourself, "That'll teach her a lesson, smug bitch," and experience a complicated feeling that combines revenge with meanness, and definitely some pleasure – but it feels dark. You can't tell anyone. It's not something you're proud of. It's your naughty secret. This jealousy is fed by further jealousy and you continue to compete with your neighbour and justify your behaviour. She features strongly in your imagination and takes on a larger-than-life position in your mind. You give the episode obsessive, inappropriate attention. She is now associated with all sorts of negative thoughts and feelings, so your mind often gets disturbed by her. This makes you even angrier.

Utilising the constructive antidotes and a big dollop of mindfulness, you could take a different approach to your feelings of jealousy.

You recognise the feeling of jealousy you have for your neighbour through mindfulness of feelings, thoughts and emotions, so you are aware of what feels nice and what doesn't. Then you remind yourself of how destructive jealousy is because it makes you feel unpleasant and it takes over your mind. You want to change the way you feel, so you consider the constructive antidotes. 'Feeling happy for her' is what you want to feel, but you need to feel something else as well to support that feeling.

You consider some of the rough things that you know have happened to her. Her boyfriend left her for a younger woman. Thinking about this makes you feel sad for her and you experience empathy – perhaps something similar has happened to you or to someone you care about. You realise you don't really want her to suffer – this is compassion. So empathy and compassion come to the aid of feeling happy for her, which you start to do. You may find you have to pretend to yourself a bit at first – you acknowledge that thinking, "It's great that she's got a new car!" sometimes makes you want to vomit, but you decide that it's definitely a better way to feel. Nevertheless, you say it through gritted teeth. You put it into action, say the words aloud or in your head, and really encourage yourself to feel happy for her by focusing on the good feelings from your heart and intensifying them. It's as if you're radiating those good feelings and sending them her way. You then acknowledge that your mind is calm and peaceful. She has helped you in your practice of emotional intelligence. If you didn't have *her in your life, you wouldn't be able to practise these positive emotions.*

Bingo! Emotional intelligence meets ethics.

This example can be clearly understood by transforming the Six Steps to Emotional Hell into the Seven Steps to Emotional Heaven. Contrast the typical trail of destructive mental events to a managed approach using your emotional rescue nurses.

From reaction to response: The Seven Steps to Emotional Heaven

The Seven Steps to Emotional Heaven originate from Buddhist teachings on training the mind to work with our emotions. Buddhism needs to be understood as a detailed and systematic approach to mind-training – there's nothing mystical about it, really; it's not magical thinking at all. It's closer to science than religion in many ways. Now, let's consider the alternative approach.

In this case, let's stay with the emotion of jealousy. Perhaps you can apply a scenario of an argument from your own experience.

Step One: Identify the feeling. Not that it will change, nor that it needs to change, and not that you rather resent realising that your feelings are negative (that's pride, by the way), but so that you can identify and understand what you're feeling (in this example, jealousy).

Step Two: Recognise whether the feeling is destructive or not. Jealousy is clearly destructive. I have heard people say that jealousy can be pleasant because it may lead to passion, arousing a desire that has cooled due to familiarity. But the passion is the positive here, while the jealousy is definitely not good. (It's interesting how emotions have their own little journeys and can evolve from one to another.)

Step Three: You *have to* want *to make changes to yourself.* This seems obvious, but it is key. People who say, "Well, that's just the way I am," like Popeye, falter here. Change will happen if you recognise the benefits of change and understand the flexibility of your 'self'. You're like a recipe for a healthy soup – a better you will emerge if some of the bitter or greasy ingredients are left out and replaced with healthier options.

Step Four: But replaced with what? You need to know what the antidote is to your disturbing emotion, or what technique you're going to put into place, otherwise you'll get as frustrated as the carrot left out of that soup. (Time to call on your nursing team and let them minister to your needs.)

Step Five: Once you know the constructive antidote/emotional technique, you have to put it into practice – a mind-changing action. You replace jealousy with feeling happy for someone and Bob's your uncle, hey presto! Of course, this takes time. When you first try this it may be through gritted teeth because of the unfamiliarity with the feeling, but, amazingly, with practice it actually starts to feel good. You could call it an acquired taste. It's an aspiration that you are transforming into an achievement.

Step Six: When you try the positive constructive antidote, you need to be aware of the more pleasant feeling, so you need to generate it, like you're blowing air onto a tiny flame. This encourages you to practise it again and again. Neuroscience agrees.

Step Seven: Finally, utilise mindfulness to *be aware of your improved state of mind*, and how the process worked. This is mindfulness 'off the cushion' – pure awareness of your mental, emotional, verbal and/or physical actions. However, you might also want to practise mindfulness of the breath, relaxing into a calm and stable state of mind. Acknowledging this pleasant state of mind seals the deal for you and ensures your practice will continue.

To help you identify the emotions that seem to arise so effortlessly in your mind as destructive habits, try the Wheel of Destructive Emotions exercise.

The Wheel of Destructive Emotions

The Wheel of Destructive Emotions allows you to identify which destructive emotions need to be worked on most, with antidote emotions to increase your wellbeing and peace of mind. It is simple and enjoyable in the same kind of way that doing one of those magazine personality tests are (let's face it, we all love thinking about ourselves).

Try working with this list of emotions to begin with (though if you are aware of any other destructive emotions that visit you regularly, you can substitute in those):

- Anger
- Pride
- Discontentment
- Jealousy
- Low self-esteem
- Fear and anxiety
- Judgement
- Greed and/or laziness

The wheel is divided into eight sections, so label each wedge with one of the eight emotions you have chosen to focus on. Rank the level of destructiveness of each wedge of emotions out of 10, with 10 being the most destructive: do this in a detached and objective way, as if you are identifying clothes in your wardrobe that just don't suit you any more, so you need to throw them out.

When you've finished ranking each wedge, number and colour/shade in the wheel to visually clarify the areas that are in most need of attention. If you ranked anger with a 5, for example, you would only colour half the wedge. The point is that the most 'full' wedge requires the most attention. This will change as your practice changes, and you can then focus on your next most difficult emotion. The following figure shows an example wheel.

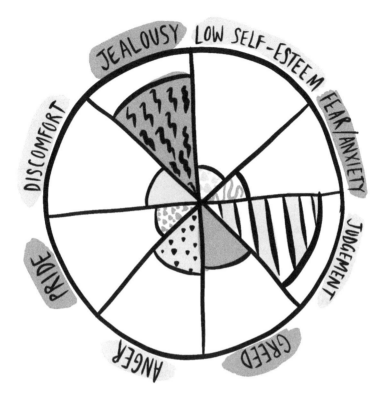

The Wheel of Destructive Emotions.

The wheel may change at different times in your life as the emotions you have focused on become subdued while others rise to the surface, like bubbles from the bottom of a pond, so this is a useful exercise to revisit. So embrace your inner child, get out your coloured pencils and enjoy.

How to be emotionally intelligent

The term 'emotional intelligence' was coined in 1990 by psychologists Peter Salovey and John D Mayer as "a form of social intelligence that involves the ability to monitor one's own and others' feelings and emotions, to discriminate among them, and to use this information to guide one's thinking and actions". The concept of emotional intelligence has reached many areas of society – it was a very popular topic for my Wellseeing Consultancy in schools. (Who wouldn't want to stop crying and fighting in schools? And that's just among the teachers.)

Psychologist Daniel Goleman researched the EQ (emotional quotient) of leaders and identified it as being more important than IQ (intelligence quotient) in terms of successful socialisation. He went on to create five emotional competencies. These five competencies provide an effective, simple guide that fits well with the practice of mindfulness:

- **Self-awareness:** Knowing your emotions
- **Handling feelings:** Managing your emotions
- **Utilising emotions in the service of a goal:** Motivating yourself
- **Empathy:** Recognising emotions in others
- **Social competence:** Handling relationships

Goleman's five emotional competencies magnify the role of others in our practice, and this is where ethics meets emotional intelligence. They form the perfect marriage, supporting and nourishing each other on the path of spiritual development.

Self-awareness leads us to be intelligent about how we utilise our emotions (which covers the first two competencies). If we're angry about an injustice, it is intelligent to consider how that anger can best be utilised. If we point the finger outwards and blame others, it's due to our egos getting rather miffed, which leads to aggressive and combative behaviour. However, if we direct our anger by engaging in rational and compassionate action, then we're more likely to achieve our goals. So the third, fourth and fifth competencies encompass 'including our enemies' in our own growth rather than excluding them. Skilful engagement with others is an advanced practice.

A great example of motivating oneself in the pursuit of a goal by utilising our emotions is non-violent protest, most famously adopted by Mahatma Gandhi. *Ahimsa* means the rejection of violence mentally, emotionally and physically. Martin Luther King, Jr, was later motivated by this concept to fight for social equality in a way that fitted with his Christian principles.

"Nonviolence means avoiding not only external violence but also internal violence of spirit. You not only refuse to shoot a man, but you refuse to hate him."

Martin Luther King, Jr

Stride Toward Freedom

Protest is most effective when it is non-violent. It encourages respect and does not open itself to censure. Our protests may not be so ambitious, but they can nevertheless achieve goals rather than inflame problems. It is not an easy road, but our spiritual qualities are important and will outlast any tyranny.

Meditations for working with the emotions

How can we practise being mindful if no one upsets us? If everything is perfect, how can we develop our minds? Understanding the interdependence of human beings is a vital aspect of accepting, tolerating and understanding the behaviour of others, because without others we cannot practise. We need others to be the 'pains in our arses' in order to develop as human beings and engage with a spiritual path.

When we practise managing our emotions meditations, we are more likely to be able to actuate this 'off the cushion'. Here, I share a few meditations on working with the emotions.

 **LISTEN**

Emotional Transformation meditation

This is a guided meditation on activating the Seven Steps to Emotional Heaven. We simply notice events, especially the feelings that arise with them, and let them go. We soon start to recognise that stress arises in direct relation to our thoughts and emotions, as we can identify, with practice, the unpleasant feelings of tightening, temperature fluctuations and pain.

Visualisation meditations

These three meditations utilise visual imagery that can help you disperse destructive thoughts and their accompanying emotions. They are similar in nature to mindfulness of the breath (refer to Chapter 2), but they use visual imagery to achieve the same stabilisation of the mind.

 LISTEN

Thought Clouds, Counting and Thoughts as Visitors meditations

 LISTEN

"What If…" meditation

Try this meditation for those difficult events that are in your past but still trouble you.

It's nice to end this meditation with some white light/black smoke breathing (which I describe in more detail in Chapter 10):

- Visualise yourself breathing in pure healing light from a benign source (the universe/the Buddha/God/the sun) and, as you breathe out, visualise your disturbing emotions and feelings as black smoke, disappearing into the depths of the earth where they dissolve and harm no one.
- Fill yourself with light.

Other practices for managing the emotions involve taking deep breaths and walking away until you feel calm, then using listening and counselling skills – this works well if you're *not* emotionally involved with someone who is throwing a tantrum or being really difficult. If you are emotionally involved, then view it as the perfect opportunity for practising emotional intelligence and take particular care of your words and actions. The person may know you well and try to push your buttons, so they are offering you a great chance to change.

Going with the flow

Understanding ourselves leads to much greater peace of mind. And the irony of this practice is that, by some kind of psychological miracle, when we let go of our grasping (whether we are grasping onto comparisons, what we think we want or feeling hard done by) we start to attract better outcomes for ourselves. People seem nicer. Opportunities arise. Things don't go wrong as much, and when they do go wrong, we manage with far less drama. This isn't science; this is the experience of mindfulness practitioners. It isn't religion either, because no prayers, supplications or offerings are required.

Every being on this planet is living in a volatile world, unable to control what happens to them and being thrown like a ball in the hands of a toddler from one accidental breakage to another. Our flourishing depends on our ability to go with the flow and deal with each situation calmly. Otherwise, we are constantly reacting and digging ourselves into quagmires of disturbing thoughts and emotions.

Going with the flow conjures a river that cannot and should not be dammed, because it knows where it is going and does not want to become a stagnant pond, eddying in circles with scum floating on the surface. It is glorious in its movement, and the sludge, twigs and weeds get stuck at the banks, while the pure crashing water keeps flowing. It's not just that life is like a river, but that we are rivers too.

In mindfulness practice, regularly reminding ourselves of the Three Marks of Existence (which I introduced in Chapter 4) enables us to embrace what happens to us mindfully and deal with it more effectively.

Here, I talk about the Three Marks of Existence in greater detail. To recap, they are:

- **Impermanence:** Everything and everyone is impermanent
- **Dissatisfaction/suffering:** We all experience feeling dissatisfied and experience suffering, both mental and physical
- **No soul:** There's nothing about us that is solid and fixed

The Buddha observed that these marks are universal aspects of life on earth and that they apply to every sentient being. If we contemplate these three truths in our meditations and during our everyday lives, then we will gradually let go of behaviours that oppose the way things are, which can relieve us from unnecessary suffering and wasted energy.

Our egos are basically flipping out about being mortal and so they grasp onto anything permanent that helps us feel secure, but trying to maintain a safe status quo can cause so much distress. Reminding ourselves regularly of the Three Marks helps us to limit our grasping and allow things to be as they are, rather than try to force things to be what we want them to be (such as a relationship, a friendship, a job, our family). Letting go of what no longer serves us is a powerful quality of the inner self: an intuitive knowing that something no longer works. We all know that the more we grasp onto a relationship, the more the other person feels constrained. Understanding that letting go is more likely to lead to a relationship continuing is one of those brilliant ironies.

Use these concepts to stretch your mind, untangle some knots and really question their meaning. Do the Three Marks of Existence make sense? Are they *right*, in your view? "Test it like gold," as the Lamas say.

Mark One: Impermanence

We live as if we are a permanent fixture here on earth; we seek to surround ourselves with a sense of permanence. But we are not permanent. We will age. We will experience problems and sickness, and we will eventually die. Other than our consciousnesses, nothing about us continues – and even our consciousness is changing all the time. It is a mental continuum. Physically, we're maturing and decaying, and mentally and emotionally we are immature and wildly chasing happiness. But if we die as the exact same person that we were as children, what would we have learned from our precious life?

Take away the concept that life is a joyride and apply the concept that life is a cosmic university, and you're faced with a more rewarding approach to life. The more we learn about our inner worlds, the fewer mistakes we make and, ironically, the more life *will* be a joyride.

When the Dalai Lama says the purpose of our lives is to be happy (a famous fridge magnet quotation), he is not promoting hedonism or materialism. He is promoting what brings us *genuine* happiness.

Mark Two: Dissatisfaction/suffering

If we pretend that something out there will eventually provide us with happiness, we will find we have even more problems. The search may bring temporary solutions, but even the richest, most gorgeous and gifted people will die and die alone, without anything to take with them. Finito.

Of course, we may be surrounded by sources of happiness: a loving partner, children that bring us joy well into old age, a job that brings us satisfaction, and so on. This mark does not require us to deny life's pleasures but to be realistic about them. The only source of genuine happiness is inside us – a deep well of inner resources we can use to transform the most difficult situations we encounter into opportunities for spiritual development. And what could be more difficult than death? And on a more pragmatic note, it also means less falling out with the family. What's not to like?

Mark Three: No soul

Mindfulness is about presence: being present without being influenced. A person who is present is changing physically, mentally and emotionally all the time, so it is very logical to conclude that there is nothing about us that will last forever – and the same applies to our understanding of having a soul. The four applications of mindfulness are meditations on the body, feelings, mind and phenomena (which I discuss in Chapter 4), which enable us to observe changes in our experience of our 'selves' and understand deeply this concept of the ever-changing self. It doesn't mean that we don't exist, just that we don't exist in the way we *think* we do – a way that keeps us grasping onto the idea of permanence and looking into the future all the time for material happiness to further solidify our sense of self.

It is only when our egos stop grasping and we let go of our desire for something that we think will bring us happiness (which may also change into something else when we get it, thus continuing the cycle of suffering) that we achieve happiness.

The proper way of defining the 'no soul' concept is to say that nothing inherently exists from its own side, but in terms of how it interacts with a being. Tomes have been written on this concept of what Buddhists call 'emptiness' – which isn't quite what it seems, but the translations are difficult. Think about a mug of tea. Does the mug call itself a mug? If an ant arrives and starts its ascent up the attractive china slope, does it think, "Oh, a mug of tea… what an attractive china slope." What is tea? Is it the leaves, the tea bag, the milk, the water or the sugar? Is it found in one sip? When the tea is cold and undrinkable, is it still tea? Does the mug of tea perceive itself to exist? Does it exist from its own side? *It exists in terms of how it interacts with a being.* It is empty of inherent existence.

Now, apply this argument to yourself. If this seems challenging, here's my version.

I'm 'Ondy'. It's my label and I respond to it. I can see that I have existed by looking at photos ranging from when I was a baby to my present self. I don't remember being a baby, but I accept this continuous flow of the person labelled Ondy. So, conventionally, I do exist and will continue to exist until I die, still labelled Ondy.

But who and what is Ondy? Am I the lithe young girl, the hopeful young woman, the wife playing at domestic bliss, the devoted mother, the indulgent grandmother, the writer, the actor, the teacher?

Am I the Ondy who was loyal and passionate, jealous and dogmatic, funny and generous, or Ondy as she is now, with slightly more of the qualities of loyalty and generosity of spirit and less of the undesirable attributes (in my view)?

Will the Ondy who got up this morning be the same Ondy that goes to bed tonight? Science tells me that, physically, pretty much everything about me will have decayed and changed. Certainly, I will be affected by my experiences today, which will lead me to self-analyse, have regrets, feel grateful, say prayers and mantras, and wish for all beings to be happy before I fall asleep, like a good Buddhist does. And so it goes. Even a quiet, uneventful day will leave new imprints on my mind and change 'me'.

Does everyone view me the same way – as a loyal friend, a formidable enemy, the old woman next door? Who is right?

And when my body is on that cold final bed, will I still be Ondy or will something have flown the coop, leaving the concept of Ondy as just a memory in other peoples' minds?

Remember, you do exist in a conventional, 'I'm Ondy' kind of way, but ultimately you don't. You are empty of inherent existence.

The benefits of mind transformation

"True love is the desire to maintain the happiness of all beings impartially, regardless of whether we like them or not."

Yongdzin Ling Rinpoche

'In Search of a Meaningful Life' in Becoming Buddha, edited by Renuka Singh[11]

It's easy to have compassion for those who are innocent victims of physical, mental and emotional abuse, but it's not so easy to have compassion for those who are the perpetrators of harm. We feel compassion for the innocent victims, but we don't see the story behind the perpetrators.

Have you ever witnessed the awful sight of people banging on the doors of a police van and screaming abuse at the culprit when a criminal is taken to or from a court hearing? The people are filled with outrage. It's like being present at a public hanging.

This is a minefield of emotional distress. Of course we have to protect the innocent, but are we ever in a position to justify hatred and want revenge? What is the result? Our minds remain disturbed, so the perpetrator achieves more destruction, as a ripple outwards from the original deed. We become angry and hateful, and we want someone to pay, which prolongs these disturbing feelings long past the actual event. Is the cause of our hatred the perpetrator or something that lies within us? Of course we must abhor the crime, but we must also take care with our attitude towards the criminal.

The perpetrator gives us an opportunity to develop our compassion as much as for the victim. If we are motivated by the wish for revenge, our inner selves are in great danger. Those who are able to transform their hatred into compassion are healed by their compassion.

---

11   Yongdzin Ling Rinpoche was one of my teachers who I had the great fortune of meeting in 1983, when I went to India on a pilgrimage shortly before he passed. In recent years I met his reincarnation in South India at his monastery.

No one is ever healed by hatred.

As I consider this, I remember that the Arabic word for 'forgiveness' has the same meaning as the word for 'freedom.'

If destructive emotions can lead to constructive emotions then they have been beneficial. It is when destructive emotions embed themselves in our consciousness and become more intense that we are in danger. We are not naïve about a desperately damaged individual, but we need to be mindful of their effects on us.

My story – my fabulous career

During my career as a school teacher, I was a bit of a maverick. While balancing subject teaching in a few different departments, I was also contributing to educational publications on moral issues and Personal, Social and Health Education (PSHE). I helped with the creation of lesson material, as well as teaching these subjects alongside Religious Studies. It kind of went with that territory. A job was created to address the fairly new phenomenon of PSHE, and it was a step up in terms of financial reward and position. Many of the staff thought I was an obvious choice (well, I was the only candidate). I was interviewed, but I didn't get the job. A bit of a wind blew through the staff room.

A short while later the job was advertised again, this time with more money. A male woodwork teacher applied for the post and, defiantly, I resubmitted my application form. We were both interviewed, and he got the job. There was now a hurricane blowing through the staff room.

On examining why I was overlooked, I had to arrive at the same conclusion as many others in the staff room: I was a woman. This was the 1990s and, although it doesn't seem long ago, sexism was still very much alive. I wrestled with my ideas on karma and not causing suffering, but I also felt a deep sense of injustice.

The union rep, one of my staunch allies and a dear friend, brought in a union solicitor to speak to me. I aired my reservations to her about taking it to a tribunal, and I remember her response vividly. It has stayed with me: "You would not be doing this for yourself, Ondy, but for your daughter. Do you want her to experience sex discrimination?" My daughter was then six. I won the tribunal, bought a new car and my first dishwasher, and took the family on a weekend trip to London. But I did not get the job. I like to think that I was influenced by the emotional competencies and was utilising my emotions in pursuit of a goal. But it wasn't easy.

Mindful choices

Ultimately, there are no wrong ways or right ways, just mindful choices. Generating constructive emotions makes us happier.

I have heard on my training courses that compassion is considered a weakness – perhaps good for women who have children, but harmful to men who need to be 'strong'. It's easy to be hateful but hard to be compassionate, so where does the real strength lie?

A consideration of what it means to be strong is important here. If strength means you can exert control, then you're lost. It's an ego-based attribute. All religions teach this, but it gets very misconstrued in interpretation. The principal advice in Buddhism and in mindfulness practice is not to harm others (deliberately).

Without mindfulness, managing to train our minds is impossible. Most of the time we are just led wherever our thoughts take us, like donkeys by carrots. Being able to disentangle ourselves from the spider's web of mental activity is essential if we are to grow as people and have lives where we feel we have some understanding of who we are and why we think the way we do.

Mindfulness is key to our self-awareness and self-esteem. Meditation, both mindful and analytical, helps us to soften our views and releases us from emotional obsessions.

Reflections

- Do you find destructive emotions isolating?
- How do you feel about the statement that 'not working with your mind to transform your destructive emotions is the waste of a lifetime'?
- Have you experienced the physical effects of your destructive emotions? Do you think they can cause illness?
- How do you feel about the statement that 'you can't change most external events; all you can do is change how you manage them'?

Authentic mindfulness

- Justifying our judgements and prejudices is the work of the ego.
- We all benefit from ancient wisdom, so acknowledge who helps you. See the connections, and be grateful.

Spiritual integrity

- Trust your inner self. Don't look to others to feel good about yourself.
- The spiritual path is for life, not just for when we think we need it. Spiritual development is a practical path, but we need to be creative in our approach. Utilise your talents and skills.
- Take it easy. Slowly, slowly. There's no rush, but don't give up.
- Enjoy the transformation and recognise it for what it is.

I have put this beautiful mindful house on the market for you. I've laid out all its attributes and now I implore you to please buy this. It's such a long-term investment, I would hope that you now have no misgivings and are eager to take up residence.

Chapter 7

Reasons to Be Good

∘ ∘ ∘

"By following purely secular ethics, we will become more easy-going, empathetic, and judicious people. Then there is a chance for the twenty-first century to be a century of peace, a century of dialogue, and a century of a more caring, responsible, and empathetic human race."

The Dalai Lama

An Appeal to the World

If humanity needs to be taught *anything* it is why and how to be good. Personal ethics starts with the mind and ends with our actions – not only our responses to the big life and death crises in our lives, but also our everyday attitudes to the world around us (the office gossip, the jealousy among friends or siblings, the casual attitude to sexual relationships). Understanding that interdependence is universal, and that with every choice we make there is a consequence – as well as understanding how our minds operate – offers us the opportunity to have a personal moral code that can guide us in all situations, socially and professionally, simply because it makes sense.

This has nothing to do with faith. No leap of faith is required because it is just good psychology, which means we can feel it improving our mental wellbeing. While religions recognise the importance of morality and can give us guidance, without inner conviction we may stray and justify the straying, like a smug cat creeping home with its tail between its legs after a few nights on the tiles.

This is a natural progression from mindfully managing our thoughts and emotions, because being good will just *happen* if we're managing our destructive inner tendencies and habits. Our home-grown moral code will guide us to ripen on the vine like saintly grapes because it is arrived at through mindfulness rather than being externally imposed.

In this chapter, I consider *why* developing this inner moral code is so important, before turning to *how* to actualise this in Chapter 8.

Destructive emotions harm everyone

"We do not see the world as it is but as we are."

Mark Williams and Danny Penman

Mindfulness: A Practical Guide to Finding Peace in a Frantic World

When we become aware of, and start managing, our emotional tendencies, we realise that it is not external causes but our emotional *reactions* that lead to our actions. For instance, no matter how irritating our child/partner/cat/dog/neighbour is at dawn on a Saturday morning, they're not *causing* us to shout at them that they are ruining our life. Anger is the culprit – that inner hooligan. Remember, we are not our emotions, but if we are dominated by an emotion we will act upon it. In this case, we might respond with our great big mouths and hurl abuse at those who are disturbing our lovely lie-in. If we get even more wound up, we might do something physical, like launch a cushion, throw a plate or bang on a wall.

Such a response may lead to three (and possibly four) unfavourable outcomes:

- There will be a reaction. Someone will be offended, hurt, upset or cross, and there will be some kind of fall-out and probably retaliation.

- Shouting abuse feels bad (and gives us a sore throat and raised blood pressure).

- We create a habit that may lead to increasingly destructive outcomes.

- We might break something – a plate, a leg, a heart.

When we realise that these are the likely outcomes, we can recognise that it would be wise to engage with our emotional intelligence and mindfulness – otherwise, it's bad for others, bad for ourselves and potentially bad for our cushions.

Being rational, calm and in control of our emotions leads to better outcomes. Can you remember when a parent/teacher verbally abused you? How did you react? In contrast, what about when a parent/teacher had a caring and respectful discussion with you about a difficult issue? What was the outcome?

Ruling with fear is an outdated (and now widely illegal) idea. If you hit someone because they offended you, they may immediately shut down and withdraw, which can make you feel like you're in charge: you have exerted your authority. But what actually happens is that the withdrawal festers into something quite destructive, which can damage relationships and reputations. If you're a parent that physically hurts a child then, at the very least, they will learn to distrust and fear you, which may mean that secrets and lies fester at the heart of your relationship. Your influence on them may well cause them to hit their own children or partners later in life. This is the cyclic nature of abuse.

You can see the effects of fear and power in autocracies and theocracies. It's called oppression and it's an unhealthy way to rule. If respect comes through fear, then it's not genuine respect.

When I worked in an inner city for a charitable organisation, I learned of a family that had been fighting each other over generations. The people on each side no longer remembered the original reasons for their shared animosity; they just knew that they hated each other. It had always been that way. Seriously? Perhaps an outing to see *West Side Story* would help.

Genuine regret and the wish to resolve issues requires moral conviction. Sometimes people apologise just to get themselves out of a sticky situation, but to look inwards and mindfully consider if we've made a mistake and got something wrong – and then apologise with the intention of not doing that thing again – takes the kind of strength you cannot acquire in the gym.

Malevolent people have huge egos because they crave the recognition that would give them stability and self-esteem. But it is this factor that makes them weak people – lacking in a sense of inner refuge.

Somewhere within their conditioning they have become damaged people. Unfortunately, with powerful egos they can cause a lot of destruction to others, although ultimately they are mostly damaging themselves. If we give people power, we must take care we do not then become powerless.

If we can see that when we do something that feels bad, the action stems from our lack of self-esteem, we may feel more motivated to change. But if we behave badly because we rationalise that we have to stick up for ourselves and that the fault lies with the perpetrator, then really we become like them. They win twice. They have hurt us and we are compromised. Working with our emotions gives us the most effective weapon – the wisdom to cut through the ignorance of our confusion and self-doubt.

The Finding Inner Refuge meditation examines our reliance on external objects and brings us to self-reliance.

 **LISTEN**

Finding Inner Refuge meditation

Disarming the ego

Being good enables us to see more clearly. As we slice through the layers of our defensive egos by managing our emotions and empowering our innate goodness, we start to recognise that the way in which we view others and the world is just our personal perspective, coloured by our conditioning. The way one person sees the world is not how everyone sees it. Understanding this enables us to use mindfulness to *disarm the ego*: our inner self gently advises rather than orders us, diplomatically taking charge, while mindfulness enables us to recollect our core values and why we need to be in charge, tenderly revealing our inherently good nature.

To illustrate how mindfulness can work in this way, I share a fictional example – the story of Beryl.

Beryl has a PhD and lectures at a university. She is well-respected and knowledgeable within her subject area. But Beryl can't settle. She is not a contented woman. She feels this inner urge to prove herself and rise above the status she has been designated. Due to never feeling completely acknowledged or recognised by others for her achievements, she develops an attitude to others that supports her ego's view of what is happening to her.

Her ego has a cynical view of others – especially those she perceives as being rewarded for things she should have been rewarded for. This cynicism ripples out into her world so that she generally feels that humanity is quite ignorant and decadent. The effect of this is that people don't feel completely comfortable with her; they feel less than her, and some of them are wary. She's quite intimidating, so some people in her professional peer group become guarded and restrained around her. Beryl never gets invited to parties or dinners because people think she feels above that, and she's too difficult, and so her ego develops a bitter aspect to its armour, leading her to sit on her high horse, contemplating humanity as if everyone is beneath her. Beryl's ego is isolating her and her cynicism leads her to criticise and condemn humanity generally.

Actually, Beryl has a very good heart, but she finds it increasingly difficult to express her feelings as she has alienated so many people. She looks at the world through a cloudy lens, and so she sees clouds. It is not reality. It is her *reality.*

Let's give this a happy ending!

One day, Beryl is told to go on a mindfulness course; resentfully, she attends. At first she is difficult and inflexible, but she has a mini awakening of sorts during her third meditation and she smiles at her discussion partner. This is just the beginning for Beryl; gradually, over weeks and months, her ego is disarmed, her intelligence is engaged, and she changes so much that people hardly recognise her.

Her reality changes and her ego is in check, so even when problems arise she manages them in a way that increases her emotional intelligence and her ability to relate to others. And so she lives happily ever after (amen).

Beryl found her way back home to her good heart, which had always been there, waiting to be nurtured, but had been conditioned by a big, fat ego. Beryl had to disarm her ego and discover her good heart herself, because if someone had come up to her with their whopping self-righteous boots on and stomped all over her ego, it would have risen up even stronger.

We all know deep down that the ego's approach to managing ethical issues doesn't *really* work – and unless we manage to disarm the ego with the support of our inner selves, the ego will return to manipulate us.

Imagine if you had an argument with a friend or family member ten years ago that was never resolved. It won't go away because your ego won't let it, so it remains an uncomfortable memory. Unless you find a way to resolve things as best you can, it will remain in your consciousness. It might also affect you physically – unsaid things may lead to a problem with your throat, chest or voice; or perhaps if you swallowed your anger then you may have trouble with your digestion. This is a holistic view, where there is a link between your body and mind.

We don't always get the chance to resolve our issues, but it helps to do the best we can. We can turn to our inner selves for guidance, taking care that we are not fooling ourselves by allowing our ego to shout the loudest. Mindfulness meditation can help here – creating a pool of calm, stabilising spaciousness from which that quiet voice of wisdom can surface.

It requires both sides to heal, and if the other partner in an emotional crime doesn't want to know, there's very little we can do – except to keep them in our hearts. Don't think of them as toxic; think of them as friends enabling us to deeply work on our emotions and ethics. And try not to permanently shut the door on anyone.

Our mindful awareness enables the inner self to jump right over the ego and make a stand. It is never painless. Whenever we are involved in an argument (and who hasn't been), we want to be proved right, so the ego does everything it can to justify itself. Once the immediate fire of the incident dies down, we can start to look at how we contributed to the situation and how we might resolve it.

Guilt is a terribly destructive emotion that eats away at us and achieves nothing, but regret is an important emotion. Regret is guilt's mindful sibling – it allows us to resolve, undo or make amends for something and move on.

Managing our emotions makes being good a walk in the park. The puppy is trained, so the owner can smell the roses.

Successful meditation relies on our ethics

The foundation for all successful meditation is pure morality, so even our meditation depends on good ethics. We know what it's like when we try to meditate and something keeps bothering us. It could be as simple and everyday as an argument with someone. It just keeps niggling at us, going round and round in our heads, buzzing like a fly captured in a glass. It's the cause of many a sleepless night – that time when we are left alone with our thoughts. When this happens, it's the ego that is trying to drown out the inner self, but neither will rest until the issue is resolved.

We might justify our actions as far as we can – this is when the ego has the upper hand. Or we might just bury the episode and change our attitude to the person we argued with by ignoring them, or leaving them out of our lives – there are many means to temporarily avoid something unpleasant. That's still the work of the ego. And by 'temporary' I don't mean a limited amount of time, I just mean that everything that happens to us *is* temporary. So, the unresolved argument continues until death do us part, with the seeds firmly planted in our consciousness. At death, the relationship will end, along with the argument, but the effects of the argument leave a stain on our consciousness. It sticks, like a mental Post-it note, small but significant, until a future time when the causes and conditions come together, karma ripens and the result of the anger is experienced.

When a meditation practitioner is about to enter a long meditation retreat, where they aim to utilise mindfulness to develop pure concentration, they are advised to put their emotional burdens to bed, resolve issues and enter the retreat with as clean a conscience as they can. If they don't, it will affect their progress.

In his wonderful book *Genuine Happiness: Meditation as the Path to Fulfillment*, the great meditator and contemplative teacher, Professor B. Alan Wallace, outlines the six traditional inner and outer requisites for a meditation retreat aimed at mind-training.

We need:

- A suitable environment
- Few desires
- Contentment
- A simple lifestyle
- Pure ethical discipline
- To avoid obsession with fantasies

All these requisites are logical, but the sixth recommendation requires some discussion. How much time do we spend doing this internal activity? How much energy does it take, and how much good does it achieve? The obsessive mind is the inner tormentor and is fuelled by attachment. We are desperate to find more and more to satisfy ourselves, so we fantasise – about winning the lottery, about a dream holiday, about owning a holiday home… you name it. It doesn't really harm anyone, but if we become *obsessed* then we will suffer when we don't get the result – we will always live in hope for the future. Sometimes fantasies can get us through a terrible experience – for example, prisoners fantasising about home – but for most of us it means we can't see what we already have.

This kind of obsession can also lead to addictions like gambling, which definitely does harm yourself and others.

Turning back to the list of inner and outer meditation retreat requisites, Alan describes the fifth recommendation, pure ethical discipline, as follows:

> "[A]voiding engaging in deeds that are detrimental to your own or others' wellbeing. In the major Western religions – Judaism, Christianity and Islam – ethics is imposed on humanity by an outside, divine authority. That is not in the spirit of Buddhism. Ethics derives naturally from the pursuit of genuine happiness, from training and refining the mind, and exploring reality."

The secret of successful meditation is diligence and developing a feeling of joy through the experience of meditation. If our minds purify through ethical practice then this wish to meditate, and the experience of joy, will happen naturally, like sunshine appearing when the clouds naturally part. No effort is required. By maintaining pure ethical discipline, we are on track to a calm and contented mind – and we cannot find genuine happiness without practising pure morality and exploring what we understand to be reality. And this is what the Dalai Lama means by being easy-going, empathetic and judicious.

Goodness feels good because goodness is home

Nobody wants to be considered bad, but we do wander into the Badlands sometimes, possibly flirting with the libertine glamour of being a bad boy/girl. The notion of rebelling fits well in our teens when we are exploring who we are and who we want to be. While we are more likely to rebel *against* being right and proper rather than *towards* a holier way of life, it does happen – but you need to be a real spiritual rebel to take that direction.

A BBC Four documentary released in 2021 about a community of Trappist monks in Leicestershire, UK (*Brotherhood: The Inner Life of*

Monks) illustrates the appeal of a life of silence and reflection. One of the monks explained that when you take away TV, social media, music – all those things that distract us – you can find God everywhere, in everything. Maybe that sounds dull, particularly for a teenager encountering a massive array of social opportunities, but making space for silence and reflection in our lives will bring us closer to home – that place within us that can provide us with nourishment if only we let it. It may not sound exciting, but this sense of home offers a bigger high than any intoxicant can provide, and is our source of peace and contentment: the well of wellbeing from which we can draw.

We do not need to be monks or nuns to take inner refuge. Distracting stimulation is everywhere: unnecessary music in lifts, sound systems on beaches and groups of people drunkenly revelling ("Look at me, I'm happy!" they seem to be saying rather desperately). Are we afraid of silence, perhaps?

The Mindfulness in Schools Project states many positive statistics gained through studies and pilot groups on the effect of mindfulness on children and teenagers. In its 2012 report *Evidence for the Impact of Mindfulness on Children and Young People*, the report's author, Professor Katherine Weare, says:

> "[A]dolescents who are mindful, either through their character or through learning, tend to experience greater well-being, and that being more mindful tends to accompany more positive emotions, greater popularity and having more friends, and less negative emotion and anxiety."

If all teenagers are offered meditation and mindfulness (and some schools in the UK are already doing so), it will be so useful in their search for identity and resilience. Remembering to go inwards to ground oneself, to take deep breaths and to become self-aware would nip in the bud any thoughts of *destructive* rebellion that may threaten their sense of self – whether that is against themselves (through self-harm or drug abuse), or against others who appear different to them. Empowering young people with the gift of silence will build their resilience.

Of course, there is nothing wrong with healthy and constructive rebellion. We don't want a society of bricks that are just like every other brick (in the wall), but neither do we want a society that has no foundation, no roof, no refuge. Just recognising that goodness is our heart-home – our inner guide – will draw us inwards every time we face a moral dilemma and make spiritual rebels of us all.

Malala Yousafzai is a Pakistani activist. As a schoolgirl, she was shot in the head in October 2012 by a Taliban gunman for daring to attend school and promoting secular education. Miraculously surviving, she now continues to fight for the right of girls to receive education. Malala was awarded the Nobel Peace Prize in 2014 and is the youngest person to have been shown this honour. She recognised that the outer rules of her society were at odds with her own inner guidance and so became a spiritual rebel.

Finding our heart-homes of inner goodness is like finding a rare jewel. It guides us staunchly through our lives. Buddhists talk of our 'inherent goodness', meaning that we are pure but defiled by destructive emotions that separate us from our goodness over countless lives. As humans we are naturally motivated to find our heart-homes – not the love of our life or the house of our dreams, but the place we can rest. If we do something we consider bad, then we have strayed far from home, and there will be no rest until we return safely.

Goodness brings inner peace and genuine happiness

By having a clear conscience, we are gifting ourselves serenity. The irony is that it is dependent on our relationships with others. The significance of this point is vital. We are not islands – our happiness is completely bound up with our relationships with others. Yes, happiness comes from within, but in our conventional lives we are all interdependent.

Our destructive emotions lead us to react rather than respond. We never calmly throw something at someone, nor scream at someone while feeling empathy and compassion. The fire of those feelings of anger and hatred are doused with the water of rational behaviour, helping us avoid harmful actions of speech and body. Making the connection from goodness to constructive emotions like empathy, compassion and equanimity increases our ability to experience inner peace and happiness.

The qualities that shape inner and outer peace are secular in nature – no prayers to chant, or rituals observed – there's no faith necessary, just emotional intelligence and mindfulness.

We're aiming to clean up our consciousness by listening to that whispering voice when we feel uncomfortable about our actions. If we do something that keeps nagging at us, or we keep trying to justify something we did that we know was a bit iffy, then our minds become disturbed, so we are aiming for a totally pure consciousness, without disturbances. Having a clean conscience is exactly that.

Inner goodness leads to outer peace

"People spit blood over religion."

Mohamedou Ould Slahi

My Brother's Keeper[12]

A world living in peace and harmony must be everyone's fantasy of the perfect world. John Lennon's song 'Imagine' became an anthem for world peace in many countries, yet it is controversial because it suggests that religion itself is the cause of most conflict in the world.

But perhaps it is not religion per se that causes conflict, nor the original religious founders, but the *leaders* within religions that use it to push their own agendas.

---

12   My Brother's Keeper is a short British film made by The Guardian and follows the story of Guantánamo guard Steve Wood and Mohamedou Ould Slahi when they meet up many years after Slahi's incarceration.

Some religious leaders exploit their own charisma and powerful egos to recruit others in their quest for power and domination. A person who lacks their own moral compass is easily drawn into ideas about what is good and what is right, which may lead them to justify violence and conflict. If people can look to their constructive qualities and their heart-homes rather than make decisions based on fear, insecurity and paranoia (and the desperate wish to stay in with the 'strongest'), then their lives will avoid the torment and eventual confusion that comes from being led by others.

There is a dangerous maxim that doing something violent or bad for the greater good outweighs the moral balance. We can look to moral wars – such as the Crusades – and blush at the ignorance of it, and we can look to the Second World War, when to stand back and be walked all over by the Nazis may seem a ridiculous decision. Yet even in the Second World War, there were Quakers and pacifists who protested against the use of violence to end violence.

Consequentialism states that an otherwise morally objectionable action can be justified if it results in a positive outcome. Leaders need mindfulness in their decision-making, as this area is the greyest of all the grey shades – and a 'just war' can be more about justification than what is right.

"An eye for an eye leaves the whole world blind."

Mahatma Gandhi[13]

Having clear personal ethics can support personal choices and decisions. Motivation is key during disagreements, wars and violent events. Instead of seeing the other side as all evil, try seeing the other side as brothers and sisters caught up in battle, all wanting happiness and deluded about how to get it. It is a tragedy that we are not yet at

---

13   This quotation is from the film Gandhi (1982), about the life of Mahatma Gandhi. The film was an end-of-term treat in my Religious Studies lessons – I showed it so many times, I can recollect almost every one of Gandhi's famous remarks. The Gandhi family believes the quote to be authentic, but there is no formal proof of its use by the Indian leader.

the point in human evolution when we recognise that there is nothing to gain by violence and everything to gain through love, kindness and respect. Simply put, the world will be a better place to live in if we work on our minds.

In his book, *Guantánamo Diary*, Mohamedou Ould Slahi tells of the inhumane treatment he received at the hands of the American military after his detainment as a suspect after the terrible terrorist act of 9/11. His book was made into a film, *The Mauritanian*. Although never charged with a crime, Mohamedou was subjected to torture and solitary confinement. In the latter part of his incarceration, he built a relationship with his guard, Steve Wood, who believed in his innocence. Steve explains that their introduction was his *Matrix* moment: a moment when you awaken and see the illusion of conventional reality. Steve says it was impossible not to like Mohamedou. Steve's openness stemmed from his belief that he should treat prisoners "with respect like any other human being". *This* is equanimity.

Finally released after 14 years, Mohamedou says that he bears no grudge as he believes in forgiveness (remember that in Arabic, forgiveness and freedom are synonymous). As Mohamedou explains: "Being Muslim is just a way of being a good person. I believe in humanity. We don't need countries, we don't need borders."

If you have to fight, do not become brutalised. Never lose touch with your heart-home. Hurt and maim others and you will likely suffer post-traumatic stress disorder and never fully be able to remove the memories from your mind (as so many armed forces veterans testify).

We all need mindfulness with which to see the world and have our own *Matrix* moments. Hopefully, one day, everyone will be mindful so there will be no thoughts of war. This is the mindful awareness we need, because we are not programmed to harm others. Our survival as a species depends more on getting on with others, rather than killing them.

Trust yourself to be good

The Buddha taught that we must pursue our own enlightenment and be guided by our inner voice. Before his death he gave one final teaching to his order of monks:

> "This is my last advice to you. All component things in the world are changeable. They are not lasting. Work hard to gain your own liberation."
>
> **The Buddha**
>
> *Mahāparinibbāna Sutta*

His last words say more than they seem – *look to oneself*. You have guidance, but look to yourself.

I learned this myself from my own spiritual guide, who, when I asked him what I should do on one occasion, knowing that I now had all the psychological tools, told me, "I trust your inner guru. Do what you think is right." Of course, this led to many personal mistakes, but through reflection and self-analysis I eventually came to trust myself. Not my ego, but my 'inner guru'.

My story – my role as a teacher of Buddhism

I was privileged to be offered a teaching role in a meditation retreat centre in Dharamshala, India, the seat of the Dalai Lama and home to a large Tibetan refugee community. I spent three months there teaching the hundreds of visitors that signed up for retreats. The introductory retreats were ten days long and incorporated teaching and meditation sessions. They were pretty intense but hugely popular, and still are. One of my most profound teaching/learning experiences was to be faced with a large contingent who had come to India after serving their time in the Israeli Army. I am not one to shy away from challenging arguments, and our discussions on non-violence were often intense and troubling. As a teacher of Buddhism, I could not agree with any of their arguments about how complicated their fight was. To a genuinely practising Buddhist, it's simple. I have never witnessed such an array of painful and tormented attitudes and responses to the experience of war and conflict. All students were able to have a ten-minute private interview with the teacher to ask any questions about their practice and understanding, and to get the personal touch. The stories I heard were incredibly moving and I learned so much. Many of these interviews felt like confessionals. Some focused on family problems of alcoholism and depression – issues that had led to damaged and dysfunctional families, directly due to the consequences of their persecution in the Second World War. Weighted down by their own suffering, parents brought up children with many problems who were still searching for some kind of release and inner peace.

Some were conscripted into the army to fight in Israel's conflict with Palestine, forced to fight whether they wanted to or not. When they ended their stint, they were paid well and it was customary for many of them to take time out and visit India for recuperation. Many recuperated by getting out of their heads for as long as possible in order to forget the brutality they had seen and taken part in. Others came on meditation courses to reconnect with their inner selves. One woman who I became close to because she was a mother, like me (most of them were young travellers), explained her loss and despair due to her son committing suicide. He was sensitive and loving, and when he was conscripted he asked to be a driver... anything except a fighter. He was refused, so rather than becoming a killer of others, he killed himself.

Reflections

- Do you agree that a troubled mind cannot settle on or off the cushion? How do you deal with ethical nagging in your head?
- Our true home is not an external place, but an inner refuge. Where is yours?
- Ethical choices lead to genuine peace and contentment – if we lack personal ethics, we can face a conflicted life.
- No perpetrator of a crime is wicked. The *act* may be wicked, but the person who committed it is simply deluded.
- How we think and behave has a powerful influence on others.

If you're feeling all saintly, a little giddy with good intentions, motivated to spread the word and be part of the mindfulness revolution, then the next chapter will be the petrol in your engine.

Chapter 8

How to Be Good

'o o o

> "I am not a saint, unless you think of a saint as a sinner who keeps on trying."
>
> *Nelson Mandela[14]*

How do we love a noisy neighbour? *How* do we love the litter droppers and needy complainers in our towns? *How* do we love the serial killer and the terrorist (and should we)?

Being 'good' is central to all religions. What isn't always so clear is *how* to be good. Jesus famously told us to love our neighbour, but he didn't tell us how. We all know from experience that having a great neighbour helps us to live in harmony with others, but when the lovely house you've bought comes with a selfish neighbour who prevents you from even sitting outside in your own garden because of all the noise pollution, then what's love got to do with it?

Being good isn't about doing as we're told, sticking to the rules and following orders. Nor is it about being *seen* to be good – which is just pride and not genuine goodness at all. Being good is really about setting up an internal alarm system so that we can know that our conscience is clear. Without it, we would struggle to find our inherent goodness.

How to be good deserves its own chapter to consider how easy it is to fall into unethical traps, and how we need strong inner guidance to manoeuvre around all the tricky games our egos play with us.

---

14   Nelson Mandela said this during a speech at the Baker Institute at Rice University, Houston, US.

We need to be able to navigate spiritual challenges, while trying to practise mindfulness as ethically as possible.

What mindfulness gives us, with its varied approach to aspects of the self, and the unplanned arrival and departure of thoughts and emotions, is a very clear guide on how to handle every aspect of what goes on inside us – it offers a veritable treasure chest of mental tools!

Practising mindfulness without moralising

Until everyone in the world takes up mindfulness (I'm an idealist), we can't assume that others will respond to us in a mindful way. On the other hand, I have had many experiences with those who are evangelically mindful, and their enthusiasm is rewarding to see. When we start practising mindfulness, we can feel as if we have found the elixir of life, but this can become rather irritating to others: no one likes to be told that the way they live is inferior because they haven't found what you have. You can become a mindfulness fanatic!

My longer mindfulness training courses are weekly three-hour sessions for eight weeks, which allows time for the practice to settle and integrate into people's lives. I always include circle time for sharing experiences during my sessions. Everyone in the group takes it in turns to share how they managed (or not) to be mindful in the previous week. People find these sessions rewarding as we talk practically about how we can transform incidents in the home and at work that may have previously upset them.

How people manage to turn incidents into personal growth and wisdom through the practice of mindfulness is evidence of the healing nature of mind training. I've witnessed some spine-tingling moments – the sessions can be very emotional. But I often notice that when people describe situations in which they found themselves being mindful, it is common for them to say things like, "I was being very mindful, but they weren't," or "That wasn't very mindful of them, was it?"

When we hear ourselves saying things like this, we have to remember to 'look in the mirror', as a Buddhist would say. Rather than judging, we need to see our own reflections in others – by recognising their faults, we see our own.

As mindfulness practitioners, we open ourselves up to scrutiny. There's nothing some people like better than to trip others up on their own morals. I have been in an argument with someone who knows I'm trying hard not to get angry "because I'm a Buddhist", and when I do, they laugh or have a mean little smile on their faces because they've managed to press my buttons. Which, of course, winds me up even more. Changing mental and emotional habits takes a long, long time.

I like to witness how good people can be without any kind of training. Some people are so naturally empathetic and caring, it takes my breath away. Now me… I needed training.

If you really buy into your spiritual practice, then you have to learn to be patient with yourself – and patient with others.

Meditating using the lines of the Buddhist prayer *The Four Immeasurables* is a beautiful inclusive practice that helps us practise mindfulness without moralising, and dissolves any inclination towards meanness of spirit. We metaphorically hold hands with all sentient beings. We are neither in front of them nor behind them, but alongside all humanity, recognising that we are equal in our wish for happiness and to be free from suffering.

 LISTEN

The Four Immeasurables meditation

If you say this prayer daily, I guarantee that your heart will expand and your tendencies for meanness and pettiness will diminish. It's like a miracle drug, so be prepared. Your ego will hate you for it, but your inner self will glow.

Being aware of ego-games

The ego tricks us, manipulates us and tries to win points. It's been doing it forever so it's very powerful, and sometimes we fall into habits that we think are about being good but are actually motivated by selfishness and wishing to feel superior to others. If this is the case, we're not holding hands here, we're slapping people down.

Look out for the following behaviours the ego can use to play games with us.

Self-righteousness

Self-righteousness is a big problem when we become mindfulness practitioners. We want to avoid being a self-righteous do-gooder ("I've found something that is amazing and you haven't, so I'm a superior being"; "I am blessed. I am special. Just look at my halo").

If we begin to feel that we are better than others, we can turn to some constructive antidotes for help (refer to Chapter 6). Equanimity and compassion, two of these antidotes, go a long way to equalise ourselves with others – but if it's just an exercise in the appearance of humility, it won't pass muster and we'll still subconsciously feel better than others.

Pity

Genuine compassion is not pity. It doesn't look down on others. It sees all others as equal. Those who believe in rebirth have a useful way of seeing all beings as equal in their quest for happiness and their wish not to suffer. We circle from life to life and no one at any time knows where they're going or where they came from. People who are rich, successful and beautiful in this life may have come from a terrible previous incarnation or be on the way to something unpleasant, so it's impossible to know what anyone has been through or what they face. It's therefore hard to know who to pity, but we can offer compassion regardless.

If we find ourselves looking down on someone, then that is the time for us to practise compassion. Don't think that you could never be in that person's situation – none of us are immune to events that can turn our world upside down.

Being judgemental

Being judgemental is a natural tendency. But if we don't know someone's back story, how can we judge them? If we haven't been through what they have been through, how can we say we would have behaved any better? I have said myself many times, "Well, if I'd known about *that*, I wouldn't have said what I did." We don't get the script of anyone else's life, and yet we're surprised when we find out that someone who did something morally reprehensible had something painful happen to them first.

Our default position is to compare ourselves to others in order to feel better about ourselves. We use others as a measure of our own worth, and even if we tend to feel worse about ourselves due to low self-esteem, being judgemental is still an ego game. It's also a powerful way for us to justify our behaviour. We either feel good because we are like others or better than them, or we feel bad because we think others are better than us.

In the practice of being good, relying on our inner self is wiser than measuring our worth against others – just remember to give others the freedom to do the same.

Divisiveness

The practice of equanimity is very profound and effective at combatting divisiveness. The term 'equanimity' is not well known, but it is the foundation of mindfulness practice.

Equanimity means not having attachments or aversions. It's an advanced practice that is extremely difficult to put into action. It's natural to have attachments to our friends and family, and equally natural to have aversion towards people who we believe to be morally deficient; however, unless we are able to view humanity as equal to us in every way, we will be living with an irrational assessment of our place in the world. Without equanimity, we are always divisive in our views of others.

Saying unkind things about a person for our own benefit is a common tactic that we use indiscriminately without considering the harm it does. People on social media are guilty of divisive speech (slander) and gossip on a daily basis. In the practice of Right Speech (as advised by the Buddha), slander and gossip are cited as harmful, along with lying and abusive speech. The reason this harmful behaviour is so common is because we are titillated by others' lives and become voyeurs – anonymously getting our kicks from their mistakes.

Divisiveness is bedded in with anger, hostility, attachment and ignorance. We want to cause problems between people for varying selfish reasons. We can be a sad bunch of misguided fools, can't we?

LISTEN

Equanimity on Friends, Strangers and Enemies meditation

The Equanimity Meditation on Friends, Strangers and Enemies is a very powerful technique for overcoming hostility and fostering a more expansive view of the world. This practice takes us from being childish human beings to real grown-ups.

The practice of contemplating the Buddhist concept of the Three Marks of Existence supports this reflection: everything is impermanent; we are all subject to suffering and dissatisfaction; and none of us carry anything in us that is unchanging (the 'no soul' concept, discussed in more depth in Chapter 6).

Piety

Piety describes the quality of being very devout and religious, but it can also describe a state of mind that feels religiously or spiritually *superior* to others. I believe the antidote to such forms of piety is to keep our feet on the ground – to check that we're not turning into someone who thinks we have all the answers. Yes, we have managed to get access to some ancient and profound wisdom. Yes, we are able to put this wisdom into action. No – we still do not have all the answers and we all make a lot of mistakes.

One of our biggest problems is knowing a little about something, but never everything, and never enough – and yet still thinking we know best. The popular Indian parable about six blind men and an elephant illustrates this well.

In ancient India, a king asked a wise man to teach him about absolute truth. The wise man asked for an elephant to be brought to court and invited six blind men, who had never come across an elephant before, to tell the king what an elephant was. Each blind man was led to a different part of the elephant's body – the ear, the trunk, the tusk, the leg, the belly and the side. They described the elephant based on their limited experience, with each of their descriptions differing wildly from each other's, arguing about who was right. Of course, the king could see that each man had only a part of the elephant to describe – none of them could see the whole picture.[15]

Humans have a tendency to claim absolute truth and ignore other people's limited and subjective experiences, even though they may be equally true.

Feeling smug about our beliefs often comes with identifying with a group that feels self-righteous too – wanting to be in with the 'in' crowd, rather than feeling like an outsider. Friendship and acceptance bring us such joy, but this joy isn't worth it if it comes at the expense of our values. Eventually, we will become conflicted by the 'we're better than other people' view.

---

15   There is a wonderful BBC Radio 4 documentary inspired by this parable, Touching the Elephant, about blind people meeting and touching an elephant for the first time: www.youtube.com/watch?v=dYt-ENAufqqQ.

Before we align with any group, we should be grounded in our practice and not subject to just another phony ego-mask – something we put on to fit in. Spiritual materialism is common among people who become religious fundamentalists – people who wear their religion like badges of honour, totally convinced of their 'rightness'. Beware.

Considering the temptations of stuff and fun

"Getting and spending, we lay waste our powers."

William Wordsworth

The World Is Too Much with Us

In our Western society, who isn't materialistic or hedonistic to some extent? We get bombarded with products and pastimes that can make life more pleasant and enjoyable. The danger arises when we place our faith in these products and pursuits in the hope that they will bring us genuine happiness. They become our religion! However, they are the antithesis of spiritual happiness because they mislead us down a path towards external gratification.

We all experience being caught up on the hedonic treadmill sometimes – the never-ending pursuit of anything that is new and shiny and promises even greater comfort and enjoyment. But we also know, deep down, that it is superficial, temporary and doesn't nourish us or change us for the better. Happiness achieved through the acquisition of stuff and the pursuit of pleasure is totally dependent on external stimuli, which is why they cannot be a source of genuine happiness. When our stuff gets old, fades or is lost, or the drink and drugs wear off, they leave us feeling empty and hollow. They can encourage destructive emotions like discontentment, greed, envy and pride, and lead us back to square one on the spiritual path – a hamster on a wheel again!

Think about the competitive nature of owning houses and cars, and looking good – as if they are signs of success. Think about the desperation of getting drunk or high with friends, and how that feels afterwards when we are alone. There is the appearance of friendship and fun, but the pleasure can be very self-centred. Pleasure isn't necessarily hedonism, but if we become attached to it as a way of achieving fulfilment then we are in trouble. Some religions advise us not to take intoxicants simply because we become unable to be mindful, which allows our emotions to take over. Furthermore, being drunk affects others through the careless things we say and do (which also affects our karma).

Moderation is key. If we are fortunate to have enough, we can moderate our desires rather than feed them. Feeding our desires just leads to more desires, so the itch is never soothed. We can consider what is necessary and what is superfluous to our needs. We can reward ourselves, and even indulge ourselves, but with a nod towards an occasional treat rather than as a regular habit.

Moderating our desires means we are content with less, with our lives and minds less cluttered. People find a sense of relief when they simplify their lives. Any wealthy person will tell you that having a big house and a fancy car is very nice, but it's not the answer to life's dissatisfaction.

The greatest danger of pursuing a life of self-gratification is that it can lead to crime – actions that harm others. Fraud, theft and murder occur as the result of greed, desire and envy, all of which stem from the common misconception that we will be happier if we get more stuff and control what we own. Our inner self feels the tension, and even a lesser crime, such as lying to get our own way, will feel wrong.

"When everything that matters can be bought and sold, when commitments can be broken because they are no longer to our advantage, when shopping becomes salvation and advertising slogans become our litany, when our worth is measured by how much we earn and spend, then the market is destroying the very virtues on which in the long run it depends."

Jonathan Sacks

'Morals and Markets' in Applied Ethics: Critical Concepts in Philosophy

Reflecting on sexual behaviour

In the Buddha's Noble Eightfold Path of Right Action, the ways of harming others are stealing, killing and sexual misconduct. Sexual misconduct is included in the Buddha's teachings because it harms others – physically, emotionally and mentally. We're sashaying through a very sensitive time concerning sexual behaviour, so it's helpful to consider our own behaviour, as well as the behaviour of those we love.

Sex between consenting adults can be fun and fulfilling. But casual sex, with someone whose name you don't even know, has the potential to become a kind of human abuse because it may lead to disrespect and contempt. This is not me being a prude or killjoy. We may objectify someone as a commodity, much in the same way as we objectify a beer. If you're going to be casual, be sincere and respectful: these are people, not pints.

Having an affair may feel tantalising to spice up a humdrum life, rather than struggle with the boredom of a long marriage where the passion has died. But before we take that passion-fuelled move, perhaps we can think about the other person in our partnership, and the other person's partner – step into their shoes and ponder the deceit and infidelity that we would need to practise to keep the liaison secret. Plus, the consequences are pretty dire. We hurt, we deceive, we lie and cheat, and families get broken. All for temporary thrills and a few orgasms.

Considering an affair requires objective examination. Ask yourself: is your desire just boredom? Are you trying to feel young again? Do you feel taken for granted? Have you considered the consequences?

Bearing in mind that everything is impermanent, it is natural that we may reach a point in a relationship where we have had enough. The relationship has run its course and we want to move on. Perhaps there is aggression or an unequal power share, or maybe it just doesn't work anymore. Perhaps you can separate as kindly as possible. If there are no children involved, you will only hurt one another. But if you have children then you will be damaging their lives to some degree, so it is essential to consider the break-up before you make the move to shack up. If you are having an affair and are still married with children, you are essentially destroying the family. There will be consequences.

How about porn? Honestly, how does that work for you? Is it helping you respect others? Does it gratify you or lead to self-hatred on some level? Are you now objectifying your sexual partner? How does that make you both feel? Do you put pressure on a partner to have sex in a certain way to fulfil the pornographic details of some video you've watched? Does porn seem like loving sex to you now?

Sexual harassment... are you guilty? The #MeToo movement highlighted the hidden sexual harassment that men have long exerted over women. I accepted it as a way of life in the '60s and '70s (and later, too). Men standing too close to you and looking at your tits. Men brushing past you and squeezing your arm/bum/hand/thigh. Men getting you to sit on their laps at parties. The list is endless.

It is normal in some cultures for men to consider that women are their possessions, but that is not in line with any moral code or mindful attitude in any belief system. The old patriarchal ways of viewing women have to change, which puts the male of the species in a challenging position. Men may feel that sexual power is all they have over women, as their power diminishes in so many other areas of life. They may feel that they need to exert physical strength through sexual violence in order to assert themselves – to feel like big, strong men. But anyone who abuses, rapes, degrades, uses and hurts another for sexual gratification is a long way away from being strong and miles away from their heart-home.

As a society, we need to see through all this bravado as a desperate plea for recognition. There should be no passion without compassion; no lust without trust. (Perhaps that's a good slogan for a tee-shirt. If so, give one to every secondary school student.)

How to be a good person within this framework of self-discipline is a challenge when we have to monitor the biological instincts of our human natures. Contemplating some of the points I have made and the ideas I have referred to will test many of us. It *is* about self-discipline, and in a society that champions the rights of the individual, it can seem counterintuitive when compared to the overall hedonistic messaging we are bombarded with. So, take care out there. The world is not a nightclub.

Valuing others

In our practice to be good people and better ourselves, it is useful to remind ourselves that other people offer us opportunities to grow. If we can hold back from judging others, refrain from trying to get the upper hand when someone is trying to belittle us, and generally do what we think is right, regardless of the reactions of others, then we are doing well.

Valuing others is about recognising the worth of every human being, regardless of how unreasonable and self-centred they appear to be. No one can judge a life by its external appearance. Consider social media: the more successful we become, the more we are in danger of being vilified by someone who doesn't give a monkey's what we feel and is frankly resentful of our success. Anonymity emboldens people to express hatred without being held to account. Using social media to put others down is cowardly and a very sad reflection of where we might be as people. Belittling someone says much more about the perpetrator than the victim.

Every experience we have with other people can be utilised to better ourselves as human beings. Life provides us with what we need to grow, and if we don't grow, we'll continue getting that experience served to us. The person who mugs you and leaves you for dead still deserves your compassion because they're not good, they're not happy and they're creating even more pain for themselves. We wouldn't want a baby to suffer because it didn't know how to change its own nappy, so why would we want anyone to suffer just because they don't know how to change their minds and their lives? They just don't *know* that being good leads to happiness.

Our lives and future lives are created by the good we intend and the good we do. They're created by our kindness, regardless of whether people return that to us; our wish to help, not to hinder or harm; and the healthy regard we have for all beings, including animals, insects, birds and fish. Value all and you will discover that the respect you give to others is eventually returned to you. Your immediate reward will be the deep sense of rightness you hold in your heart.

My story – compassion in action

When I left teaching to open a centre for wellbeing – the business venture I had dreamed up during my latter years of teaching – I was full of good intentions. To say I was naïve is an understatement, but I was motivated to bring spirituality to the masses. The idea was that the centre would have a Buddhist heart and a secular brain. Trying to combine both passions in the same building proved to be one of the biggest challenges I had yet taken on. While it operated, I was able to attract enough people who shared my vision and put in a great deal of time and effort to help make it work. The Buddhist group was an expansion of the one I had started with the encouragement of my Tibetan teacher who had founded the Institute and now headed a worldwide organisation.

I invited many teachers and therapists to visit and work at the centre. Thanks to my links to the early days at the Institute, I knew a lot of senior Buddhists who had since become respected teachers in their own right.

During their teaching visits, it was usual for these teachers to stay with my family because we knew them all as friends and members of our spiritual peer group. After we left the Institute, our family rented a big old house in a village. Neatly tucked away in the countryside, the village earned the local nickname of 'Dingly Dell', like a childhood fairy-tale place from a bygone age.

On one occasion, an American nun was on a teaching visit. She was a very humble and quiet person, but she had a startling intellect alongside a soft-spoken tenderness, which had a wonderful influence on us.

Our behaviour was always modified by visiting 'sangha'[16] who brought out the best in us. My kids were also on their best behaviour as they had learned to be highly respectful of those who were ordained (and they appreciated the mountains of goodies and delectables available so that I could offer the best I could to a Buddhist teacher – a Buddhist practice). One morning, we were all getting up when it became apparent to my partner and I that we had been burgled. We managed to get the family out of the door on their way to school before we addressed what had happened. We called the police. "Unbelievable. Here, in Dingly Dell? How did they get in?" (Probably through the 'back back door' as we called it, in our utility room, which we often forgot to lock.)

The burglar had taken a laptop, some credit cards and a little cash from both our wallets. When the police arrived they found us unexpectedly calm, having processed it together. As they brushed our house with white fingerprint powder, our Victim Liaison Officer spoke to us. "You must be feeling terrible – violated," she empathetically suggested. Our nun, who was hanging up her washing above the old range, said, "He must have really needed the money. Maybe it was an addict." My partner said, "He could have taken much more. Anyway, it's our karma. We must have done something awful ourselves in a past life." And I said, "At least he didn't leave a mess. It was a very neat burglary." The Officer was pretty astonished... not at our sexist assumptions that it must have been a man, but because this was not the usual response to burglary. She of course noted the nun's robes, and she must have known that there was a large Buddhist community in the area. She said, "That's the most sympathetic response I've ever heard. You probably don't need me then." And we didn't.

We never did get to the bottom of the burglary, although we had our suspicions. But we had managed to transform a very difficult situation into a positive one – definitely with the help of the right influence in the room. Our friend was objective and rational and guided our thoughts towards compassion.

---

16   'Sangha', in Buddhist Sanskrit terminology, is used to describe the Buddhist community, especially those who are ordained and most importantly, who have realisations.

Understanding what we mean by love

The Greeks have many words for love (well, they would, wouldn't they). Here are some of them:

- Eros – romantic, physical desire
- Phylia – close, trusting friendship
- Storge – family ties and affection
- Xenia – hospitality between different cultures and seeing visitors as friends
- Agape – unconditional love for others, especially if they are suffering

In mindfulness practice, it is useful to recognise that all these loving relationships will be tested, and that some may lead to hatred, especially in the case of romantic love. This is due to impermanence (one of the Marks of Existence, explained in Chapter 6) and our out-of-control emotional reactions.

It is only 'agape' that compares to the kind of love that Jesus was talking about in his 'love thy neighbour' teaching, and we can dislike our neighbour but still love them. We can deal with any bad treatment from other human beings if we can forgive them and understand that they are coming from places far from their heart-homes, and so are lost in ignorance. We are all like lost children, and we all want to find our way home again. Cultivate compassion all the way.

Loving-kindness is a quality that extends warmth and good wishes to all beings, and we can expand this into having compassion for all beings. But first of all, we need to have love for ourselves. This quality of self-love and self-compassion has been noticeably missing in a society prone to self-hatred, out of mistaken religious guilt or simple negative conditioning.

 **LISTEN**

Self-love and Self-compassion meditation

Once we have healed any negative attitudes towards ourselves, we can genuinely extend love and compassion to others. Someone who hates others firstly hates themselves. That's how interconnected we are – if we haven't been shown how to deal with our own pain, we might take our pain out on others.

Being supported by Inner Management

In an attempt to cross-fertilise, and being a teacher of religions and recognising their commonalities, I created and taught a series of 'Inner Management' courses that explored the three main areas found in all religions. I refer to them in the Preface:

- Life has meaning and purpose
- Goodness brings rewards
- There is life after death

Here they are explained in greater detail.

Life has meaning and purpose

Identifying our strengths and what we have to offer can answer the question, "What is my purpose on earth?"

Most of us will live a potpourri kind of life, smelling the various petals of inspiration at different times or as opportunities arise, while some people may have a vocation – something that they are especially capable of fulfilling or delivering. You may be fortunate enough to have a talent for art or music, for example. But no matter our skills or talents, our prime purpose is our spiritual development. If we climb to the top of our career tree but have walked over others, and generally been self-interested along the way, then we die having achieved very little.

Goodness brings rewards

Doing good leads to the reward of not only feeling better within ourselves, but also to better outcomes in our lives, such as more positive relationships, and experiencing the trust and respect that others have for us. These are the genuine rewards of living a virtuous life and they are self-driven.

If you believe in an afterlife then you're onto a winner. Rewards come in the form of an afterlife that brings peace and an end to suffering, or perhaps in being reborn to continue one's spiritual path. Your good and bad deeds in this life lead to the nature of your future lives.

This beautiful Buddhist contemplation describes the eventual rewards of good deeds performed out of loving-kindness towards others:

You will have sweet dreams, fall asleep easily, and awaken with a smile.
The gods and angels will love and protect you.
Men and women will love you.
Weapons won't be able to harm you.
People will welcome you wherever you go.
You'll have pleasant thoughts.
Your mind will become very quiet.
Animals will love you.
Your voice will become pleasant to listen to.
Your babies will be happy in the womb.
Your children will grow up happy.
If you fall off a cliff, a tree will always be there to catch you.
Your countenance will be serene and your eyes shiny.
You will become awakened.[17]

Who wouldn't want a tree to always be there to catch you?

Acts of kindness are linked to increased feelings of wellbeing.[18] It makes sense – helping others improves our networks so we become more sociable, less isolated and more active.

---

17   This Buddhist contemplation is from the book Moral Issues in Six Religions, to which I contributed the Buddhism section.

18   Mental Health Foundation. Kindness Matters guide. www.mentalhealth.org.uk/campaigns/kindness/kindness-matters-guide.

It also impacts on our sense of self-esteem. Evidence suggests that when we help others, it can actually make changes in the brain that are linked with happiness – all those happy blobs light up and the sad blobs go to sleep. So, we're only a few lifetimes away from building up enough good to become that serene and shiny person.

There is life after death

If you believe that you're just walking meat, without spirit, consciousness or soul, then when you're dead, you're dead. What lies beyond for you may be something you don't give a fig about. How that impacts on your moral behaviour may depend on many things, such as the imprints on your consciousness and your conditioning. If you've been a 'giver' then you leave behind rewards for others, regardless of your beliefs, which in itself is noble. However, many people do believe in life after death, which supports their moral code.

A belief in life after death broadens our world-view, so we can see the eternal interdependence of all things. It helps us to be a good person because we see the single amidst the whole, the eternal spider's-web microcosm within the macrocosm, and our relationship with others becomes like our relationship with ourselves.

If you have a sound spiritual practice, then it doesn't matter what you believe. Perhaps you can see that a belief in life after death can help and support you in this life – or maybe you are more open to the idea of an afterlife now. It does help us make sense of some of the more insane events that happen in a single lifetime of a sentient being – considering that the cause of a tragedy in this life may stem from causes created in previous lives. It also gives us the impetus to take responsibility for future lives and take great care of how we walk on this planet in this life. It's a large world-view that deserves consideration.

Becoming aware of the value of rules and laws

Mindfulness enables us to follow a personal set of moral guidelines from which we do not divert. This is the person-centred approach to goodness, instead of some religious traditions where moral rules are imposed by an external divine being.

The Golden Rule is a basic but profound motto for how to live morally and is shared by all belief systems in their own words. Generally, it is understood as 'treat others as you would wish to be treated yourself.'

We can go a step further by practising the Platinum Rule (originally proposed by Dave Kerpen in his book *The Art of People*), which takes into account the feelings of others: "Treat others how *they* would like to be treated." The focus shifts from 'this is what I want, so I'll give everyone the same thing' to 'let me first understand what others want, and then I'll give it to them.'

There are many sources of religious wisdom that point to unity, as reflected in the Golden and Platinum rules – in other words, we are all the same. When we practise meditation, we become aware of the thoughts and emotions that dominate us and are often the source of a lot of struggle and disturbance. We get used to this disturbance (just like we get used to mosquitos on holiday), but no matter how small and insignificant an emotion seems, it can cause us a lot of problems.

Add mindfulness to any religious practice and we find out *how* to live by the Golden and Platinum Rules and so lose the divisiveness that exists in different belief systems.

Buddhists traditionally keep five vows (not to kill, steal, lie, commit sexual misconduct or take intoxicants) so that they harm no one, and thus protect their own consciousness.

The rules are there to help us get on, and surely *understanding* our minds and why we have conflicts is another viable route towards living in harmony. This is working with what we have in common, rather than what separates us.

The mindfulness route – recognising that our inner disturbances are dealt with by pointing the finger *inwards*, at ourselves – is more likely to result in harmony with others, rather than an external set of religious rules where we are just told what to do without necessarily understanding why.

If our chosen religion guides us, then we will be better religious practitioners (though not necessarily better people). If our religion seeks to convert others, we may have many problems. Our mission is not to force others to be like us, but to change ourselves into being the best we can be.

At the root of all these vows and rules is one simple guideline: do not harm others.

Considering your role models carefully

How are we able to discern if our spiritual guide (if we have one) is the real thing? This is not easy. I can talk about this from experience because I almost became a follower of a religious teacher as opposed to a practitioner of a religion. There is a huge difference. We have to be very alert and use all our discriminating wisdom to understand that if we go against a majority (such as the people who follow a charismatic religious teacher), we may be isolated and feel attacked by those we call our friends and neighbours. They may then become our enemies and wish to harm us. We could even be victimised and suffer the hatred of an entire social group. This path requires great courage and a sense of inner conviction.

In a professional environment, someone who exposes unethical behaviour is called a whistle-blower. This is not a pleasant role as they may suffer terrible victimisation from the herd, who may feel the need to discredit them due to professional and financial pressure. But to say nothing would definitely affect their peace of mind because their awareness of unethical behaviour will have been alerted.

Cult leaders who appear to be speaking words of wisdom and compassion may also be motivated to acquire power and control in this world. Spiritual power is said to be one of the last negative states of mind in the progress of a human being towards enlightenment. If you have spiritual power, it can corrupt you.

Courage is such a vital quality in our battle with the ego. The last temptation of Jesus was that he could do and have all he wanted and succumb to his ego's desires for power, fame and greed if he worshipped

Satan instead of God. The story is a wonderful example of the fragility of the mind unless our motivation is pure. Jesus defeated these destructive influences through his inner wisdom and compassion.

This is similar to the final temptation of the Buddha before his enlightenment. 'Maras' (obstructive spirit forces) tried to seduce him into giving up his pursuit of enlightenment. When he was able to dismiss these forces as delusions, he finally attained nirvana.

In testing any spiritual guides, we need to remove all external influences – especially those from other people. Cult followers succumb to a kind of hypnosis. They may be primarily motivated by wanting goodness and freedom to prevail in society, but they are seduced into thinking that such outcomes can only arise from their guide... no one else.

The well-used phrase, "Well, [my spiritual guide] says...", is something we all need to be wary of. And if you are the one saying it, then *you* need to be very wary of whom you are handing your autonomy to.

Doing good work

Mindful work means putting ethics and values before personal gain. It also means we need to have a strong sense of who we are.

American psychologist Howard Gardner defines 'good work'[19] as follows:

- Work of high quality
- Work that matters to society
- Work that enhances the lives of others
- Work that is conducted in an ethical manner

He suggests we employ what he calls the '3 Es' to assess whether we are doing good work:

- Is it of an *excellent* quality (the best I can do)? – this pleases ourselves

---

19   For more on 'good work', visit: www.thegoodproject.org.

- Is it *engaging*? – of benefit to others
- Is it *ethical*? – morally sound and not harming others

We all want to be seen to be ethical at work, but we are often guilty of bending the rules in order to get a pay rise or a promotion, revealing that ambition sometimes overrides ethics.

In relation to the people we serve, we are not always fortunate enough to have an ethical boss. The Buddhist step on the Noble Eightfold Path that relates to work is called 'Right Livelihood'. Again, the premise is to engage in work that brings benefit to others, not harm. But if we have a leader who is self-serving, then our ethics may become compromised.

We are led by others for many reasons: to fit in, to earn more money, to belong, to avoid victimisation, to be on the winning side, and so on. If our motivation is clear then we are less likely to be led blindly. Mindful followership is a great quality and leadership qualities will emerge more readily from the many rather than the few if we have unshakeable ethical values.

Having good motivation

If we return to the Dalai Lama's description of spiritual qualities in the Preface (love, compassion, patience, tolerance, forgiveness, contentment, responsibility and harmony), we can see that being good also relies on developing these qualities. So can a destructive emotion ever be good? In an interview with Noriyuki Ueda (entitled 'The (Justifiably) Angry Marxist'[20]), the Dalai Lama says, "Anger that is motivated by compassion or a desire to correct social justice, and does not seek to harm the other person, is a good anger that is worth having."

To have good motivation is essential, but 'the road to hell is paved with good intentions', as the saying goes, so checking on our intentions is key to our conduct. Justifying doing something that is harmful to others for the greater good, for instance, is probably at the basis of much violence and conflict. Constantly checking in with our motivation enables us to avoid getting caught up in harming others.

---

20   https://tricycle.org/trikedaily/justifiably-angry-marxist-interview-dalai-lama/

Ethical mindfulness

To conclude, *incorporating* mindfulness into how to be good is vital to support our ethical values.

Ethical mindfulness in our everyday lives can be explained as:

- **Ethics of restraint:** With mindfulness, we become aware of our tendencies and hold ourselves back from saying and doing things that are harmful to others.

- **Ethics of virtue:** We practise thinking, saying and doing things that will benefit others – being kind, complimenting others, showing sensitivity and offering help when needed. This sits beautifully with practising the constructive emotions (turn to Chapter 6 for more on these).

- **Ethics of altruism:** We consider the whole world as a place for our practice – not confined to just those we are close to, but so that we recognise unity with every human being.

Ethical misconduct starts with the mind. It ends with actions, causes problems and unhappiness to ourselves and others, and ultimately harms society. Mindfully managing our thoughts and emotions will help the process of self-assessing our tendencies and conditioning, and lead us towards restraining our behaviour in our practice of being good. It's not about ending fun, it's about ending confusion and finding genuine peace of mind.

Reflections

- From all these tools and ideas around being good, which one sits most comfortably with you?
- Do you find it important to extend love and compassion to yourself? Is that hard or easy?
- What approach works best for you in the suggestions on how to be good at work?
- What's your drug in terms of temptation? Does reading this chapter make you want to change something to simplify and clean up your life, or not?

Authentic mindfulness

- Do-gooders are those who do good in order *to be seen* to be doing good.
- Check that feelings of pity don't take root and instead transform them into empathy and compassion.
- You can follow people on Twitter, but don't *follow* them. Take no one as your inner boss except yourself. Trust your inner guide.
- There's a great rule in Buddhism: if someone wants to know about what you know, they have to ask three times. This is to ensure that they are really interested. It's the complete opposite of trying to convert others. You can take a horse to water.... Converting, preaching and acting like you've 'got it' only alienates others.

Spiritual integrity

- Being good sounds like being god. That's because being good does bring you closer to godliness. Feel the power of your potential saint or buddha nature within and rejoice. Hallelujah!
- The more you feel part of something bigger, the more your ego

humbles itself.

- ○ Be aware that your life holds meaning and purpose and remind yourself of your good work every day.

- ○ If you slip up and do something morally questionable, don't let it be a burden. Acknowledge it, regret it and, if you need to, apologise for it and move on.

- ○ Rules and laws are there to protect your mind as well as protecting society.

Lead by example, but relax with your humanity. Don't give yourself a hard time and people will warm to you. No one likes a know-it-all. It's so ironic really, isn't it? We think that by changing the external world we can achieve happiness, but the very opposite is true.

Chapter 9

Wellseeing through Mindful Eyes

∘ ∘ ∘

"The mind is its own place, and in itself can make a heaven of hell, a hell of heaven."

John Milton

Paradise Lost

By now, hopefully, you will feel equipped to manage a whole host of issues and social situations through the practices of emotional intelligence and personal ethics. You must be feeling pretty saintly as you glide through the world on your mindfully oiled skates. You may recognise how all these practices segue into each other – goodness naturally arising from emotion management; empathy and compassion neatly leading you into principled speech and actions. Now, you're relating to others with awareness and humility, your inner light ablaze like a spiritual Fitbit, counting all those mindful steps.

So what's left in the mental aerobics programme? Seeing into our selves is a lot like peeling an onion. There are layers and layers, but no central core.

Managing thoughts and emotions was the first layer. Exploring personal ethics was the second. The focus of this chapter is the third layer, in which we take a look at our ingrained attitudes, and how the way we look at the world colours our experience. This provides us with insight into how we can see through mindful eyes and how 'wellseeing' is the window into 'wellbeing'. Chapter 10 then provides a guide to *practising* wellseeing.

Wellseeing for wellbeing

'Wellbeing' is the term used to describe the interconnected health of body, mind and spirit. It is a holistic view that recognises how the mind inextricably links to our body and our spirit. I chose to call my consultancy business Wellseeing Consultancy: for me, the term 'wellseeing' points to the principle cause of our wellbeing, because no matter what life throws at us, we can deal with it, manage it, gain resilience and inner fortitude from it – and ultimately spiritually benefit from it – if we are *aware*. I wasn't suggesting my consultancy was an alternative to Specsavers. My aim was to highlight that a mistaken view of reality will get in the way of our happiness and wellbeing, because we look out with these visual sense objects (our eyes!) that are utterly coloured by mistaken views and mental attitudes, thus stimulating confusion.

Mental attitudes arise from our mistaken perception of reality. By calling my consultancy Wellseeing Consultancy, I was drawing attention to the fact that our limited, concretised view of reality is the principal cause of our problems, and that if we address that, then our problems will diminish.

Well*being* as a label is everywhere. Physical, emotional and mental wellbeing has become our modern pursuit, which is undeniably a healthy path to tread.

The promotion of a healthy lifestyle – one that encourages a nutritious diet and regular exercise as a natural route to finding genuine happiness – can be seen wherever you look, crossing politics and business as well as being on a rich menu of evening classes and weekend courses. We are shaking off the ghosts of old aspirations that failed to deliver on the post-war 1950s dream – the house, the car, family life – as the gateway to happiness, and we seem genuinely relieved to exorcise them, as they never dealt with the reality of being human anyway.

In a world that struggles with so many social issues, the signpost now points to individual wellbeing as the route to fulfilling human potential – which is definitely more realistic and more attainable. This does not mean that the goal of having a satisfying family life is dead, just that our expectations are more realistic (we are *aware*), and our individual wellbeing is more likely to be the route towards fulfilling that dream anyway.

The art of wellseeing – changing our attitudes

Mindfulness has become a recognised and effective method for finding wellbeing. It is used to manage anxiety, depression, post-traumatic stress disorder, general levels of stress and other negative assaults on our wellbeing. It became well-known through the work of Jon Kabat-Zinn and later practitioners, who were able to support their practices with ground-breaking research in neuroscientific discoveries. Originally, seen as a therapeutic tool, mindfulness is responsible for several relatively new, scientifically based psychological treatments:

- **MBSR:** Mindfulness-Based Stress Reduction – to manage stress
- **DBT:** Dialectical Behaviour Therapy – for treating borderline personality disorder
- **MBCT:** Mindfulness-Based Cognitive Therapy – for managing depression
- **ACT:** Acceptance and Commitment Therapy – for managing relationship issues

The UK's marvellous heroine of wellbeing, the NHS, has introduced mindfulness to support a wide variety of health and wellbeing initiatives. I have trained health workers across the spectrum in hospitals in North West England to integrate mindfulness into their lives in order to support their mental health.

Extensive research (the INSEAD Business School is a good place to start to find out more about such studies; search 'mindfulness') has even won over the world of business through the findings that mindfulness brings these benefits:

- Reduces stress and helps people cope with pressure
- Helps with anxiety

- Helps with numerous medical disorders
- Helps with relationship issues
- Enhances an overall sense of wellbeing
- Increases focus and concentration, including the ability to deal with distractions
- Supports creativity and avoiding negative thought patterns

With consideration, it is not difficult to see how mindfulness and meditation practice lead to these benefits. Humans have learned that the best way to defeat an enemy is to get to know it and find out its weaknesses. Stress is our main enemy in our 21st century lives, and we can only get to know its effects on us, and its triggers, through mindful awareness.

Having a mindful attitude to our lives means keeping an open and curious mind. If mindfulness meditation is all about being in the here and now, then being mindful in our everyday lives means taking that attitude to our experiences. It's like having the mind of a child – full of innocence and wonder – coupled with qualities of compassion and wisdom. With a mindful attitude, our brushes with the unpleasantness of life can give us new depths of loving-kindness towards others, rather than us tightening and closing up to keep others out.

This doesn't mean that we have to accept bad behaviour; instead, having a mindful attitude encourages us to contemplate how our own view contributes to our experience. We can't wait for *others* to change, but we can mindfully effect change by altering the way *we* see things.

Here's an example scenario from one of my attendees on the Wellseeing Leadership Programme training days on 'Mindful Attitudes', and one that does not seem to be unusual:

Valerie goes home every evening to be greeted by her husband sitting in front of the TV. He has a manual job and is strictly 9–5 in his working habits. When I say 'greeted', I don't mean that he greets her. She just sees him sitting there. She makes herself a cup of tea and sits in the open plan kitchen adjacent to the living room.

Val doesn't consider herself to be an angry person, but she is quietly irritated by the habits of her husband. She secretly harbours the view that he has become lazy and expects to be waited on. She goes through the motions of asking him about his day and what he wants for dinner. He grunts a bit and says he'll leave dinner to her, and he asks if she picked up any beer on her way home.

Val smoulders with a deep feeling of swirling smoke in her belly. Her face goes tight and her throat swells. She considers how patient she is, and what she has to put up with every day. She looks at her husband with narrow eyes and a sense of loathing emerges.

In the training days, we work on managing thoughts and emotions through changing our view. Val has considered leaving her husband, but this just feels sad to her. She remembers how they used to be and wonders when she started to view him in such a negative light.

As part of my courses, I give the trainees homework – usually to practise some meditation, but also to develop a new way of dealing with an everyday situation mindfully. Val decides to work mindfully with her irritation – which she acknowledges is a form of repressed anger – and to try to see her husband's positive attributes.

Val buys a bottle of wine and a ready meal from the supermarket on her way home from work. When she gets in, she kisses her husband, which surprises him. She goes back to the kitchen to make herself a cup of tea. While she is drinking it, she considers her husband – his hard job that is starting to make his back hurt; how he has patiently put up with family life, even though he wanted to travel. She considers him mindfully, and instead of irritation she starts to feel a warm flood of compassion for him. At dinner, her husband picks up on her feelings and they talk more than usual. Something starts to melt.

Nothing changed except Val's view – and that changed everything.

When she told us this, everyone in the room felt the hairs rise on the back of their necks: a sure sign of having touched something deep and profound. Val was crying by the end of the story, and several other people were too, such was their level of empathy. Releasing emotional distress can have that effect.

Understanding that we can change the way we view things is a common hypothesis for many contemporary psychological models. It's ancient wisdom meets modern psychology. Of course, no one will ever change through osmosis. Change has to come from within us. If you are of the opinion that you have always been a certain way (negative, grumpy, pessimistic) and you are too old to change (dogs, tricks and things), or you expect others to just put up with who you are ("You should know me by now!"), then you will find this hard. Your ego is in control, with both hands gripping tight on the steering wheel.

The first step in any therapy or personal development programme is to consider that you *don't* have to stay the same, and that you might just become a better person, with a more rewarding life, if you attempt to change.

I've met many managers and leaders who can't imagine why they would wish to change a single hair on their bodies. They are the people who turn up late to your training session, never having checked what room it is in, still eating their lunch and proclaiming that they're only attending because they have to. Their attitudes are ingrained through status and power and the expectation that everyone will put up with them because they're the boss; a view that is enabled by the people around them who are just trying to have an easy life. Whatever your viewpoint, you will recognise this stubbornly entitled person somewhere in your life experience. The fact that they are stuck with a self that refuses to budge because their ego is so scared is definitely worthy of compassion, but you have to be careful not to become the victim of their inner monsters.

Unfortunately, attitudes of superiority and inferiority are woven into the very fabric of societies – class, caste, race, gender – and they're what we're clothed in on our arrival into this world. So changing inborn attitudes may be our toughest hurdle.

In his book *One of Them: An Eton College Memoir*, Musa Okwonga talks of the conditioning that is entitlement and how this can affect a whole society:

"I look at the most confident people in my year and I realise that the greatest gift that has been bestowed upon them is that of shameless-ness. Shamelessness is the superpower of a certain section of the English upper classes. While so many other people in the country are hamstrung by the deference and social embarrassment they have been taught since birth, the upper classes calmly parade on through the streets and boardrooms to claim the spoils. They don't learn shameless-ness at Eton, but this is where they perfect it."

Mental attitudes towards ourselves, the world around us and life itself can help us or hinder us. We don't have to go to a public school to become confident, nor be born into an 'inferior' class to learn humility. Mindfulness can help us be aware of everything that is colouring our view. And how courageous if we are someone who is entitled but can still feel equal to others; or if we are practising not feeling resentment or jealousy when we compare ourselves to others. Wherever we sit – in a Mercedes-Benz or on a bike – we can tinker with our mental attitudes.

Unwellseeing leads to unwellbeing

The Buddha taught that until we are enlightened and have destroyed the ego, we are all mentally ill to some degree. Even this idea is a challenge to us, as we mostly consider ourselves to be 'normal'. But normality is many shades of grey, and none of us 'normal' beings see things as they really are (just like the blind men in the parable about the elephant in Chapter 8).

Let's consider some of the self-limiting mental attitudes that can cloud our vision and negatively affect our wellness – our 'sicknesses'.

Negative thinking

Negative thinking combines pessimism with catastrophic thinking, all based on fear and insecurity. Someone who approaches life through these ominous, cloud-filled lenses always expects the worst thing to happen and that things will go wrong. If they are looking for a parking space, they will have already decided before they hit the car park that there will be no spaces left for them. If they go for a job interview, they will already be prepared for failure. Their minds are dominated by fear, worry and anxiety, and this creates a mindset that feels heavy and can lead to depression. Pessimism is the default mental attitude, but catastrophic thinking is its powerful upgrade.

Catastrophic thinking often happens in those dark, wakeful hours between midnight and dawn. It can be pre-empted by a genuine concern. Your daughter has not come home yet and she should have been home half an hour ago. I use this example because it is a rational worry – we all watch the news. Our minds go to the worst-case scenario, so we imagine the worst and then feel the worst. Sometimes, we feel almost obliged to worry as a parent – and if we don't worry, then we worry that there must be something wrong with us. But most likely, your daughter will come home.

In 2021, there was a surge of protest concerning the safety of women on the streets, especially in cities. Justifiable anger that strives to change the law and protect women from violence and sexual assault is a mindful approach, so this is not to deny the importance of challenging existing views and attitudes, but to moderate our catastrophic 'what if' thinking and be rational instead.

Catastrophic and negative thinking hold us in dark places and their attitude to life is that everything will go wrong and bad things will happen. Usually, this is not how things happen during a lifetime. It is much more of a seesaw kind of experience, as we learn to walk round holes in the road or try to negotiate a way through challenges. People who have the strength to deal with challenging experiences are not negative or catastrophic thinkers. They have their inner light to guide them and reassure them that nothing is permanent, and they will get through. They are positive thinkers.

You can replace negative thoughts with positive thoughts, and dissolve catastrophic thinking through rational analysis. Ask yourself: "Is there anything I can do about this?" If there is, do it. If there isn't, why worry? You achieve nothing, may make yourself ill and will worry others around you.

Some people think that if they expect the worst, the reality will turn out to be something better, and this makes them feel better. Hey, it's not for me to preach – if it works for you, then carry on – but always expecting the worst can be depressing, not only for you but for those you love. Self-fulfilling prophecies demonstrate how powerful the mind can be. If you think something is going to happen, you can 'will' it to happen. It's when expectation meets self-righteousness – "I told you so!" – that sense of knowing it will be bad, and being glad you can tell others that you were right. I'm reminded of the epitaph on comic actor and writer Spike Milligan's tombstone: "I told you I was ill." I bow down to the master of black humour.

We all think negatively sometimes. We can recognise this through mindfulness and gently lift ourselves out of this dark place. Without mindfulness, we will think that negativity is who we are, and more feelings of fear and shame will dominate. The first step in mindfulness practice is to see that we are not our thoughts – it is the first wonderfully liberating realisation. The second step is to understand that we can change the way we think, and so begins our practice.

Negative thinking is a habit. If you can recognise it, whatever its roots, you can work with it.

High expectations

Worldly success is measured by external standards, yet it is virtually impossible to measure what one learns spiritually in a lifetime (which is all that really matters). Because Western society places so much emphasis on achievements, goals and material successes, we aim unnecessarily high and unrealistically expect worldly fruits to drop from the trees of plenty into our sweaty palms. But our expectations need to be rooted in reality – we are aspiring saints, but not yet enlightened. Our expectations might be more achievable if we make them spiritual objectives by measuring our worth internally rather than conventionally.

Perhaps the most genuinely successful people are those who transform disappointing outcomes into positive experiences, increasing their resilience and adding miles to their spiritual progress.

Anxiety and worry

Two states of mind link with negative and catastrophic thinking. They are most commonly associated with being dealt with through mindfulness practice because they are the mental attitudes that oppose presence. Worries place themselves in the future: "What if?" is the starting point. ("What if I get sick, how will I pay the mortgage?" "What if the car is stolen? I won't be able to get to work." And so it goes on.) Anxieties are past-based and usually focus on things that have happened and we can't change – but we can't stop thinking about them.

Mindfulness meditation brings us to the present, and focuses our mind on what is actually happening now. It is reality-based. Mindfulness in our everyday life brings our minds to the present, reining us in on a short leash to experience the NOW. Whenever we are future- or past-focused in a way that is disturbing our peace of mind, practising mindfulness is like your gran gently slapping your cheek, encouraging you to stop being so daft and grow up.

Depression

This mental bully is like having our head filled with, and surrounded by, smog. It gets into every part of us, affecting our physical health and our ability to connect with our inner self. When the mind is in hell, the body is too, and to lift ourselves out of this disease is a struggle. Antidepressants help people who regularly experience depression, but mindfulness is one of the most effective natural remedies. Depression can hit us at different times in our lives, and it can take the form of us just being mildly but continually unhappy or take us to the extreme of self-harming and feeling suicidal. Mindfulness helps in that we can observe our state of mind and take action – positive, healthy action.

I have suffered from depression: the kind of depression that kept me in bed with the duvet over my head. In those times I forced myself to repeat, "May no other being ever feel this pain." It helped, because mental illness self-obsesses. When we move our attention to others, it loses its grip and the clouds disperse a little. And for me, as a Buddhist practitioner, I could reassure myself that even in times of great emotional pain I was able to think of others.

The link between mind and body is at its most obvious in depression. Our body language and our ways of speaking express our depression. It impacts our posture and energy levels. Exercise becomes hard, if not impossible, to engage in. We may eat too much or too little, or turn to alcohol or substance abuse. Being mindful of this, we can adjust our posture, lift our voices and take care to at least go for a daily walk and manage our diet. I make this sound easy, but to actually do these things takes huge effort of course, and we won't respond kindly to remonstrations to 'get a grip.' The effort has to come from within.

Certain therapeutic methods (such as psychotherapy and neuro-linguistic programming) offer positive psychology as part of their training. All these therapies are based on the premise that the brain can be manipulated and changed (neuroplasticity) by changing the thoughts and actions of our body, speech and mind.

Depression that comes and goes may be considered a healthy response to a world that is so loaded with negativity, but if it lingers and is accompanied by anxiety then we have a problem that needs addressing. There is a difference between low mood states and clinical depression.

The need for spiritual support, and awareness of our inner light, could never be more necessary, as no external measures can genuinely help those of us who have become disillusioned with being human. Depression, self-harm and suicide are not always expressions of self-hatred, but articulate the loathing of being human. Never was the time more perfect for gifting ourselves the tools to deal with depression, anxiety and stress.

Depression, of course, is something that can accompany grief, so we need to be mindful if, and when, we find ourselves in a tragic state of loss. People and animals we love will die – it is a side-effect of being mortal. Grief can possess our minds and keep us in a dark place as we try to deal with our loss. Grief is not a destructive emotion because it is sadness, and that is a healthy response to loss, but we have to take care that we have coping methods and support, and that grief does not turn into depression.

The problem with grief is that it becomes past-fixated, because there appears to be no future without that loved one. If you have a spiritual perspective, religious or not, and consider that you may meet the person or pet again in another dimension or realm, this will help you. It may also help you to consider how they have helped you grow as a person and all the positives that they brought during their life – their legacy to the world.

Cynicism and scepticism

The positive, largely unknown root of cynicism comes from the ancient Greeks. For the Cynics, the purpose of life was to live virtuously and in harmony with nature. Cynics could gain happiness through disciplined moral training and by living in a way that was natural, rejecting all the conventional routes to happiness such as gaining wealth, power and fame. Instead, they led a simple life free from all possessions.

Buddhism and secular mindfulness align very well with the Cynics' approach to life. However, *cynicism* (a moralistic and judgemental view) developed as a negative attitude towards those who did not live in accordance with the values of the Cynics. The compassion was missing, you see.

Scepticism is when we are in a state of suspicion and disbelief that hampers what is actually possible. It is cynicism's sister act, in that there is a level of negative judgement at work. It can affect outcomes due to its ability to deflate ideas and projects. It is born from disappointment in our limited view of others and the world around us, so it needs balancing with an uplifting dose of optimism.

Stress

Stress is when we feel we're being pushed too far and we're not coping with what's being asked of us. It's the adverse reaction we have to excessive pressures, usually in our working lives, and that includes stay-at-home parents raising children. We experience burnout and have depleted energy, and if we suffer from stress too often, it will undoubtedly trigger physical illness. High blood pressure, back pain, heart problems and digestive issues are all associated with stress. Stress can have a negative effect on our relationships too. Our tolerance levels are different, but it is a mistake to think we don't each have a stress threshold.

Unfortunately, the speediest remedy is reliance on excessive use of alcohol and drugs to deaden the pain, but this reliance only adds to the continuity of stress. Alcohol and drugs deplete our energy levels so only work as a short-term solution, offering a short period in which to forget and avoid stress, which ultimately doesn't help at all.

Having a healthy attitude to work means creating more and more positive work environments as we wise up to tedious, outdated '9–5' structures. Rather than seeing work as something to tolerate in order to make a living, we can take a different attitude to work and create flexible workplaces and employment structures. The word 'work' has a somewhat onerous meaning in the English language, but other cultures have translations that mean 'nourishment for life' or 'life's meaning', which give the word a much more positive profile.

While stress is more accurately 'distress', conversely there is a positive kind of stress called *eustress*. It's when pressure inspires us to be creative – when we become energised by what's expected of us and discover our hidden strengths and talents. We work better with others to succeed and, here's the important point, it is occasional and it is rewarded.

It's great to be challenged. It brings out the human qualities of personal growth and strength. But the challenge has to be achievable, otherwise we feel set up to fail. Eustress can easily fall into stress if we are not mindful of what is actually achievable.

If we take the stress out of work, we can create a new template for fulfilling and meaningful occupations. It doesn't have to be philanthropic work, but our motivation, our relationships and our ethics will be the reward.

My story – ego-games

Long before Buddhism entered my life, I hung out with a group of youthful intellectuals who shared the idea that the only intelligent way to view a large part of society was to be cynical about them. How my friends and I laughed at the ignorance and ineptitude of social climbers and political self-servers. A new girlfriend of one of this group of friends was listening to us pontificating one evening. She was drying her hair by the fire, having rejected my hair dryer, and I watched as she let her hair cascade into a natural waterfall of curls. She was so pretty. She started to argue with us, and her counter-attack that challenged our view – reminding us that it was not the only view on the subject – left its impression on me. Her voice was new and fresh to me and felt annoyingly right. But there was no way I would have admitted that at the time.

Reflecting on that encounter many years later, having begun to deal with my ego and face my shortcomings in my Buddhist practice, I realised that she was one of my first teachers. She had unknowingly challenged my sense of identity and yet awakened my inner self, who was whispering to me. The unwholesome emotions of jealousy and pride were obstacles to my wellseeing, although I lacked the self-awareness to realise that then. These attitudes had helped me to feel superior, clever, witty and cultured in my youth. What an incredible shock it was to recognise that these cynical views were my sicknesses, contributing to my low self-esteem and inauthenticity of being.

I began to feel a little better when I understood that I had these attitudes because I was insecure and disappointed with many of the aspects of life that had seemed so important in my youth. You see, I just did not yet understand the power of compassion.

Now, I am a little kinder to myself, as I have learned that actually the root of cynicism meant to live simply, denounce worldly pursuits and throw scorn on those who didn't. I was halfway there, but I needed some constructive antidotes to adjust my view. It was so easy to compare myself to others and find them lacking, but I had never really noticed how my words could hurt my target. I only saw the admiration of my appreciative audience when I was sarcastic and trying to be clever. Ahh, Buddhism, you have ruined my comedic skills. How hard it is to be a comedian without taking the piss out of others.

The view of emptiness – the ultimate antidote

"Recalling it differently, as we were bound to, what was it, in fact, we saw? Which one among us has the truth of it now? And which one shall be the judge? The truth is, of course, that there is no pure truth, only the moody accounts of witnesses."

Laurie Lee

Cider with Rosie

The view of emptiness is central to Buddhist practice. It is so profound that many great scholars of Buddhism have written extensively on the subject. For Buddhists, the term 'wisdom' is applied to this way of viewing our reality, which is why I refer to it earlier in the book as being no ordinary wisdom. Buddhists try to integrate emptiness into their everyday practice, and indeed their motivation for practising mindfulness meditation is to attain this realisation of the true nature of reality, famously described as nirvana. It's not a place you go to, but an unconditioned and egoless view of reality. It is not ignorance; it is the 'pure truth', its antithesis. When you attain nirvana you become liberated from your ego and then you will experience the bliss of this mental state that is emotionless.

If you understand what Laurie Lee is saying then you'll get that emptiness is not so hard to understand, although it is very difficult to practise. If you can but get a small taste of what emptiness means, it will support you when other techniques fail.

If you know someone who proclaims to be Buddhist, utter the words, "It is all empty" to them. You'll get some respect, and it might start a very interesting conversation!

The emptiness of conditioned existence

Conditioning isn't just what we do to our hair to make it silky smooth, or when we need to oil a car engine to make it purr. I'm talking about when people are influenced in such a profound way by past experiences and the habits they've formed that their minds are shaped purely according to their life experiences (Chapter 3 digs into conditioning in more detail).

Imagine the conventional experience of an individual human being (let's call them Everyperson).

Everyperson sees the world as an external place. They are at the centre, and are the most important person. Their views are right, and if everyone agreed with them then the world would be a better place. They see everything and everyone with the view of whether they like them or not, and try to avoid things and people they don't like. Everyperson thinks that to be happy they must get as much of the stuff that they like as possible, and avoid the stuff they don't like. When people are nice to them and admire their strengths, it makes them feel good; when they are criticised, they feel down and depressed. The way Everyperson reacts to life is to measure every experience against what they think is good or bad, right or wrong, intelligent or stupid. Their view is conditioned. Their conditioning comes from influences that have been impressed upon them since they were born – from their family, who raised them a certain way, to their friends and colleagues, whose approval they seek. Everything they do and everything they experience is a result of their mental attitudes to life that have arisen through this conditioning. Consequently, their life is an emotional rollercoaster, and they feel that they are constantly firefighting. Happiness always seems to be just beyond where they are now.

Every one of us relates to everything through our own conditioning and tendencies. Our egos build a view of ourselves and the world we live in. This leads to barriers – prejudices and judgements. We form attachments to the things that help us feel better about ourselves, and develop an aversion towards all the rest. If something doesn't affect us, we just ignore it or give it random, occasional consideration. In Buddhism, this is called *ego-grasping* because we are painting a view of reality that supports our poor old egos. It is a mistaken view of existence because there is actually nothing that we grasp onto that has any permanent, inbuilt aspect to it. Grasping onto our egos, and our way of seeing things as being right, is labelled by Buddhists as 'ignorance'. This is what Laurie Lee meant when he described people's way of seeing things as 'moody accounts'. Ignorance here doesn't mean we're stupid; instead, we're merely unaware of how things actually are – unaware of the fact that we are creating our own reality based on what our ego has created for us. We are unaware of the role our ego is playing in creating our *life*. It is as if we are asleep.

Now let's imagine that Everyperson is a mindfulness practitioner and has accepted that they might be very similar to everyone else, not better or worse than others. Let's say that Everyperson is practising the view of emptiness.

Everyperson tries to see the world as a mirror of their inner reality. They recognise their interdependence with everything and so consequently feel themselves to be one of many, rather than the only important one. Although they have preferences, they recognise that everything is subject to change, and everyone is worthy of respect and love as we are all equally searching for happiness. Everyperson likes to encounter pleasing things, but they accept when things go a different way – they try to go with the flow. They know that to be happy is more about contentment and inner peace. They love it when people are nice to them and admire them, but if they don't, they try to rationally consider what is happening, put right what they can and let go of what they can't change. Their equanimity isn't affected. They recognise their conditioning and try to be aware of it. By meditating and practising mindfulness, Everyperson can see that they project onto their experiences and that they won't always be right. Their outlook is mindful, and they deal with negative mental attitudes as they arise and as they recognise them. They regularly connect with their inner self through meditation and reflection, and remind themselves of its power and its presence whenever they feel the need to withdraw, take stock and replenish.

Everyperson is having the same life but their view of life is different. One is with the conventional view and one is with the view of emptiness. Understanding that our entire experience of life is due to the conditioned way we see it, underpins the concept of wellseeing. If you assess that you like the way you see the world and it works for you, then so be it. But if you consider how your experience of life might be altered for the better if you developed awareness, then I'm right behind you, kiddo.

Seeing with wisdom

The practice of developing the view of emptiness, or seeing with wisdom, requires extensive meditation, but in a gradual way we can all work towards this understanding. Consider an example of how conditioning and ego-grasping leads to problems:

Billy grows up in Manchester. He and his family support Manchester United. In fact, lot of people in his street support Manchester United. One of the team's greatest adversaries is the other Manchester team… Manchester City. Manchester United win a lot and Billy develops the view that they are the best team. One day, Manchester City win. Billy is heartbroken. His ego is grasping at his team being the best. He is conditioned to think so. His family and neighbours are supporters. A Manchester City fan taunts him that Manchester City are the best team. This angers Billy. His ego is under attack. This leads to a big punch-up and many people are hurt, as they join in like sheep. (Sound familiar?)

Manchester United are not the best team, otherwise this would be a constant. Players change, times change, financial support changes, so there is nothing permanent about Manchester United. But Billy has attached himself to the label of Manchester United and any attack on them is an attack on his ego. He is also unable to consider that things and times change. He doesn't understand emptiness.

Emptiness refers to the fact that nothing exists in a concrete way. There is no 'inherent' Manchester United. The team is in a state of change all the time, just as we all are. The players, the manager… they're always changing. Everything about us changes and, because change can threaten our ego, we are constantly trying to hold on to a view of ourselves, others and everything we experience as permanent. If we can integrate this view of emptiness and impermanence into our lives, we can see that this is the truth of our reality. Impermanence isn't a belief; it's how things are.

The spiritual view

Applying the view of emptiness means that whenever something happens to upset us, we can stand back and recognise that we are only seeing the experience from our own perspective: how we perceive it to be. It is an illusion to think that it is the reality. We are shackled by our ego's projection of what is happening – be that the end of a relationship, receiving an award or buying our dream house.

Of course, things do exist conventionally, but our interpretation of them is conditioned. Whether we think something is good or bad is totally dependent on our projections of what is good and what is bad. The house we fall in love with can end up being the house we're desperate to leave. It's not inherent in the house, but in our view.

The spiritual practitioner tries to see everything from this perspective and applies the view of emptiness to everything that takes place. They know that by subduing their egos, their inner self will be empowered and they'll cope better with difficulties.

Applying the view of emptiness each day to our experiences gives us freedom from narrow, polluted ways of thinking. When we do this, we are becoming more of an inner being than an outer being. Simply using mindfulness to be aware of our projections and our conditioning loosens our grip on ego-grasping and will lead us to this wisdom. As I keep saying, merely using mindfulness as a stress reduction and relaxation tool is the waste of a mega gizmo.

Reflections

- In your own experience of stress, can you recognise its negative effect on your life, and how to deal with it effectively so that it doesn't bring you *un*wellbeing?
- How do you feel about the idea that our attitudes can be our sicknesses?
- Is the view of emptiness and conditioned existence resonating with you, or confusing you?
- Are you clear on how seeing through mindful eyes brings wellbeing?

You don't have to be a Buddhist to develop wellseeing because by practising mindfulness, your ignorance will naturally melt away like ice in the warmth of the sun.

Chapter 10

How to Be Wellseeing

o o o

"It is high time we realise that it is pointless to praise the light and preach it if nobody can see it. It is much more needful to teach people the art of seeing."

Carl Jung

Psychology and Alchemy[21]

Our *unwellseeing* is the thoughts and emotions that fill us with negativity and obstruct our view. By replacing these murky visitors with healthy residents, ethically guided and altruistic, the light is naturally revealed. It is important to realise that without being in the darkness of difficult emotions, we would not have been able to find the light.

In Buddhism, the lotus is a symbol for enlightenment, because it grows out of mud and through shadowy water before it emerges into the sunlight above. We have to go through the darkness to find the light.

Holding our hand to ensure that we don't get lost is our inner guide – that reassuring presence that illuminates the path, no matter how challenging it might be.

Here, I explore how being mindful of *how* our mental attitudes influence our experience can free us to see more clearly, transforming scary woods into peaceful glades, frogs into princes and hells into heavens. Mindful analysis helps us to see the truth of our existence and can transform our insular approach to life into one that is unified and fulfilling. Slowly, slowly, gently, gently.

---

21   This Jung quote was also quoted in relationship to Buddhist practice in Radmila Moacanin's 2003 book The Essence of Jung's Psychology and Tibetan Buddhism.

Combining the practice of mindfulness with compatible psychological models encourages self-awareness and mental transformation, so I share several examples from the work of psychologists in this chapter. The more ways we have to understand our behaviours and why we think the way we do, the more we are able to progress towards good self-esteem and achieve a more authentic way of being. It's like having a team of specialists working with us: we need all the help we can get.

So, how can we ensure that our way of seeing the world – the very attitudes and conditioning that we bring to our experience – is healthy? How can we access the light and become *wellseeing*?

What is the light?

This 'light' that Jung referred to brings us to ideas of spirituality. He believed in God within, and that our relationship with God is an internal thing. When he talks about the higher self, he is referring to 'unity with God' and that if we know how, we can contact that light and learn how to see well. This does not have to have a God label, either – I use a variety of labels that mean the same thing but are not religious. Our experience will be the same, but our interpretation will link with our own beliefs.

How does one see this light? The answer is simple. Do the practices in this book and your heart will open up like a flower. Inside will be the most perfect pair of spiritual spectacles you could ever imagine. Rose-tinted, of course. No prescription required.

There is nothing self-delusional or superficial about being spiritual. The ego hurts like hell as we recognise the way we have blundered through life and all the terrible errors we have made. We also have to accept that we will continue blundering through the rest of it – perhaps more mindfully, but embarrassingly imperfectly. This is true spirituality because we embrace humility. We do not need forgiveness from an outside authority, but we do need to forgive ourselves.

We have to take responsibility for our own life and go into DIY self-analysis on a regular basis. It's grounded and messy, and the wonderful experiences of feeling connected to something divine are rare and don't come to order. Insights, dreams and visions come unexpected-ly – not necessarily in our darkest hours, and hardly ever when we ask for them.

The spiritual method of changing the way we see things lies in our practices. We can choose to be present; challenge our thoughts and emotions; keep an eye on our inner storytelling; embrace humanity in all its diversity; forgive; have compassion, respect and feel a small part of something much bigger – or we can choose another way. Finding what works for you will depend on how well you've related to this book.

I think the negative view of spirituality is just a misunderstanding of what it actually is. This negative attitude has crept into our social fabric and woven its way into some kind of collective opinion for those now wary of religion. Being rational and guided by science seems the only option for the intelligent and sensible, but unfortunately it has also morphed into a superior attitude that ridicules those who say they meditate, or have an interest in an 'Eastern' religion. Spirituality is too often linked with magical thinking and therefore deemed irrational and superstitious.

It is not uncommon for the elderly or terminally ill to find faith as they approach death, because they are suddenly faced with mortality and the unknown. It is also common for people to lose their faith due to disillusionment, or to find faith during a crisis. Perhaps the word 'faith' itself is the problem. 'A leap of faith' is a strange expression. It suggests a lack of evidence and therefore a need to take a deep breath and believe in something to keep us sane (perhaps the term 'belief' itself has also become tarnished?).

I'm not much of a believer, personally, but what attracted me to Buddhism was the continual instruction by my teachers to 'check up' or 'test it like gold' – meaning 'see if it works in your mind'. Don't rely on faith; rely on the evidence of your practice. In other words, the only faith you need is in your own potential.

When I first told good friends that I had become a Buddhist, it was as if I'd died and they were mourning the loss of their funny friend. They kept looking for signs that I'd joined a cult – was I wearing orange clothes, had I given up alcohol/smoking weed/dancing? The headteacher told the staff at my leaving do that it was a terrible waste, me moving into a Buddhist monastery.

With today's mindfulness revolution, those attitudes have evolved, but if mindfulness is separated from its spiritual dimension we may still face the big questions of meaning and purpose. That fully opened lotus flower in our hearts gives us a home; a base; something that comes from within us and is not dependent on anything external. We don't have to have faith in anything except our own potential for growth and change.

We have an opportunity as a species to combine the extraordinary knowledge found in science with the profound wisdom of our religious systems and transform our world-view so that it works not for organised religion, but for disorganised us.

Meditation is a wonderful source of insight. It literally is the road to our inner wisdom and compassion. Our journey there takes us beyond the darkness and into the light. Seeing the light begs the question, "What is the darkness?"

In meditation practice, we experience that the inner darkness we carry can transform through mindful awareness. One powerful meditation focuses on breathing out black smoke and breathing in white light. It is a visualisation practice that is not strictly mindfulness, but it helps us symbolically let go of our shadow energy – the dark thoughts and emotions that follow us around uninvited – and be purified by the power of light. Light is a universal symbol of positivity and all we're doing in this practice is empowering ourselves to release all of the heavy emotional baggage we carry and to just open ourselves to a moment of lightness – in both its meanings.

This meditation was requested by, and created for, victims of domestic abuse.

 **LISTEN**

Cleansing and Creating a Safe Space meditation

If you are ill, angry or grief-stricken, you can practise this meditation. You can practise it just to let go of a stressful day. Be creative with it. Make a strong motivation and stay with breathing in and out gently, focusing on the whole experience or aspects of it whenever you wish. You don't have to be able to see a particular result; just believe in the practice and – like we know a dog can hear a whistle that we can't – consider that transformation is happening.

Many people love this meditation, but some don't, as they find it smacks of godliness. In my training, I sometimes encounter people who are highly suspicious that I might be trying to convert them. If I introduce a meditation on light then they actually guffaw – they have a strong reaction to practices that could link with religion. They engage with the neuroscientific explanations of the practices, but literally withdraw from any suggestion that consciousness is not about the brain.

The compassion factor

Buddhism teaches that the main obstacles to developing compassion are cynicism, pity, pride and cruelty. To illustrate this teaching, I use the example of how we might react when faced with a homeless person – smelly, dishevelled and definitely high on something:

- **With cynicism:** "What a burden on society. He's brought it all on himself. I'm not supporting his nasty habit. He'll just take my money and shoot it up his veins."

- **With pity:** "Oh how awful. Thank goodness I am not like him. He's clearly weak. Not like me. Poor, poor inferior person."

- **With pride:** "I cannot understand how anyone could let themselves get so low. That would never happen to me."

- **With cruelty:** "He should be put away where he can rot in hell for all I care. I hope he dies tonight so we can clean up the streets. All homeless people are a blot on society."

There's no room for compassion with these ways of seeing. It's like trying to keep a deer alive in a cage full of lions. Contrast this with utilising the constructive antidotes of empathy, equanimity and compassion (and a hefty dollop of courage) to destroy the destructive thoughts and emotions:

- "Poor guy. I wonder what his story is?"
  You're immediately generating compassion and accompanying this with equanimity. You avoid a judgemental approach and show empathy by wondering about his story – which could so easily be your story.

- "I'm not going to give him money, but I'll get him a hot drink. Maybe some soup. Or I can ask what people know about him."
  You're not stupid, so you're not going to practise 'idiot compassion' – giving without wisdom and not helping anyone. But you want to help him and so you engage with your compassion and empathy by wishing to do something practical that will help him. It takes courage to engage as we are often scared of people who are strange to us (and strangers). It also takes some level of judgement, which in this case is sensible.

- "I really hope he finds better luck."
  You are generating love and compassion without judgement. You want him to be happy and free from suffering and you are avoiding thoughts of superiority.

- "Can I help?"
  You are generating the altruistic wish to be of benefit to him.

- "I can at the very least wish him well, because I know this can happen to anyone. We are all only a few steps away from homelessness."
  You have no time and nothing to give him, but you wish him no harm and hope he will be okay. This is also generating love and compassion. There's strong empathy here as you consider the volatile nature of life.

The more we engage with difficult and challenging experiences, the more we will grow, and this is a powerful way of learning how other beings help us grow spiritually. Just walking down a street and seeing someone in need can help you grow. No one will see this, and no one will know, but it has happened. This is a spiritual event – a positive glow stamped on your consciousness.

We can consider which constructive attitude would benefit us, and maybe even the homeless man. He is offering us an opportunity to grow our compassion, so he is a true friend to us. It is only *our choice* to see him as an enemy or stranger. Try this compassion exercise and see how it makes you feel. Notice your first tendency, kick it out of your head and say the antidote words (try the ones suggested, or others that work for you). Even if they grate, say them and really look at that person.

LISTEN

Giving and Taking meditation

This is an extension of the white light/black smoke meditation that focuses on helping others rather than oneself. You take in and dissolve someone else's darkness, and replace it with light, both within yourself and the other person. It is an ancient, traditional Tibetan Buddhist meditation that is so powerful that it was kept secret in Tibet for only a few yogi(ni)s to practise, as the teachers feared ordinary folk would find it too difficult to understand.

Powerfully feeding your creative imagination will help you to develop stronger and stronger experiences. You will not necessarily achieve your intention of relieving someone's suffering in 'real' life, although prayer can be very powerful, and it is a form of prayer, but the effect on your mind will be inexpressibly powerful. Recognise that this is of mutual benefit as the person you are imagining is helping you develop love and compassion, which is crucial for this meditation to avoid pride.

This practice helps you understand how others help you grow spiritually. Don't be afraid of taking in smoke – this is a transforma-tional meditation because you are *changing* the smoke, through your compassion, into light. None of these practices should weigh you down with others' pain and sickness. That is not at all what the practice is about. It is a practice of ethical altruism.

Social intelligence

Social aptitude means knowing how to get the best out of people and shared encounters. Through our own personal observations and common sense, we can judge that diplomacy and not bullying opens up conversations and new relationships. If we are mindful, we will know through experience, and being witness to others' experiences, that if we act wisely in relationships we will get the best out of them.

When we are intelligent not only *about* our social relationships but also *within* them, then we are socially intelligent. If we are snappy, grumpy, bad tempered and mean, then people close up and learn to distrust us. If we listen, practise empathy and compassion, and show sincere interest in others, then the opposite is true. In our conversations with others we too often listen in order to *speak*, not to actually *hear* and understand others.

If we always come away from conversations and interactions to find our inner critic noting the faults we found in others, then we are missing the positive opportunities. And if it's not what *they* did wrong, then we focus on what *we* did wrong because we are conditioned to take things personally. If someone says or does something unpleasant, we tend to think it's aimed at us ("It's not *my* fault" or "I don't know why she's looking at me like that. *I* didn't do anything."). But it is usually nothing to do with us, and more to do with them.

These everyday situations are opportunities for us to stand back and be an observer to our own tendencies so we can respond appropriately, rather than taking on the role of becoming a perpetrator or a victim of someone else's issues.

Mindful intelligence

How intelligent are you feeling? Let's bring emotional intelligence and social intelligence under the one umbrella of mindful intelligence. The mindful awareness we practise brings in awareness of thoughts and emotions, awareness of how we interact with others, and awareness of how to adapt to situations mindfully so that we get the best out of ourselves, others and events.

Mindfulness is all about presence, and when you are fully present with someone who is talking to you, then you take everything in that they are trying to communicate. There is no distraction from your mobile device, or from someone else you would rather be talking to, or from somewhere else you would rather be – just full focus on your companion. That tiny bubble of you and them offers you a massive opportunity for spiritual progress.

Compare the unmindful way of communicating that is so common. You haven't got time; you've got one eye on your phone; you judge that this person has nothing to offer you; your eyes are on other people in the room because you're scared of missing out on something better. With unmindful communication, you give the other person a version of listening that isn't hearing much at all of what they're trying to communicate with you.

If you are having a conversation that involves conflicting ideas, then the ego will be there, almost ready to punch your companion in the face (metaphorically speaking, of course). Dealing with issues with your ego defence mechanism might initially make you feel strong, but the long-term effect is a lack of genuine communication with others who could enhance your life.

People don't want to have to engage in combat when they meet us. They are also looking for companionship and friendship based on good communication. We all have to accept faults in others as they need to accept ours. I know we don't think we're the ones at fault, but we all contribute to the mass misunderstandings in communication. If we indulge our egos and allow them to run rampant with other egos, we may repeat our bad habits and never fully open our hearts to others. Due to our tendencies to have aversion or attraction for others, we can be so selective that we might miss someone right in front of us who can give us so much. Don't welcome the initial buzz we feel when we get the better of others – it is just our low self-esteem feeling better because the ego is judging others and reinforcing our destructive mental habits.

Mindful listening

We can help ourselves by developing mindful communication skills that support our spiritual practice. In our conversations with others, a mindful technique is to consider how attentive our listening is. There are many times when our conversations tend to focus on self-expression and we're not really interested in the other person's input. This can have the effect of blocking others as they soon grow tired of engaging and trying to be heard, so the conversation becomes one-sided.

If people sit passively when someone is talking, they may be trying to be polite but not personally getting anything out of the conversation. If someone is listening to someone else talking their heads off, any interjection is simply used as a jumping-off point for the talker to find another topic on which to talk about themselves. Many of us know what that feels like: we feel unheard, unappreciated and, quite frankly, a bit bored.

Practising listening skills doesn't mean we're a passive participant in a conversation – it means we'll hear more, empathise more, be able to share life experiences and encourage more meaningful dialogue as the talker feels more and more relaxed, more heard, and therefore more likely to listen to us. If we really attend to what others are saying, we achieve better mutual understanding.

Let's take a look at some typical types of listening that we can all relate to:

- **Passive listening:** We mutter answers that are non-committal and vague like, "Yeah, yeah" or "I see." Our ears are involved but our minds are elsewhere.

"I'm involved in something more interesting and I'm going to take in the bare minimum and ignore your wittering on."

- **Selective listening:** We only focus on what is relevant to us, and we're not interested in how others are feeling. This can feel analytical to the speaker and therefore alienating, as instead of encouraging them to open up, we are closing them down with uncomfortable silences and by being quite detached.
  "What you're saying is this, but it only reinforces my points which are actually the correct ones. I'm not sure there's any point, as far as I'm concerned, in even replying."

- **Attentive listening:** This type of listening engages with the whole person and makes them feel heard. But unless we include an empathic attitude, we may lack compassion and put the speaker into a position of inferiority to us.
  "I get what you're saying, but I don't necessarily agree with you, or even like you. You're clearly not as insightful as me."

- **Mindful listening:** Once we include empathy and compassion, we are mindfully listening. It really requires a change in the attitude of the listener. Here, we fully immerse ourselves in the speaker's perspective, becoming aware of the speaker's feelings, emotions, values and beliefs. To achieve this requires acceptance of the person, not just what they are saying.
  "I hear what you're saying and I understand the emotional impact this has had on you. I want to respond to you in a way that makes you feel fully understood because I value you, and recognise you have something to communicate that is important to you."

We can't be this empathically attentive in all our conversations, but instead of taking loved ones for granted we could build bridges if we try a more empathic approach. I have seen how useful mindful listening has been for parents with teenage children, and vice versa!

In an emotionally explosive situation, managing a conversation by listening mindfully can transform an outcome. We need to:

- Be sensitive to the emotional state of the other person
- Be able to reflect back to check we have understood properly and that we understand the other person's feelings
- Try not to interrupt
- Be willing to let hurtful comments go and to understand why these are being said
- Pay attention
- Try to keep the discussion going by asking open-ended questions rather than closed questions with only 'yes' or 'no' answers

Mindful listening takes the tension out of a situation by trying to create a win-win discussion rather than an argument that results in alienation and resentment. If we have empathy and compassion through mindfulness, we can fully focus on what's being presented to us and therefore increase the other person's confidence. We're telling them that what they have to say is important and we're not there to judge them. In this way we can forge a bond that will reduce all the stress and tension, build trust, and engage us in continued communication that is open and honest.

How many times has someone said to you, "You're not listening!"? As a parent, the challenge is to allow your children to become themselves, not just your echo. Tough, I know. Attachment gets in the way here. Children are great when they adore you, but when their own personality and character start to develop, it is natural for them to reject their former role models. We have an idea about who they are and we like it that way, but as they grow and develop independence and their own ideas, we can lose their respect if we don't change too.

Being wary of giving advice and 'solutions'

When something awful happens, such as a break-up, we all know how irritating it can be to be told that it's a good thing because now we can find someone who really loves us, or wants to travel with us/go to university with us… and so on. Our egos reject their platitudes. So, we must be careful to maintain empathy and compassion when we give advice and when listening to others.

Giving advice and offering solutions are thorny actions, and should only be embarked on if requested. "If you want my advice…" is usually perceived as someone else saying they know better than you, and actually you don't want their advice: this is a path of self-learning. Offering solutions to someone's issues has empathic motivation but the other person probably just wants to be heard and doesn't want to know what you think would solve their problem. Being a fixer may have good intentions but does not necessarily bring about a positive result.

We can mistake being a problem-solver with being kind. Often, being a problem-solver for others just means that we want to put the problem to bed and move on to something more pleasant and fun, or *feel* like a good friend. Or feel superior.

With a mindful approach, we are returning to the idea of the Platinum Rule: treating others as they would wish to be treated.

A touch of philosophy

This Taoist tale is a great philosophical way of seeing life. Taoist philosophy views life as being a constant interplay between good and bad, and that bad comes out of good, and good comes out of bad. (Think of the well-known yin-yang symbol.)

There was an old man who had an only son. The only other thing in his life that was important was his horse. One day the horse escaped from the field and went missing. The villagers heard about this and felt sorry for the poor old man. They came to see him, saying, "We're so sorry you lost your horse. What bad luck." The old man smiled and replied, "It's not necessarily bad luck."

A few days later the horse returned, bringing with him a wild herd. The old man and his son captured all the horses and filled their field with them. The villagers returned and said, "Oh, what great good fortune." The old man smiled and replied, "Not necessarily."

The son was very taken with a white stallion in the herd. One day he mounted him and went riding. The stallion was too strong for him and the boy went flying. He broke his leg in several places. The villagers again came by to express their sympathy. "Oh, how awful. He'll never walk properly again. What bad luck." The old man just smiled and said, "Not necessarily."

A few weeks later, war was declared, and soldiers came to the village to conscript all the able-bodied. All, that is, except the old man's son, whose leg was too damaged...

Acceptance of life's difficulties and understanding impermanence, one of the Three Marks of Existence (explored more in Chapter 6), enables us to be philosophical about life and accept its challenges rather than pushing against them and getting upset about the inevitable. We'll experience a more equanimous life with fewer ups and downs, and more realistic expectations.

There are many wise sayings that come from antiquity. The wisdom of the ages – it's all there, tucked into the corners of civilisation.

Learning optimism

"A pessimist is one who makes difficulties out of opportunities, and an optimist is one who makes opportunities of difficulties."

Attributed to Harry S. Truman, 33rd President of the United States

Positive thinking and positive psychology are not the same, but they are close friends. If we think that by saying that something will happen will make it happen, we may soon become despondent at the outcome. But if we create the causes for something to happen, and accompany those actions with self-belief, then we will more likely succeed in our aims.

Hundreds of studies show that optimists do much better in education, work and socially. They are generally healthier, age better and live longer. Pessimists give up more easily and get depressed more often. In his book *Learned Optimism*, American psychologist Martin Seligman[22] claims that people living in the shadow of pessimism can effect change in their lives just by learning to be more optimistic.

Seligman claims that because we have learned to see things in a particular way, we can also *unlearn* these ways of seeing. Learned optimism offers the same message as mindfulness practice. Through our awareness of how our egos have built in pessimism as a defence mechanism against the frustrations and disappointments we experience in life, we can apply mindfulness by pointing the finger inwards and making positive changes to our psychological habits. It's about taking responsibility for our happiness. It requires effort, and if we have settled into ruts of low self-esteem then the internal workload will not be easy, because we will have learned helplessness.

Learned helplessness, learned pessimism and learned optimism suggest that you have taken a particular way of seeing because it seems to work for you. But only learned optimism is constructive. Imagine how liberating it would be to learn a way of seeing that makes us feel better about ourselves and the world we live in. The psychology of "What's right with me?" rather than "What's wrong with me?" does not lie in fluffy positive phrases or by visualising victory, but in *the way we think about causes*, which prepares us for positive outcomes.

We're not indulging in empty phrases but recognising how we can make things happen, not through attracting positive vibes but by creating the cause for a positive outcome. It is the idea that a talent for joy, like any other, can be cultivated. In contrast with learned helplessness, optimism is learned by consciously challenging any negative self-talk.

The charitable organisation Centre for Confidence and Well-being, in Glasgow, UK, came up with a useful exercise that can support our mental efforts to learn to see the best in life and in ourselves. It's called The Three Pats Technique. Of course, the patting is mental – you don't literally have to reach for your back to pat it.

---

22 Martin Seligman's book The Optimistic Child is also worth looking at for his comparison between positive psychology and learned optimism.

You're complimenting your mind, and empowering your inner self in a mindful way.

- Each evening, remember three good things you have done or three good things that have happened (it works better if you have been an active participant in the good thing).

- Run through the day in your mind and identify these three things (more if you want) and mentally enjoy them and compliment yourself on them.

Practising this technique every night for at least a month resulted in more resilient mental health for participants.

Our negativity bias – a tendency to register negative experiences more easily than positive ones, and to dwell on negative events – means that we feel and remember the one bad thing that happened in a given day, rather than any of the good things. Turning our attention to the good things is one way to change our mental habits.

Games we play

Canadian psychiatrist Eric Berne developed the transactional analysis model in the 1960s, in his book *Games People Play: The Psychology of Human Relationships*. It aims to promote healthy personal change in order to reach our highest human potential. Austrian psychoanalyst Sigmund Freud influenced Berne, but his approach was significantly unique.

Transactional analysis requires us to consider how the influences on our ways of thinking have shaped us. Berne very much promoted the healthy ego and this model encourages us to consider what voices we carry in our heads that lead to unhealthy ways of thinking – in this way, it is very much in line with mindfulness practices as we become super aware of our conditioning.

Consider the voices you may hear in your head (each one an aspect of your conditioned ego):

- Life as taught – your parents' voice
- Life as thought – your grown-up adult voice
- Life as felt – your child's voice

Berne asks us to check up on who is in your head with you – who is telling you off, telling you not to be stupid, crying out for help, blaming your brother, for example.

He refers to the ego games you play that justify your attitudes and ways of thinking. Were you taught to think a certain way and are still trying to please a parental voice? Do you still have your helpless child's voice screaming "life's not fair" in your head? Or can you develop an adult voice that takes responsibility for your own actions and is guided by your inner self?

An ego game is a way of behaving that is not authentically you but has been powerfully influenced by significant others in your childhood. Or perhaps you wear a mask that you think will impress others because you learned that this type of behaviour impressed your parents. We all act inauthentically to some extent to fit in, but it can also lead to a pathological tendency to lie when we have a weak view of ourselves.

As a parent, I blanch at the thought of how I have influenced my children. I was a devoted mother and did everything I could to support them, but it is only with distance that I can see that, however well-intentioned, my own conditioning and ego states affected their conditioning.

Do you hear your mother or father in your own words to your children? Don't beat yourself up for your mistakes – remember, we are only human and doing our best, but be aware. Counselling can help us understand why we are what we are.

Toxic behaviour

When we get stressed, we often revert to ways of behaving that we learned in childhood. It's always useful to consider our tendencies, and American family therapist Virginia Satir introduced five different behavioural tendencies.[23]

Do you identify with any of these tendencies – or are you maybe a combination, depending on the situation?

- Blamer – points the finger outwards
- Placater – hates any kind of conflict
- Distractor – avoids confrontation
- Computer – removes themselves emotionally
- Leveller – is open and honest (tells it like it is)

Satir describes the leveller as a healthy tendency in stressful situations. Levellers will address the issue and are most likely to support constructive outcomes.

The attributes of a leveller include:

- Open body language
- Open listening
- Honesty in communication
- Objectivity
- Adult to adult conversation and no 'games'
- Disarming not defensive
- Rapport

We can learn to be a leveller if we weren't born with this tendency.

One exercise that floored me when considering these behavioural types was to ask myself if I was a difficult person. Until then I had always considered myself to be easy to get on with, but the more I considered it, the more I found that I was only easy to deal with in certain situations. In some relationships I was, quite honestly, a bit of a nightmare. I used to think of myself as being direct, but my lack of diplomacy didn't bring out the best in others at all.

If we are mindful, then we are most likely to be objective and to

---

23   Satir's Transformational Systemic Therapy, also known as the Satir Growth Model, emphasises engaging the inner self, and analysing a person's situation and choices. Her books Making Contact and The New Peoplemaking are great places to start if you want to find out more about her work.

avoid the pitfalls of repeating destructive modes of behaviour due to destructive ways of thinking. We will be aware.

Seeing with wisdom

If we take the Buddhist practice of emptiness (refer to Chapter 9 for more on the view of emptiness) on a walk with us through woods, in a park, or wherever nature helps us be still, then we can get a taste of non-duality – the 'oneness' between us and the world. There is no object to see, no subject doing the seeing, just unity. This is the experience of emptiness. This is the art of seeing, perfected. Meditation is the best way to get to grips with this challenging concept, and it's well worth the effort.

This is an analytical meditation that aims to help us see the emptiness of things.

 LISTEN

Emptiness meditation

Now we can apply this same analysis to ourselves. This meditation on the self can be a little unnerving, but the aim is to liberate us into a way of being that sees the emptiness in everything.

 LISTEN

Emptiness of the Self meditation

The aim is not to deny our conventional existence. We do exist but we are a construct, just like the mug in the audio meditation. This is our conventional reality. We are here, we have a name and we are living a life. The aim is to destroy the ego's grasping onto a solid idea of the self that will not move from its identity and which causes so many problems for us, because we are frightened to take on anything that challenges this sense of a solid identity. Releasing this ego-grasping enables us to enjoy life with more freedom from attachment and aversion – to go more with the flow of life and with our ability to change for the better.

Applying the view of emptiness to someone we have strong attachment or aversion to needn't diminish the passion and enjoyment we share with them, or leave us stuck in feelings of anger and hatred; instead, a more realistic view of another person allows us to develop acceptance, forgiveness and compassion. The other person is also subject to impermanence.

My story – believing what you want to believe

When I was pregnant with my daughter, I felt the urge to bring back some personal creativity into my life. I had managed to incorporate singing in a band into my working life, which gave me a buzz. I don't think the world of soul music suffered much when I left, but it was so much fun while it lasted. Having been to drama school, with the focus of much of my early life on acting and performance, I was a little starved of creative expression.

Storytelling was coming into vogue at that time. In Cumbria I emerged as a credible storyteller but, ever the teacher, I focused on learning. So, with some wonderful encouragement and support from a primary school headteacher I knew, I began a side career that would suit a mainly full-time mum for a few years.

My idea was to create characters and transform into them, in front of the children, to tell a story in character. Then we would do drama workshops for the rest of the school day. It was popular, and I adored my largely open-minded audiences who lapped up the characters of Dr Mahabindibhaji, The Jelly Baby Elf, Krazy Kate from Kansas, Shaz (the ShagBag... obviously that was my secret name for her!), Aunty Mo and Professor Sofia Sofine. There was also The Boss – a credible male chauvinist for secondary schools. These characters were extreme, very un-PC

– that not being a thing back in the early '90s – and funny. The outfits, makeup and accessories were wonderfully imagined and created by my most artistic neighbour.

The children were mainly primary school age, but a 10/11-year-old is not an easy win. My show was to stand in front of them and tell them that I had invited a much more interesting friend to tell the story. With a table full of stuff, which ranged from fluorescent glitter hairspray and magical hats (such as a giant foam ten-gallon hat with an arrow through it), I would then gradually transform in front of their eyes. In character, I would tell my stories – moral tales with lots of hilarity – for their entertainment (and education). Then later, after they had returned to their classrooms, I would change back into myself and meet them for workshops.

What amazed me was the children's total belief that the character had left and now I was there instead. Some of them even told me that they'd seen the character leaving, and even what car they were driving. Even though they'd watched me change in front of their very eyes, they had suspended their belief, totally engaging with another character. This was a common phenomenon in those years.

I travelled all over Cumbria, weaving in workshops with supply teaching and part-time teaching work. I did over 50 workshops before finally focusing on my centre for wellbeing. In all that time, the children's ability to believe in what they wanted to believe and tell themselves that the characters I'd created were real, and not just me acting, provided me with a great insight into the power of the mind and the presence of emptiness.

Interdependence

We don't exist as islands. We can't even survive in isolation. We all need each other: for food and shelter, work and family, meaning and purpose. We need to understand that others connect with us to teach us how to be fully human and develop our full potential. When we realise this interdependence, we look at the world from a different perspective.

It's how ancient civilisations may have felt when they discovered that their land was not solitary but connected to many others. 'We' are a 'whole' coming together due to a constant interplay between us and the world we live in that changes moment by moment.

Reflections

○ This chapter offers various psychological tools to help you. Is there one that you relate to best?

○ Identify your own positive and negative habits – at least one of each. Would you like to change the negative one? Why is the positive one constructive?

○ Are you able to integrate empathy and compassion into your everyday behaviours? Are there any risks to this, in your view?

○ How do you describe living wisely?

Authentic mindfulness

○ It's wise to view conventional reality as merely your projection because this helps dissolve your destructive tendencies.

○ Seeing things from the perspective of others removes the clouds from your eyes.

○ Being an activist for a big cause often stops you from seeing what's in front of your nose. For example, if you want a healthy environment, start with your own garden.

○ A beginner's mind that is open and pliable is more effective than the mind of someone who thinks they're special because they know a little.

○ Mindfulness can be applied to every aspect of your inner development because awareness is both self-awareness *and* other-awareness.

Spiritual integrity

- ○ It's not what you achieve that is important, but what your intention is in trying to achieve something.

- ○ Being the light is being someone who gives to the world.

- ○ Be positive, but don't beat yourself up if you can't see the positive. Sit with the negative feeling instead and know it for what it is.

- ○ Practising compassion towards the self and others is a spiritual path, regardless of your beliefs.

- ○ Being motivated to develop your spiritual self means that, in practice, you develop constructive qualities and become self-reflective.

It takes time to change our ego-centred view. It is a deeply rooted instinct to plump everything up with our projection of how things exist, which is a view that's so entrenched that it's important we go at this gently.

Chapter 11

The Spiritual Warrior

∘ ∘ ∘

"All you need to know is that the future is completely open
and we are writing it moment to moment."

Ascribed to Pema Chödrön

The term 'spiritual warrior' originated in Tibetan Buddhism as "one who is spiritually brave" and reassuringly has nothing to do with wearing physical, clunky armour. The 'war' is against our own ignorance and aggression, and to fight them, despite all the influences around us, requires boldness and unwavering inner conviction. I like the term because it has a different dynamic to the passive view of modest monks – eyes cast downward, ineffably humble. I guess I like it because I am a doer, not a sitter.

By activating all the inner practices of mindfulness explored in this book, we have a chance to make changes at an individual level and then, as mindful spiritual warriors, create our perfect world – walking this earth in order to protect the vulnerable and make changes that will form the wholesome roots of a future world. And that has to be the ultimate act of rebellion in a world dominated by materialism and hedonism.

If we all sing from the same mindful hymn sheet, we have a chance to succeed because of our united wish for equanimity. That unity lies in the recognition that we are all inherently good and that by being mindful of our conditioning – those habits we harbour unintentionally – and by managing our volatile egos, we can become marvellous human beings. Why this isn't the aim of any government must be because it's so radical, it's revolutionary!

Considering the questions of world issues and dealing with all the 'isms' (sexism, racism, and so on) in a mindful way will help us to be prepared for being a spiritual warrior, because we need courage in a world that too frequently appears a bit sleazy, if not downright degenerate. In this chapter, I will approach some world problems one by one and ponder how we might utilise mindfulness in each area. But first, I consider how and why it is meaningful for us to live in ways that can lead to positive external changes in the world. And it's always important to remember that this doesn't happen overnight, or over one lifetime; it happens over many. Our goal is what might be termed 'long-term.'

The force is with us

How can working on changing ourselves affect the external world – how might it affect climate change, racism, poverty, war? Good question, because it will be very frustrating to be doing all the right things for all the right reasons, only to find that you seem to be living amongst barbarians who aren't prepared to change anything about their lifestyles – as if the world is theirs to suck up, savour the spoils and regurgitate the remains.

The premise of Buddhist psychology is that problems can't be solved by making new rules and regulations that act as preventative measures. The source of our problems lies within us. If we lack ethical values, then no rule will get in the way of us doing what we want. Giving precedence to pleasure and materialistic concerns will increase our unwholesome thoughts and emotions, resulting in corruption, crime and injustice. Our external world will reflect our inner world.

I hear some of you thinking, "Oh, come on, mindfulness is for personal use, it cannot possibly change the world, so what is the point? Is it reasonable to expect us to stand firm in our views and our mindful way of life when it seems we're surrounded by some very selfish and delusional people? Wouldn't it be easier to just blend in, go with what's mainstream and to heck with all this saintliness?" If it doesn't sit right because your heart's not in it, you'll feel out of balance and your ego will become dominant – like a big bully in your body, spitting fury at your inner hero and your outer world. It can even lead to physical ill-health.

You know me by now, ever the optimist and idealist, and so I cannot desist from sharing with you my vision of a better world in this chapter, where mindful living can lead to positive external change.

There is an assertion in Buddhism that if you imagine something, even for a moment, you are laying the ground for that event to manifest in the future. I have a little story that demonstrates this well.

A student was driving our teacher from the airport to a Buddhist centre, feeling a little nervous. For Buddhists, having responsibility for a Lama is a bit like looking after the Queen of England: nerve-racking. The student started to worry and thought, "What if I crash the car and kill the Lama?" As the thought froze inside his head, the Lama said quietly, "Do not even think it."

Many 'realised' teachers seem to develop clairvoyance en route to enlightenment. If we consider that mindfulness practices are all about interconnectedness, compassion and expanding the mind, then maybe this story doesn't seem as far-fetched as one might initially judge.

Another way of looking at this concept is to visualise and imagine the positive fruition of a project or plan in order to create the potential for this event to happen. Now, I know that many top athletes visualise themselves winning in their arena. This definitely fires them up with the strong volition to achieve that goal, but let's be realistic. If every athlete visualises winning, there's going to be some who lose, at least conventionally speaking.

Buddhist wisdom teaches that, due to the law of cause and effect, everything we think, say and do results in an effect (karma, explored more in Chapter 3). There will come a time when all the right causes and conditions arise for us to experience the effects. Because so many of us still have our 'one life' blinkers on, this often feels unbelievable. But, if we look at the apparent unfairness of life, we can start to see how the concept of karma can explain that this unfairness has nothing to do with us now, in this life; instead, it goes way back to when 'we' were truly ignorant and creating all kinds of ego-centred mischief in lifetimes loooong ago. When we come to better understand the ongoing journey of our consciousness, then we can start to get the picture.

This is the force that is with spiritual warriors, whether they are yogi(ni)s or activists. They're creating the karma to fight evil. The world is their place of learning and the people in it their allies. Their eyes are not blinkered but telescopic.

Paradise found

> "Paradise is not some kind of enchanted land filled with flowers and music. It is not some kind of spiritual Disneyland. Paradise is our primordial pure consciousness, which is free of all limitations but embodies the infinity of the divine."

> **Anam Thubten**

> *No Self, No Problem: Awakening to Our True Nature*

I thought I had found external paradise when I arrived by ferry on my first Greek island in the early 1970s. I could never have imagined anything so beautiful. We had no internet then to do the virtual tour before we arrived, just as we still have no access to what paradise looks like except in our imaginations. Is it white sand and palm trees, infinity pools and exotic cocktails? You will have your own idea of what paradise looks like.

We have made a mess of our earthly paradise – seas full of plastic, dying coral reefs and threatened species, inhospitable refugee camps and indigenous peoples losing their way of life. Does that mean the real paradise is no longer out there? And could the cause lie within our minds, muddied by materialism and hedonism, creating an earthly mess?

If we are to create an external paradise, then our minds need to be a paradise as well. This means developing a mental state that is wholly *wellseeing* (explored in chapters 9 and 10) if we are to literally see physical places transformed. This is magic. But it is practical magic and definitely not magical thinking.

The concept of a pure realm such as the Garden of Eden, Shangri-La or the state of nirvana (freedom from ignorance) is not that they are real geographical places behind waterfalls guarded by yetis, but that seeing with new eyes transforms our external reality into perfection. We could be in Brixton, Chicago or Timbuktu, yet if we transform 'the eye of our mind' we could be in paradise. Imagine the most beautiful transformation of your home-town. Visualise it now. You are creating the cause for you to live in what you imagine. Working on this visualisation can lead to finding ways to not only find internal paradise, but to be a force in creating external paradise. You have the vision.

It's not unrealistic to believe this if we have been practising mindfulness, because we can see that just by changing a point of view we can transform an external event with our wisdom and compassion. A car crash of a meeting can become a mere scratch or dent in our egos and eventually even transform into a joyful union of minds as the barriers to communication dissolve. If we become advanced drivers, mindful of potential hazards, then the eye of our mind will find the reward.

In these concluding chapters I would like to explore with you how we can achieve paradise, but only if we heed the moral warnings. Neglect our inner values, and external problems will continue. Destructive characteristics, such as greed and wanting power over others, are like weeds: stubborn and difficult to remove. Leave the tiniest shoot, and they'll return stronger than ever. By rooting out the weeds emboldened by our stressed-out egos, our inner qualities of compassion and equanimity will reveal to us a world that is indeed paradise. As well as being climate activists, we also need to be mind activists.

My story – Shiva at the Ganges

Having ended an extensive purification retreat in India, I visited Varanasi, a most revered spiritual place in India. Hindus and Buddhists alike spend time there experiencing its sacred river as well as its rituals surrounding death and rebirth.

This was 1983, and a simpler time. There was a café where you could buy a 'bhang lassi'. These drinks were sold not to get high like in the cannabis cafés of Amsterdam but to increase one's spiritual sensitivities. They were offered in three strengths – low, medium or high. Accompanied by a friend who knew his way around, I chose the medium-strength lassi. (I'm a Middle Way kind of girl.) We took a boat out onto the Ganges and I delighted in the experience of garlands of marigolds being floated out towards me by smiling children. The river was pure and fragrant, and the boats and beings on them were glowing with health and cleanliness. Then I saw a god, standing at the water's edge. It was the Hindu deity Shiva, absolutely sublime and entirely composed of blue light. I watched, transfixed by his beauty, as he gathered water. Then he disappeared into the crowd.

The next day we went back to the river, although it appeared less pure and somewhat polluted by floating bodies, as well as tourist boats. There again I recognised the 'god', but this time he was a sadhu – a wandering spiritual practitioner and a follower of Shiva (as his hair adornments confirmed). Virtually naked and garbed in rags, he was collecting water again from the sacred Ganges River.

The bhang lassi had opened doors in my mind. Perhaps, influenced by my spiritual leanings, I was able to experience an alternate reality. Was the sadhu a god that I could only see when there was no veil over my eyes?

The web of Tantra

"Tantra considers it very important to eradicate such symptoms of ego. There is no point in holding garbage-concepts of yourself. You are perfect; you just need to recognize it. According to tantra, you do not need to wait until your next life to experience heaven."

Lama Thubten Yeshe

The Bliss of Inner Fire: Heart Practice of the Six Yogas of Naropa[24]

In Buddhism, there is a specific practice where we take the future into the present in order to create the causes for it to happen. This practice is known as *Tantra*, literally meaning 'web', and it brings together all energies and unifies them. I know, pretty spacy.

We visualise deities of wisdom and compassion; we visualise pure realms where we might be reborn; and we consider how we can purify our messy humanity by contemplating that our bodies are full of rivers and streams of pure energy just crying out to be released, transforming us into a Superhuman.

Tantric deities are a fantastical bunch. Naked, red, green – some are peaceful; some are crazy looking, wrathful creatures with many heads and arms. They are the superheroes that pre-date Spiderman, Superwoman, Batman and Catwoman by miles. So don't dismiss them as weird and unbelievable. They're just Eastern images as opposed to our slightly sanitised and restrained Western versions. Why stop at one head and two pairs of limbs? Our concept of what is possible is so limited.

---

24   Lama Thubten Yeshe was my great teacher. I didn't know him for long but he literally grabbed hold of my mind and guided me on the path. He was an extraordinary man who became pivotal to bringing Tibetan Buddhism to the West. He was the spiritual founder of the Foundation for the Preservation of the Mahayana Tradition and, along with his heart (closest) disciple Lama Zopa Rinpoche, literally took the East to the West. His centres still flourish throughout the world. It was his words to me personally about writing a book on Buddhism that anyone could buy at any train station that contributed to me finally writing this book, almost 40 years later. See www.fpmt.org for a centre near you and/or access to literature and audio teachings.

The reason we can imagine all these super-powered beings, intent on saving humanity, is simply because within us all, there is that power. If we can imagine it, then we can become it. Not tomorrow, after eating three shredded wheats for breakfast, but in future lifetimes, when we will eventually be ready to be interconnected, compassionate beings with superpowers that benefit all humankind.

Tantra is considered a much faster route to enlightenment than the slower Sutra route (gradual mind training), although it's fraught with more danger, just like driving an Aston Martin compared to a safe and solid Audi. All the power of a racing car is turned on through the ignition of Tantra. A word of warning: the more potency you give a person, the more liable they are to misuse it, or blow it – hence the danger. This is why students wishing to practise Tantra are initiated by experienced and realised teachers. You cannot safely practise it without this preparatory instruction.

Tantra is often linked with sexual practices, which is not untrue but is frequently misleading. Tantric sex is about unifying female and male energies, which are spiritual vehicles for wisdom and compassion, and utilising the moment of orgasm for understanding emptiness, or 'the bliss of nirvana.' The ultimate purpose of the Tantra vehicle is the same as the Sutra vehicle (the slower Audi path), which is to become enlightened, and then help others to become enlightened. It is for the initiated and the spiritual stalwarts, not for the thrill-seekers.

With the Shangri-La meditation I share here, you are practising mindful Tantra. You are taking the future result into the present by visualising your idea of a perfect world, and the more you can imagine this perfection, the more you will create the impetus for it to happen. You are also changing your own deepest prejudices, which purifies your inner energy channels.

 **LISTEN**

Creating Shangri-La meditation

My story – the natural high of Tantra

When I first started to hear the Buddhist doctrines, I was particularly inspired by the teachings on Tantra. Unlike the grounded step-by-step path that was my newly acquired Buddhist way of life, these were ideas that really took me into an enchanted space. I remember being seated by a sunny window in the 'gompa' (Tibetan place of meditation), when I just opened my mind and experienced an extraordinary sense that fairy tales could come true. Like every other child, I had been told fairy stories about magical creatures that I soon discovered were just imaginary. We were told that Father Christmas was real. Our parents weren't liars, they just wished to prolong our innocence and the make-believe of childhood. Well, suddenly, the Lamas were giving it back to me. Having gradually let go of what I had hoped would happen in my life, and adopted cynicism as a way of coping with the loss of those dreams, I was presented with a realistic method that made sound psychological sense, and offered reassurance that dreams could come true.

The practice of Tantra takes the future into the present. So you generate yourself as a super-powered gorgeous deity, complete with all your symbolic bits and bobs and ready to bring enlightenment to all. All you have to do is believe yourself to be this right now.

That doesn't mean that you jump off a building because you think you can fly. Tantra isn't a hallucinogenic drug, but it does encourage powerful visualisation methods to make something internal real. You are aspiring to be this deity, so one day you will definitely become this deity. Maybe at death, maybe in a few future lifetimes, but it will happen. If you dedicate yourself to this practice, it is even possible to become this transformed energy system, totally purified by your practice, in one life, like the sadhu who was Shiva at the Ganges.

Mindfulness in the world

"There is no miserable place waiting for you, no hell realm, sitting and waiting like Alaska – waiting to turn you into ice-cream. But whatever you call it – hell or the suffering realms – it is something that you enter by creating a world of neurotic fantasy and believing it to be real. It sounds simple, but that's exactly what happens."

Lama Thubten Yeshe

An Introduction to Tantra

When we hear and see the terrible things that are going on in the world, it is common for us to feel helpless and that we can do nothing because we have no power or political status. We might give to a charity, or engage more actively with an aid organisation, but still, these are like temporary sticking plasters and cannot heal the root causes of the problems. Sometimes it feels like we're trying to hold back a tidal wave with a bath plug. But it is a noble human trait to have hope that sometime in the future the world will live in peace and mutual prosperity.

Every noble cause aligns with mindfulness: if we are mindful, then we will be engaged with causes that reduce suffering and seek equality. That's what we mean by 'noble'. Investing in the knowledge that things will somehow improve is the eternal human wish for a brighter future and reflected in our quest for an earthly paradise – that Shangri-La, Utopia or Garden of Eden.

If transforming our outer world starts with ourselves, let's consider some of the world issues we face and how mindfulness fits with different concerns. A mind-expanding meditation follows each little summary.

Politics

Participating in movements that oppose capitalism, totalitarianism and oppression necessitates bringing a mindful attitude to our concerns and activism and ensures that we don't get caught up in the pitfalls of greed and corruption, hatred and violence.

If mindfulness was a political movement, it would be green, with its emphasis on environmentalism, non-violence, social justice, democracy, gender equality, LGBT rights and eco-socialism, and its anti-war and anti-racism stance. On the political spectrum, the Mindfulness Party would be left-wing and aim to benefit people at every level of society rather than focusing on an elite. It would focus on the whole of society rather than economic wealth, which appears to mainly benefit the rich.

Sometimes, people use their political ideals to express hatred and violence, which is the opposite of being mindful. If every political party encompassed mindfulness, we could significantly reduce the common practices of deceit, divisiveness and hatred. Watching people in government, even within the same political party, try to destroy each other, sets a terrible example to our children.

 ## LISTEN

Creating a Mindful Society meditation

Climate change and environmentalism

It took a child to wake us up to the immediate dangers of climate change. Swedish environmental activist Greta Thunberg showed us the way with her courage, non-violent protest and persistence. Those who say there is no problem and that the topic is too complex and diverse to tackle are afraid of change. The only complexities and difficulties lie with those who oppose climate change due to having monster egos that are greedy, manipulative and self-serving. If they practised mindfulness, with all its inner methods of positive development, then they'd realise the shortcomings of their views and change. The key is in *change* – it's so hard to give up our bad habits (like lovely log burners, powerful SUVs and ridiculously cheap fashion), but if we can become more fluid with our attitudes, we can stop before it's too late.

The interdependence of our ecological system needs recognition. It really is about removing 'me and my needs' above everyone else. I would like my grandchildren to have a future, as I am sure you would. Mindfulness sees the interconnectedness of our actions and recognises that if we are destructive, we will experience destruction ourselves.

Mother Earth is in danger of dying from neglect. If we don't hold her in our collective arms and love her to bits, then we will lose her.

 LISTEN

Mindful Lifestyle Walking meditation

Racism

Racism is just taught lies. We aren't born racist; we have just been taught 'difference' and that some of us are 'better' than others. We are very suggestible creatures – as children, if we are taught that people with blue eyes are superior to people with brown eyes, we will believe it, especially if we have blue eyes, but interestingly, also if we have brown eyes.

In the '60s, the United States was in the midst of a race crisis, much as it still is today. Professor Jane Elliott,[25] a teacher and anti-racism activist, experimented with her primary students. She told them that people with brown eyes were better than people with blue eyes and made the blue-eyed students put armbands on the brown-eyed students to show them that an arbitrarily established difference could separate them and turn them against one another. The 'superior' designated ones were mean and nasty and turned against their friends. The 'inferior' ones were

---

25   Professor Jane Elliott is an American diversity educator. As a schoolteacher, she became known for her 'blue eyes/brown eyes' exercise, which she first conducted with her third-grade class the day after the assassination of Martin Luther King Jr. The compositions that the children wrote about the experience were published in a local newspaper and led to much broader media interest. The classroom exercise was filmed in 1970, becoming the documentary The Eye of the Storm. An episode of Frontline featured a reunion of the 1970 class, as well as Elliott's work with adults, in its 1985 episode 'A Class Divided'. Invitations to speak and to conduct her exercise eventually led Elliott to give up school teaching and to become a full-time public speaker against discrimination. She has directed the exercise and lectured on its effects in many places throughout the world. She also has conducted the exercise with college students, as seen in the 2001 documentary The Angry Eye.

upset and cast aside, believing in their own inferiority. She then showed them how and why they had turned against each other. The next week, she reversed the experiment with the class. Shockingly, the children were as ready as any Nazi to be the superior race, but equally, when they were taught that the difference was arbitrary, they relaxed into the glorious feeling of being unified again.

Mindfulness simply cannot align with elitism or racism. It obviously goes against all mindful aspirations and labelling.

 ## LISTEN

Everyone Is Beautiful meditation

Sexism

> "The rebalancing of genders currently underway may be the greatest achievement of this century."

Lama Tsultrim Allione

Feeding Your Demons: Ancient Wisdom for Resolving Inner Conflict[26]

The arrival of the #MeToo movement, a social movement against sexual abuse and harassment where people publicise allegations of sex crimes, is overdue. I think it is very hard for men to understand how disempowered women have been for so long.

---

26   Lama Tsultrim Allione is an American author and teacher who has studied in Tibetan Buddhism's Karma Kagyu lineage. One of her many wonderful books is Feeding Your Demons, in which she quotes Carl Jung as saying, "One does not become enlightened by imagining figures of light but by making the darkness conscious." On the book's cover, American psychotherapist Mark Epstein is quoted as describing it as "a book that Carl Jung could only have dreamed of writing".

Sexism, like racism, comes from a part of society that thinks itself superior, mainly because of conditioning, but women themselves then cement these views by having ingrained attitudes about their own gender, just like the children in Jane Elliott's anti-racism experiment. For example, I vividly remember being quite upset if I *didn't* get wolf whistles as I passed building sites in the '60s! Of course, it was embarrassing to be targeted, but if they didn't whistle that meant I was unattractive; the end of a teenage girl's self-esteem. We still have so far to go, but change is happening.

You can't practise mindfulness and be sexist – and if you are, you're getting it wrong. I have met men with impressive meditative realisations who still spout sexist nonsense. It can be so hard to destroy the ignorance of our own conditioning. Women have a job to do on themselves too – rooting out their own conditioned sexist views of themselves, as well as correcting others.

I cannot deny that religious institutions are often very sexist. The Buddha was not a social reformist, but he was revolutionary in allowing women to become ordained and practise Buddhism seriously. He said that women were as able to become enlightened as any man. Today, the Dalai Lama suggests that women are more compassionate and therefore more capable of spiritual development than men.

There is no place for sexism in mindfulness practice – against men or women. The power struggles that parents who split up have over their children often leave fathers bereft and disempowered. Causing suffering to our children because of wanting revenge is not mindful, and often women are in a position where, in this arena, they hold the power. The pendulum needs to centre, rather than just swing in the opposite direction.

 **LISTEN**

Equality of the Sexes meditation

Gender and sexuality

I played the bit part of a blind eunuch in a drama college production of *The Visit* by Friedrich Dürrenmatt, yet I can honestly say that I cannot imagine or ever know what it's like to have your balls cut off. (And if you think I'm being trivial, I have had a series of eye-watering natal disasters followed by successes, all of which were excruciating in the vaginal department.) These days one hopes that involuntary castration is relegated to the past, but gender and sexuality is currently a hot topic for discussion. However you define yourself and your sexuality is no one's business – as long as you're trying not to cause suffering to others. Revealing your true identity may cause some initial problems, but you can be sensitive and caring rather than defensive and angry. When we step away from the 'norms' of society then that huge mass of 'normals' feel threatened, and this is where prejudices arise. Parents of children with gender confusion will find some of the issues they're faced with particularly challenging and will need to be supremely mindful as they support their offspring. We all need support in letting go of our prejudices because they have been within us for such a long time.

Regardless of what your kids identify as, just imagining them having sex at all is pretty testing, let alone who with. And our kids have the same problems with their parents! The thought that we might still be 'doing it' past 40 inflames their aversion to ageing. Old fogeys should be sitting in their rocking chairs watching game shows, not online shopping for sexy lingerie or vibrators that take the strain from our arthritic hands!

Really, gender issues are irrelevant unless anything unmindful – insensitive, selfish or oppressive – is taking place. Open up your hearts and let the love flow (I feel like a '60s flower-power song is about to emerge from me). No coercion, no impositions, no bullying: just love and everything will be all right. What's considered shocking now will be normal in 20 years anyway.

I had to get the pill by regularly bunking off school and going up to London, where an enlightened clinic prevented me from getting pregnant. When my local doctor found out he called me 'wicked'. So did my mum. It wasn't their fault. They were conditioned by their past and I was disobeying all the traditional societal rules. (Actually, I was being very responsible, but not in their eyes.) When my daughter became sexually active, we talked about what would be best for her, and went along to the doctor together. What her daughter (karma dependent) will do is a visualisation practice you might like to create for her now.

Personal ethics will guide us to be aware if our sexuality threatens to break our moral codes. As our physical bodies mature, we can be emotionally thrown at the loss of childhood, so it is a time when we need strong inner refuge, without judgement. Enlightened beings may manifest as male or female deities or a combination of both. This is just symbolic representation. In reality, they are the perfect balance of both male and female energies and are therefore genderless.

 LISTEN

Gender Acceptance meditation

Health

A holistic approach to health aligns with the interconnected philosophy behind mindfulness. This doesn't mean dumping your doctor but, instead, finding ways to treat the whole person. It's commonplace now to recognise that exercise and diet are essential to good health. I can't remember the last time spinach got me excited, but I'm working on it.

Exercises that recognise emotional links in the body and respect the spiritual nature of undressing our inner bodies are wonderful ways in which to practise mindfulness. T'ai chi, yoga and other methods for healing should no longer be called 'alternative' – they are just as important as the scientific approach to healing and medicine. They all complement each other, and we are fortunate to be getting to the point that they are no longer perceived to be hippy-dippy but normal.

The 'mind, body, spirit' movement recognises that our health is holistic. We enjoy wellbeing if all three aspects of what it means to be human share equal esteem. Conventional medicine (allopathy), that is evidence-based and treats illness alone, disregarding other aspects of a human being, is starting to lose its stranglehold on healing, but we shouldn't ignore its many benefits. Homeopathic and herbal medicine are starting to gain new respect.

What is spiritual medicine? Mindfulness. We may enjoy leanings towards other spiritual practices, but to keep us grounded, mindfulness is our foundation. It's our essential daily multivitamin supplement. If we ensure that we have mental wellbeing, then our physical wellbeing will be easier to maintain, whatever the diagnosis.

 **LISTEN**

Holistic Health meditation

Global conflict

The world's authoritarians – and anyone who tries to oppress others or create war for personal power and material reward (or because of personal beliefs) – are heavily swayed by their own destructive emotions. The wish to control others is the prime influence that leads to destructive emotions and unethical behaviour. Conflict between governments is at once simple and complex because, no matter how many different views prevail, it is difficult to find truth. Instead, compassion and tolerance have to be at the heart of every government. Nothing is achieved through outdated ideas of revenge and honour, as the only honour is a compassionate heart that wins over people through kindness and respect for all. Leadership and democratic government need the support of all the mindful ways discussed in this book in order to serve and manage our countries and continents. Managing the world will then follow in a harmonious and constructive way.

The following beautiful prayer can be adapted by changing 'Cambodia' into any country you wish, or indeed by changing it into 'the world.'

A Peaceful Heart: A Prayer

The suffering of Cambodia has been deep.
From this suffering comes Great Compassion.
Great Compassion makes a Peaceful Heart.
A Peaceful Heart makes a Peaceful Person.
A Peaceful Person makes a Peaceful Family.
A Peaceful Family makes a Peaceful Community.
A Peaceful Community makes a Peaceful Nation.
And a Peaceful Nation makes a Peaceful World.
May all beings live in Happiness and Peace.

Venerable Mahā Ghosānanda[27]

Reflections

- How do you feel about the concept of Tantra?

- Are you involved in a cause? Does it make you hate the enemies of the cause or have compassion for them?

- Are you conditioned by your religion or race to look down on others of different religions or races? Can you mindfully break the cycle of hate?

- Have you managed to dig out your unconscious prejudices?

The greatest heroes are those who fight their own egos; the greatest rebels are those who reject materialism and hedonism as the 'be all and end all' of life. These heroes and rebels rely not on violent struggle but gentle disarmament. If we have to fight, fight with wisdom, compassion

---

27   Venerable Mahā Ghosānanda was a highly revered Cambodian Buddhist monk who lived during the Khmer Rouge period and post-Communist transition period. His name means 'great joyful proclaimer.'

and a mindful attitude, arming the inner self to take the moral high ground in order to win the battle against ignorance.

Chapter 12

Spiritual Warrior Training

∘ ∘ ∘

"Enlightened 'heroes' or 'warriors' are highly altruistic beings who have the wisdom to realise that by dedicating themselves to the welfare of other sentient beings, the fulfilment of their own self-interest comes automatically as a by-product."

The Dalai Lama

Illuminating the Path to Enlightenment

Recognising what we understand by spirituality is a vital aspect of mindfulness practice and religion, and turns us into spiritual warriors who recognise that the universal enemy is *self*-ignorance, not others who don't believe in what we believe. As heroes, we have the spiritual courage to face our own inner enemies and are ethically driven to prevent and avoid causing the suffering of others. Being willing to take on our own ego, and recognise that the enemy is within, is the response of a truly mature individual. To believe that the faults lie in others is the attitude of a child.

Taking responsibility for our own actions is rarely a leadership requirement, even within democracies, so we must look beyond appearance, power and status to find the person within. A spiritual warrior is an inner being, motivated by profound ideals and altruistic intentions. The war on the ego is the most heroic battle of all because it is hidden, attracting no recognition or material reward. We become a spiritual rebel when we commit to focusing on our inner life, consigning worldly concerns to second place in our consideration of what is important.

The name given to highly altruistic beings in Buddhism is 'bodhisattva'[28] It's a small word that encompasses great meaning, but basically translates to 'enlightenment being', or 'saint'. These incredible beings have transformed their humanity into something greater – a way of being that has purified weaknesses so that only strengths are now present. They've got inner self six-packs.

When you train to be a bodhisattva, you take vows to stay as long as it takes to free all beings from *samsara* (the cycle of suffering). Here is a verse from one of the Dalai Lama's favourite prayers, and a prayer that many Buddhists recite:

As long as space remains
As long as sentient beings remain
Until then may I too remain
To dispel the miseries of the world.

Shantideva
A Guide to the Bodhisattva's Way of Life

The Dalai Lama's quotation at the start of this chapter also points to another benefit of being a spiritual warrior: the advantages to oneself. It is a delicious irony in that by helping others, we help ourselves. It may seem counterintuitive; however, having read this book, perhaps you can start to understand how this works, and what the magnificent rewards are. The biggest challenge is to take that very first step away from the ego and towards your inner self.

If you are still reading, then I think you might have done that already. In this final chapter, I revisit what you may have learned from this book,

---

28   Bodhisattva is the name given to one who has delayed their personal enlightenment and final free-dom from samsara – cyclic existence – in order to benefit others. Due to their spiritual realisations, they have qualities that go beyond human limitations and have the spontaneously arising wish (bodhicitta) to help free others from suffering.

so you can take away a clear idea of what you wish to incorporate into your own spiritual training – and how.

Find yourself a teacher

A good teacher is a valuable asset – someone who is qualified and you feel comfortable with. However, be careful not to become a disciple (unless you have absolute conviction and have tested them as if they were gold), no matter how other-worldly and exotic they may appear (and perhaps *especially* if they appear other-worldly and exotic). Having several teachers is always a healthy option to gain a range of experiences and perspectives.

Take care that you understand what you're getting into. There are some rather wacky additions to pure mindfulness practice that are fashionable and exciting to the senses. Remember, that's not what you want to do. Your aim is to pacify the senses. So go and have your hot, tantric, mindful sex and enjoy it, but don't kid yourself that you are now enlightened. Check up on the teacher and test what they know before you commit yourself. You could end up thrashing around with someone you wouldn't normally even notice, just because a teacher says you should open your mind and love the one you're with.

There will always be people who wish to be seen as experts about something, especially spiritual stuff, and they might be so charismatic that they fool you. Maybe they take on the appearance of being mystical, wear Eastern gear, float about reciting unintelligible mantras and look meaningfully out into space, but it doesn't mean they know what they're talking about. So please, dear reader, become mindful of bullshit (with compassion, obviously).

The importance of community

Find yourself a community of other mindful practitioners that you relate to, preferably recommended by some of your grounded friends. This may be a local class, or a group of friends you wish to meditate with using guided meditations (and then, with experience and confidence, you can take it in turns to guide each other). Buddhist groups are usually reliable and support all the psychology, but again, you need to be sure they're not cult-like (if they have only the one 'god-teacher', then beware). Remember to check your intuition when you're in a spiritual group.

Try out YouTube and the internet for more information and support on mindfulness, and use a meditation app. Basically, don't go it alone. (I list some recommended resources at the back of the book that were reliable at the time of writing.)

My story – bodhisattva ideals

I knew nothing about Buddhism as a child, being educated in the standard spiritual fare of Great British Christian Protestantism. Dad was an atheist, but Mum lived her life by Christian ideals, much like the rest of 1950s Britain. Although not encouraged by my father to go to church, she did resuscitate her strangled beliefs in her later life.

My link with the bodhisattva ideal came very early in my life when I was still a child. My parents' friends had a large glass cabinet of ornaments, and my eye caught the smiling golden buddha with long earlobes. Mum's friend kindly asked me if I'd like to rub his belly and make a wish. Her opening of the cabinet and lifting me to reach the statue was very exciting, and I solemnly rubbed the cool gilt belly and made my wish. I have no memory of the wish or if it came true, but I still remember that occasion. I had made a subconscious connection with that image, which represented safety and happiness.

Much later, I would recognise the statue as a smiling buddha, and then later still, through my Buddhist education, I realised that it was not a buddha but a bodhisattva. Buddha statues are lean and look inwards, symbolising their renunciation of the world. Bodhisattva statues smile outwards, looking at us, and may even be surrounded by children and have fat tummies that symbolise their wealth of virtue and enormous compassion. They are not going beyond; they are staying with us.

The use of symbolism in religion is universal: it helps us understand profound ideas that cannot otherwise be easily explained. In Tibetan Buddhism, the key to connecting to our subconscious minds is through the use of symbolic imagery – whether that is a golden statue or a multi-coloured, multi-limbed deity. Imagery can help us learn to understand and work with our multi-faceted ego: all its games and all its potential.

My other childhood memory that relates intellectually to my contact with the bodhisattva ideal was a bedtime experience. My parents' bedroom was adjacent to mine, and if I was still awake when they came to bed, I could hear them talking. Sometimes the tone was light and night-time quiet, but at other times I could hear them argue. Mum would always get very emotional and I hated to hear her cry, and Dad would be barking at her or, if sodden with alcohol, behaving stupidly – laughing in a childish way or provocatively goading her. I could rarely hear the words but got used to the tone. One night, they were really going at each other and, unusually, Mum was defending herself with some assertion. My heart was pumping wildly. I longed for the row to stop and started to think about how I could make my parents happy, especially Mum. I'm a very analytical person, so I reasoned my way through what needed to happen. If I was to be happy then I needed to make Mum happy, and in order for her to be happy, I had to make Dad happy. If I needed to make Dad happy then I had to make my sister and brother happy. I kept going through this process until I realised that before I could be happy, I had to make the whole world happy. I may have had a selfish motivation, but it took me through to a logical conclusion. Much later, when I learned about the bodhisattva ideal, I recalled this childhood memory and needed little persuasion to recognise its solid-gold truth.

Start with the end result

Using the techniques you have learned in the meditation exercises, create a vision of your future self. Give yourself a generous timescale of five to ten years, and visualise yourself with your burgeoning qualities and your fulfilling environment, perhaps symbolically represented. See the people that surround you, and your place within that image.

Now reflect on the inner weapons you need to arm yourself with if you are to create the cause for this future vision to become real. You may also find it helpful to draw the aspirational vision and stick it on your fridge for inspiration.

Personalising your practice

Mindfulness can be applied to anything in life, so it's important that you feel free to personalise your practice and apply it wherever and whenever. Nothing need be excluded; nothing. Here's a few ideas to get you going, starting with the basics and gradually building on these.

The basics

A meditation practice

Create a space for yourself and decide on when you will meditate so you can make meditation a healthy habit. Ensure you incorporate mindfulness meditation into your life for 20 minutes a day. Use the listed meditations to create a meditation menu for yourself. Include some practices that challenge you, to stretch your mind. Become aware of your comfort zone and try to push its boundaries.

Everyday mindfulness

Incorporate mindful practices into your daily life – for example:

- When you're out and about, try being mindful of your surroundings. Really experience them rather than walking along absent-mindedly, absorbed in internal chatter. Remember to turn your phone to silent – and unplug your headphones.

- Extend your meditation to 'off the cushion' mindfulness by observing your thoughts and emotions during your everyday life, and start to monitor and manage them. Utilise the Wheel of Destructive Emotions exercise occasionally to identify the emotions you're going to work on first (Chapter 6).

- Enter into modest self-analysis. Notice when you get irritated or jealous – or any other negative feelings. Analyse why you feel this way. Can you turn the finger around, away from others, and point it at yourself? You can't change most external events; all you can do is change how you manage them. Aim for the least collateral damage arising from your negativity.

- Consider everything you value about yourself. Really focus on your qualities, and also the opportunities that have come your way. You might even consider how some seemingly negative situations have led you to better circumstances, or how much you learned from them. Think about your potential. You can do this in an analytical meditation or on a long reflective walk (alone).

- Practise being alone. Enjoy the opportunity to be with yourself.

Intermediate practices

Ethical practice

Start to consider your own ethical behaviour, and try to change some ingrained habits that you can now recognise as being a bit iffy. Identify some of your ways of thinking that lead to unwholesome emotions, and how that connects with your speech and actions. Consider when you are most in danger of being unethical and think about what you can put in place to protect yourself (and others) when you're tempted to fall back into old habits. Chapter 8 has helpful messages and exercises that you can use to support your inner self.

Wellseeing

Chapter 10 provides some examples of psychological models that you could try putting into practice. Which ones do you think you can use? Identify at least one that you can incorporate into your everyday life. Start to appreciate that your practice is a spiritual one, and generate a sense of healthy self-esteem that you have entered a very noble way of being. Try to develop a philosophical way of thinking to give you resilience. This might be as simple as trying to 'go with the flow', or as profound as conducting an intellectual investigation into religion and philosophy to find what works for you.

Advanced practices

Compassion

Your empathy and compassion will increase as you become used to the type of mind training you're engaging in. Compassion is the factor that can lift every action of thought, word and body to another level of being human. As your practice evolves, your everyday life will lose its focus on helping yourself and shift to how you can help others – and this leads you to feel better about yourself.

Wisdom – the view of emptiness

You can also develop the view of emptiness (refer to Chapter 9) at this stage in your practice, which can support you when you over-identify with people and situations. It helps you live harmoniously with others through everyday challenges, and it helps lift you from self-obsessed, depressive mind states. It really helps you to let go of anger and hatred if you can dissolve the experience of grasping onto anything and anyone.

Supportive Buddhist concepts

Here, I share some specifically Buddhist teachings to support you in your practice; however, they do require you to be open to certain 'truths'. The concept of our continuum of consciousness challenges the ideas around having a permanent soul and also leads us to the consideration of karma and interdependence. See what you think…

The Three Marks of Existence

The Buddha described Three Marks of Existence (or Three Universal

Truths), as explained in chapters 4 and 6:

1. Everything is impermanent, and constantly changing

2. There is suffering and dissatisfaction in life

3. We don't have a solid 'I' – a 'soul'

Which of these resonates with you? Remember them like they're your daily cuppas, arriving at intervals to give you strength. If you don't 'get' them all, don't worry; just use what does work and put the rest in the mental fridge for later.

Cause and effect

The concept of cause and effect is the actual meaning of *karma*, which translates literally to 'action' and just means that everything we do has an effect. Consider whether you can use this as a support system for what you get dished up in life and what you dish out. It doesn't really work that well if you have a one-life view, although you can see karma in global issues such as climate change. We, humanity in general, have created the causes for our changing environment.

Be aware that the term 'karma' is often used flippantly or incorrectly.

Tantra

Even without entering into a spiritual discipline with a spiritual guide, you can still incorporate the view of Tantra into your life. It is a dynamic process that creates positive and uplifting ways of thinking. Assess whether it can help you in your life, and try some of the meditations referred to in Chapter 11.

Inner self and ego

Really ensure that you understand what these mean – head to Chapter 3 for the explanations. When referring to ego, I don't mean the healthy ego that we develop as part of growing up into well-adjusted human beings, but the self-grasping and self-cherishing ego that's bent on creating an inflated and incorrect view of itself. It's our inner monster.

The inner *self* is called various names, so you might find a label that you prefer. I call mine 'buddha nature', along with all the Buddhists of the world. 'Buddha' translates to 'enlightened', so it's a nice reminder that we are inherently good and working through all the layers of self-deception that the ego presents to us.

Conditioned existence

I mention this a lot (see Chapter 3) to underline how much we live according to the influences on us. It's a key concept in Buddhism, as it points to the freedom that is 'nirvana' – freedom from ignorance. All our misunderstandings of life spring from our conditioning, and it is important to unravel the many layers of conditioning that we have as individuals. All the topics discussed in this book enable us to reflect on and be mindful of how outer influences have shaped us. Doing so frees us and leads to authenticity of being.

Interdependence

Every person we meet and every situation that presents itself to us in our life is an opportunity for self-growth. When we understand this concept, we are ready to start to understand interdependence (explained more in Chapter 10). We may feel that we have difficult circumstances but, apart from doing what is practically useful, we can see that our minds – which we use to develop ourselves and deal with anything that comes our way – are totally dependent on how we relate to others. We are dependent on others for our survival, the conditions we live in and the kindness of others.

One of the more practical ways to experience this kind of interdependence is to – before you eat any meal – consider how many different kinds of people, jobs, places and so on have been involved in the process of enabling the meal to arrive on your table. The simplest meal, like a bowl of porridge, involves the work, effort and kindness of so many others.

Key qualities

Neuroscience has recognised that generating key qualities (such as gratitude and loving-kindness) benefits our wellbeing. This is now such a widely spread idea that we can access inspiration about cultivating them from TV, magazines, self-development books and wellbeing apps. With the deeper understanding of how to utilise mindfulness and its associated practices, we can expand these qualities from shallow accessories into lifestyle essentials.

Gratitude

Gratitude is the recognition that without others we have nothing. The food we eat, our health, the bed we lie on, the entertainment we enjoy⊠ we can trace *everything* in living experience to the kindness of others. You might think, "Well, they didn't do that out of kindness to me," but, actually, they did. The very fact someone grew your food, stitched up your wound, built your bed and recorded your favourite programme is a kindness. Work with your mindful awareness of interdependence and cause and effect (karma) to generate in yourself a humungous amount of appreciation for what you have.

This quality of gratitude also abounds when we understand that we have a precious human life. We don't have to look far to see the suffering, deprivation and lack of freedom in others to know exactly what we have and what we can do with our lives.

Loving-kindness

Wanting others to be happy is a wonderful quality. If we can extend this to everyone – even the despots and those filled with hatred and anger (in fact, especially those) – we will grow spiritually and, just like those big fat tummies of the bodhisattvas, feel a swelling in us that wishes to connect to all living beings, not just those we love. Loving-kindness takes on a universal quality that we can apply to everyone wounded in the battle of life. Loving-kindness is the paracetamol of the spirit.

Generosity

Giving stuff is very kind. Giving shelter to those in need (the refugee, the traveller, the nomad, the visitor) is kinder still. Opening up our homes and our countries to others is a gesture of friendship, trust and tolerance, as we learn to live with others who have different ways to ourselves. We become a source of refuge for others, just like the spiritual teachings are a source of inner refuge for ourselves.

Giving wisdom when requested is considered to be the greatest generosity, as we are actually giving people the key to spiritual growth and ultimate freedom. Unlike missionaries, who try to force others to believe in their particular brand of wisdom, we need to give wisdom unmotivated by attempting conversion or believing one's ideas to be better than others. Generosity is a willingness to give many things – friendship, a listening ear, time, compassion. Practising generosity with mindful awareness will bring us riches beyond mere possessions.

Resilience

When we have inner resilience, we have self-esteem engendered by self-knowledge and an appreciation for our potential. And when we have developed a world-view that is meaningful and sensible, then we have resilience. No matter what life throws at us, and no matter how low we fall, we can get up and never give up.

Does religion help?

Many people have rejected religion as part of the whole spiritual package and regard it as being quite harmful. It divides us, instead of uniting us. It leads to violence and war as we try to enforce views on others, because we are told that our views are right, and others have got it wrong. We want everyone to believe the same thing. Ouch! This leads to people being *religious* but *not spiritual*, hardened by misunderstood and reinterpreted ideals that were often never even propounded by the original religious founders.

Can we be religious without being spiritual? Is this possible? If our religion negates the spiritual qualities explained in this book then perhaps we are in danger, as religious practitioners, of wearing the coat without wearing the knickers – it's all for show with nothing underneath.

For secular people, modern-day mindfulness has sweetly managed to avoid religious association through its use of scientific evidence, and focusing attention on the workings of the brain. What an incredible tool – it's for everyone, religious or not! In this way, we can become united as we increase and expand our awareness outwards from our self to others.

Having suffered centuries of patriarchal religion, and wars fought about whose belief is right or not, it now seems that religion may have run its course for many questioning, intelligent and well-educated people – so much so that many people keep their religious beliefs to themselves. Religion has gone into the closet. Sexual, racial and cultural diversity has come out – washed, dried and aired on the washing line of popular opinion – but poor old religion is relegated to the charity bag. We don't mind the soft stuff on TV comedies to give us a warm glow of goodness on a Sunday evening, but anything that seriously considers something other than this one short life is practically taboo.

When we identify with one religion, we too often reject the others. Holding on to a set of beliefs can be more about joining a club than finding the inner self, or 'God within.' There are so many pitfalls in religious practice. If the depth of the founder's message is understood clearly, then religious practice can give life incredible meaning, but too often the cultural and historical add-ons have become old Post-it notes stuck with ancient glue that just don't suit the current décor of our lives. I'm not suggesting that religion is either an obstacle (or, indeed, essential) to a spiritual life, but rather that we have thrown the baby out with the bath water. In rejecting religion, are we in danger of losing life's meaning?

The common denominator in religions is morality. There is unanimous agreement that leading a good life leads to rewards. It's just unfortunate that *how* to lead a good life is clouded by rules and regulations that disguise the original intent of the founders, and can be more about control and even create conflict between religions. If we can take the essence of a religion and remain alert to the codes of behaviour that are no longer relevant and go against contemporary wisdom, then religions and their followers can co-exist in one great spiritual support system.

The place of Buddhist psychology

'Buddha' means 'enlightened' – awake. Buddhist psychology is not about bowing down to some golden bloke with a funny hairdo. It's about the qualities all of us can achieve if we are able to acknowledge spiritual progress as being more important than anything else. When we acknowledge this, we pay respect to that quality within us all – our enlightened nature. Understanding some of the language that comes from East to West is important, otherwise we think it's all mystical mantras and smoky incense.

Although mindfulness meditation existed before the Buddha, it is strongly associated with Buddhism. Teachers of contemporary mindfulness go to great lengths to reassure their students of the non-religious nature of mindfulness, which is absolutely right. But the psychology of Buddhism is an aspect of mindfulness that is blended into the practice, and so good mindfulness teachers – those who really know what they're talking about – will have knowledge of Buddhism. An MA in Mindfulness is a great certification, but it doesn't replace the knowledge and experience of a long-term practising Buddhist.

You can separate religion from mindfulness, but you can't separate out the psychology. And the psychology of mindfulness is the psychology of Buddhism, which is why this book is interwoven with references to Buddhism.

Other factors

When we know exactly what is meant by spiritual materialism and scientific materialism, we are able to be genuine spiritual rebels – basically, avoiding the pitfalls of materialism.

Spiritual materialism

Some people's ideas of spiritual development can be quirky and sometimes downright weird. People who say they are spiritual but are really just trying on different ego-masks give spirituality a dubious image. Spiritual influencers might look the part with their robes and beads, but that doesn't mean they're the real deal.

Tibetan Buddhist meditation master Chögyam Trungpa called this dubious attitude 'spiritual materialism' – when the ego grasps onto a way of being to strengthen its sense of self (as opposed to a genuine spiritual practice, which loosens the grip of the ego). Just think of the market that exists for accessories like malas (rosary beads), essential oils, incense and candles. Some people just like to *wear* spirituality!

It's a very tricky balance to have a genuine interest in the spiritual and not just use it to spice up our lives. It can be escapism, and that can be dangerous and self-deluding. It makes us feel special and other-worldly, but it is just another costume.

Scientific materialism and neuroscience

The neuroscientists deserve a big thank you – before they did their stuff and got everyone on board the meditation train, it was cold out there.

The breakthrough came when a French-Tibetan Buddhist monk, Matthieu Ricard,[29] participated in a 12-year brain study on meditation and compassion led by neuroscientist Richard Davidson (founder of the Center for Healthy Minds) from the University of Wisconsin-Madison. The results gave Matthieu the moniker 'the world's happiest man'. Other tests followed and meditation suddenly became acceptable – so hooray for that!

It was absolutely right that meditation advocates, who had status and

---

29   Matthieu Ricard is a French writer, photographer, translator and Buddhist monk. He grew up among the personalities and ideas of French intellectual circles, and received a PhD degree in molecular genetics from the Pasteur Institute in 1972. He then decided to forsake his scientific career and instead practise Tibetan Buddhism, living mainly in the Himalayas.

recognition, engaged with science to prove the benefits. We needed the doctors, neuroscientists and behaviourists to promote meditation for wellbeing. Meditation started to get the respect it deserved, instead of being some Eastern practice that we in the West patronised. But delving into the brain brought with it both beneficial and self-limiting side effects.

Everything became about the brain. People were persuaded through science that meditation (and mindfulness, in particular) held the answers to many mental and emotional problems. And there's absolutely nothing wrong with that – until we start identifying the mind with the brain and making everything about matter.

Science has followed the evolution route to identify the stages of development of the brain. There is continuing discussion about whether we carry vintage brain cells as well as more current IKEA-type brain cells within us, but scientists agree that our survival aspect is powerful and that we're genetically coded to seek rewards; that our brains are complex computers and that "whatever we experience mentally is a result of the different combinations of neurons."[30] In this way, we're reduced to nothing more than DNA and genetic disposition.

Neuroscience has added its explanation and, as reasonable and rational as it is, has taken away the magic of human experience and reduced it to the workings of a three-pound pink mass of pudding-like substance, hammering away like an eternal engine in our heads.

Scientific materialism declares that the physical world is the only thing that exists and that nothing supernatural exists. That unless we can see something and quantify it, then there is no evidence. People's experiences of supernatural phenomena are explained away as imbalances of chemicals in the brain, heightened imagination or some kind of mental sickness. That wasn't Shiva at the Ganges, you fool – that was drugs! (See Chapter 11 for my story on Shiva at the Ganges.)

---

30   A quote from Sane New World: Taming the Mind by Ruby Wax, which I highly recommend.

The modern-day practice of mindfulness has focused on 'brain-change', or 'neuroplasticity', a powerful method for regulating mental imbalance and intentionally increasing the good chemicals in our brains to promote wellbeing and happiness.

I'm not knocking this theory, but mindfulness without spirituality is just the bath without the lovely, bubbly, warm healing water within it, not forgetting the rubber ducks and soapy sponges. And, of course, the delightful, contented, glowing baby. Mindfulness that only focuses on the brain is just an empty bath that holds no water, and no spiritual meaning.

As human beings, we need meaning and purpose in our lives, as well as status, identity and positive relationships. We're intelligent, social animals with the potential for enormous achievements that benefit humanity. For meaning and purpose, we must look beyond the brain.

Spiritual focus

The unseen spiritual benefits of mindfulness are the ones that benefit us the most. Value them. They are not there to give us material security, but to give us true guidance on the road to genuine freedom.

Ultimate meaning and purpose

Practising secular mindfulness as an antidote to some of the BIG mental health issues we suffer is a wonderful thing. Lives improve. We can manage depression and anxiety and experience life more fully. Brilliant. But for what ultimate purpose? To enjoy more hedonistic pursuits? To be better at our jobs? To manage and enjoy better relationships? Well, what else is life for? You live, then you die. Even if you have the most marvellous, balanced, creative and productive life, your reward is death.

Practising spiritual mindfulness is our insurance and, unlike the money we spend on material insurance – from laptops to life insurance – as spiritual practitioners we can be mindful that we take the practice with us when we die. It imprints on our consciousness, ready to be the cause of a very nice effect in a future life. So spiritual mindfulness is quite selfish really. It's not for your loved ones; it's for you, because you're worth it.

The importance of death within life

It's well-reported that we in the West have a very unhealthy attitude to death. We generally pretend it's not going to happen to us, and then we shut away the old, the sick and the dying. Funerals themselves literally draw curtains around the process of cremation, and burying the dead is sanitised.

The difference between Eastern and Western funeral practices highlights our Western fear of death. I was both fascinated and horrified to witness the rituals at the burning ghats in Varanasi, India. Bodies were wrapped like pieces of meat, stretched out on wooden frames and then set alight. One of my friends recounted how her boyfriend, who tragically died far too soon in India, was carried to the funeral pyre. She insisted on being a bearer and had to deal with his arm flopping down off the stretcher and into her face. A tragi-comedy in action, but oh so real, and literally in your face, making death a part of life.

It's a great support to have belief when someone dies, but too often we aren't prepared. We then make up ideas that comfort us but have no basis in reality. If the restrictions during the pandemic of 2020 gave us anything in the West, it was an appreciation of life itself, and its value. Death can happen anytime, and it will be more peaceful if we prepare for it and don't fear it. Otherwise, our experience will be like a car crash.

Life after death

The sheer fact that humanity is still chewing over life after death in all its complexity means that we not only carry a sense of our own importance, but also genuinely feel that we're here for a purpose – that life does hold meaning.

The scientific materialist view is that we are just matter – thinking meat. We can have a positive or negative effect in this life, but that is all there is. They say that there is no evidence for an afterlife, so therefore it doesn't exist.

Neuroscientists are divided and have their own ideas about the spiritual aspect of ourselves. Possibly intrigued by the interest and focus on science and the emotions, they are looking for that evidence.

"Our souls are contained within structures called microtubules which live within our brain cells. In a near-death experience, the microtubules lose their quantum state, but the information within them is not destroyed. Or, in layman's terms, the soul does not die but returns to the universe."

Dr Stuart Hameroff

'Is There Life After Death?' (an episode of the documentary series Through the Wormhole)[31]

In his book *After*, Dr Bruce Greyson, the world-leading expert on near-death experiences (when someone dies but is resuscitated, explored more in Chapter 4), proposes that the evidence from his research into this phenomenon shows that we are more than our physical bodies. He believes that this knowledge can impact how we live our lives. If we are open to the concept of near-death experiences, then we might ask, "After we die, do we stay in that warm glow forever, or is it just another temporary place of existence – a kind of reflective rest room before we move on again?"

The Buddhist view is that our consciousness is indestructible energy dependent on karmic imprints, and will move on, like a river, towards its next incarnation. We are but a product of what we think and must take responsibility for what happens to us because it is what we have created.

Authenticity and integrity

Throughout the book, I suggest ways in which you can check that your spiritual practice doesn't become just another fashion accessory; an addition to your ego-mask that helps you fit into a society that gets off on wellbeing.

---

31   Dr Stuart Hameroff and Sir Roger Penrose's Quantum Theory of Consciousness was explained by Dr Hameroff on the Science Channel's Through the Wormhole documentary series in an episode titled 'Is There Life After Death?'.

Authenticity and integrity are all about intention, and checking that you're doing things for the right reasons. They are key to your development, so it's always worth looking to see if the crafty ego is getting its way and drowning out the quiet voice of your inner self.

Reflection

Never Give Up

No matter what is going on
Never give up
Develop the heart
Too much energy in your country
Is spent developing the mind
Instead of the heart
Be compassionate
Not just to your friends
But to everyone
Be compassionate
Work for peace
In your heart and in the world
Work for peace
And I say again
Never give up
No matter what is going on around you
Never give up.

The Dalai Lama

Authentic mindfulness

- ○ Develop good habits and ditch the bad ones.
- ○ Whenever you get shouty and dogmatic, slow down, quieten down and listen to your inner voice. Recognise that your inner self is in danger of being smothered.
- ○ Remember the advice about being asked three times before you talk about your practice. And try not to proselytise.

Spiritual integrity

- ○ Try to get on with others and see their point of view.
- ○ Be guided by your inner self.
- ○ Listening is as important as speaking.
- ○ A genuine sense of humility will be your most important ally.
- ○ Be grateful for everything life sends you, and learn from it.

All the qualities in this book are inner weapons of mass ignorance destruction – they cut through ignorance and effectively destroy everything about us that is unwholesome. A physical blade or gun will never destroy suffering, only prolong it. Be gentle with yourself and think slowly, slowly. Spiritual warriors do not die on the battlefield of life; they are reborn, not through buying something new or indulging in another distraction or rejecting a way of life that feels stale, but because every day is a rebirth of a spiritual new you. If you have any pride at all, may it be a gentle, aware and spiritual pride. And may it not be as covert and self-conscious as it might have been when you started this book.

Afterword

○ ○ ○

A spiritual *warrior* is a bearer of wisdom and compassion, seeing through the ego-games and worldly ideals that exist in *samsara* (the cycle of suffering). They have so many eyes that they can look to all four corners of the world and cry with compassion at all they witness, and they have so many arms that there is room for every being to be held within them. The path of a spiritual warrior requires courage and conviction. But to walk any other path would be like circling a roundabout, taking roads signposted to happiness and finding only dead ends.

But first we need to *rebel* against what society offers us. Joining the spiritual rebellion may well be the greatest step you take in this lifetime. Its most noble attributes are that there is no uniform, no colour and no coded hand gestures you need to share with others. You do it not to belong to a club or tribe but because you have recognised the casual futility of so many worldly pursuits, and because you wish to live an authentic and meaningful life. You are a great being in this challenging world.

That's it, folks.

I hope that you now feel equipped with the tools and techniques you need to 'see well' in every aspect of life. You may have many questions about specific events or situations that are not covered in this book, but actually it is all quite simple. Be mindful (with attitude) and trust in your own inner guidance that is found in the spiritual tradition of your choice. Let being a spiritual rebel become the new rock and roll way of being for us all. May the power of your wisdom and compassion flourish like the bougainvillea on a perfectly white Greek street, and may you shine like a crazy diamond in this world and after.

More from the author

o o o

www.wellseeingconsultancy.co.uk – My professional consultancy website for training courses and events that I refer to throughout the book. See in particular The Leadership Programme.

www.ondywillson.com – My personal website offering teaching and training courses and retreats that cover every aspect of this book. This website is kindly sponsored by The Foundation for Contemplative Studies.

Apps

Insight Timer – Meditations, talks, courses and music to relieve anxiety and stress and promote mental and emotional health (free, with additional paid material). You can follow *Ondy Willson* on this app and listen to all the meditations referred to in this book.

Also by

Published work (as Andrea Willson):

Heinemann Educational Publishers

1991: *Moral Issues in Six Religions*, author of the Buddhism section

1997: *Spirituality in Focus*, author of the Buddhism section

1999: *Buddhist Temples*

1999: *What's at Issue?* (Series: 'Families')

Wellseeing Books

2009: *Ten Thousand Days of Summer: The story of the boy who would be Buddha*

This is her first book published under the diminutive form of her name.

Appendix

○ ○ ○

List of Guided Audio Meditations

Audio versions are available on the app INSIGHT TIMER. See also www.ondywillson.com for links to these and other audio meditations, as well as transcribed versions of the meditations listed in this book if you are unable to listen to the recordings.

You can also find my meditations SoundCloud and YouTube. I'll try not to be possessive if you wander off under someone else's influence as you explore the available meditations!

Chapter 2. How to Meditate

- How to Meditate: Beginner's Instruction (4 minutes)
- Full Body Scan/Mindfulness of the Body (10 minutes)
- Mindful Breathing: Ten Minutes of Clarity (10 minutes)

Chapter 3. Being Human

- My Precious Human Life (11 minutes)

Chapter 4. It's All in the Mind

- The Nature of the Mind (9 minutes)
- Impermanence and Death (13 minutes)

- Mindfulness of Feelings (24 minutes)
- Mindfulness of Phenomena (21 minutes)

Chapter 6. Managing Thoughts and Emotions

- Emotional Transformation (13 minutes)
- Thought Clouds (6 minutes)
- Counting (6 minutes)
- Thoughts as Visitors (5 minutes)
- "What If…" (11 minutes)

Chapter 7. Reasons to Be Good

- Finding Inner Refuge (21 minutes)

Chapter 8. How to Be Good

- The Four Immeasurables (9 minutes)
- Equanimity on Friends, Strangers and Enemies (21 minutes)
- Self-love and Self-compassion (15 minutes)

Chapter 10. How to Be Wellseeing

- Cleansing and Creating a Safe Space (18 minutes)
- Giving and Taking (20 minutes)
- Emptiness (15 minutes)
- Emptiness of the Self (15 minutes)

Chapter 11. The Spiritual Warrior

- Creating Shangri-La (5 minutes)
- Creating a Mindful Society (5 minutes)
- Mindful Lifestyle Walking (5 minutes)
- Everyone Is Beautiful (5 minutes)
- Equality of the Sexes (5 minutes)
- Gender Acceptance (5 minutes)
- Holistic Health (5 minutes)

References

○ ○ ○

Preface

His Holiness the Dalai Lama. *Ethics for the New Millenium*, 1999.

Part One – Talking the Walk

Chapter 2. How to Meditate

Shunryu Suzuki. *Zen Mind, Beginner's Mind*, 1970.
Joseph Campbell. *Reflections on the Art of Living: A Joseph Campbell Companion*, Diane K. Osbon (ed.), 1995.
The Buddha. *Samyutta Nikaya*.

Chapter 3. Being Human

Joseph Campbell (with Bill Moyers). *The Power of Myth*, 1988.
The Buddha. *Dhammapada*.
Margaret Mead. *Coming of Age in Samoa*, 1928.

Chapter 4. It's All in the Mind

Mahatma Gandhi. *An Autobiography: The Story of My Experiments with Truth*, 1927.
Padmasambhava. *The Tibetan Book of the Dead*.
Antoine de Saint-Exupéry. *The Little Prince*, 1943.
Charles D. Leviton and Patti Leviton. What is Guided Imagery? The Cutting-Edge Process in Mind/Body Medical Procedures. *Annals of the American Psychotherapy Association*, 2004; Vol. 7(2).
Pim van Lommel. *Consciousness Beyond Life: The Science of the*

Near-Death Experience, 2007.

Jack Kornfield. *After the Ecstasy, the Laundry: How the Heart Grows Wise on the Spiritual Path*, 2000.

Part Two – Walking the Talk

Chapter 5. Understanding Thoughts and Emotions

Rosemary Wells. *Noisy Nora*, 1973.

Jean Paul Sartre. *No Exit*, 1945.

Elisabeth Kübler-Ross. *On Death and Dying*, 1969.

Fyodor Dostoevsky. *Notes from Underground*, 1864.

Chapter 6. Managing Thoughts and Emotions

Lama Thubten Yeshe. *Mahamudra: How to Discover Our True Nature*, Robina Courtin (ed.), 2018.

Cheryl Strayed. *Wild*, 2012.

Peter Salovey and John D. Mayer. Emotional Intelligence. *Imagination, Cognition and Personality*. 1990; Vol. 9(3): 185–211.

Daniel Goleman. *Emotional Intelligence*, 1995.

Martin Luther King, Jr. *Stride Toward Freedom*, 1958.

Yongzin Ling Rinpoche. 'In Search of a Meaningful Life' in *Becoming Buddha*, Renuka Singh (ed.), 2012.

Chapter 7. Reasons to Be Good

His Holiness the Dalai Lama and Franz Alt. *An Appeal to the World: The Way to Peace in a Time of Division*, 2017.

Mark Williams and Danny Penman. *Mindfulness: A Practical Guide to Finding Peace in a Frantic World*, 2011.

B. Alan Wallace. *Genuine Happiness: Meditation as the Path to Fulfillment*, 2005.

BBC Four. *Brotherhood: The Inner Life of Monks*, 2021 (documentary).

Katherine Weare and The Mindfulness in Schools Project. *Evidence for the Impact of Mindfulness on Children and Young People*, 2012.

Gandhi, 1982 (film).

The Guardian. *My Brother's Keeper*, 2021 (short film/documentary).

Mohamedou Ould Slahi. *Guantánamo Diary*, 2015.

The Buddha. *Mahāparinibbāna Sutta*.

Chapter 8. How to Be Good

William Wordsworth. 'The World Is Too Much with Us' in *Poems, in Two Volumes*, 1807.

Jonathan Sacks. 'Morals and Markets' in *Applied Ethics: Critical Concepts in Philosophy*, *Volume V: Business and Economics*, Ruth Chadwick and Doris Schroeder (eds.), 2002.

Owen Cole (ed.). *Moral Issues in Six Religions*, 1991.

Mental Health Foundation. *Kindness Matters Guide*. https://www.mentalhealth.org.uk/campaigns/kindness/kindness-matters-guide.

Dave Kerpen. *The Art of People: The 11 Simple People Skills That Will Get You Everything You Want*, 2016.

Howard Gardner, www.thegoodproject.org.

Noriyuki Ueda. 'The (Justifiably) Angry Marxist: An Interview with the Dalai Lama', *Tricycle*. https://tricycle.org/trikedaily/justifiably-angry-marxist-interview-dalai-lama/.

Chapter 9. Wellseeing through Mindful Eyes

John Milton. *Paradise Lost*, 1667 (1674).

INSEAD, https://www.insead.edu/.

Musa Okwonga. *One of Them: An Eton College Memoir*, 2021.

Laurie Lee. *Cider with Rosie*, 1959.

Chapter 10. How to Be Wellseeing

Carl Jung. *Psychology and Alchemy*, 1944.

Radmila Moacanin. *The Essence of Jung's Psychology and Tibetan Buddhism: Western and Eastern Paths to the Heart*, 2003.

Martin Seligman. *Learned Optimism: How to Change Your Mind and*

Your Life, 1990.

Eric Berne. *Games People Play: The Psychology of Human Relationships*, 1964.

Virginia Satir. *Making Contact*, 1976.

Virginia Satir. *The New Peoplemaking*, 1988.

Chapter 11. The Spiritual Warrior

Anam Thubten. *No Self, No Problem: Awakening to Our True Nature*, 2009.

Lama Thubten Yeshe. *The Bliss of Inner Fire: Heart Practice of the Six Yogas of Naropa*, 2003.

Lama Thubten Yeshe. *An Introduction to Tantra: The Transformation of Desire*, 1987.

The Eye of the Storm, 1970 (documentary).

Frontline (documentary series). 'A Class Divided', 1985.

The Angry Eye, 2001 (documentary).

Lama Tsultrim Allione. *Feeding Your Demons: Ancient Wisdom for Resolving Inner Conflict*, 2008.

Venerable Maha Ghosananda. 'A Peaceful Heart: A Prayer' in *Step by Step*, 1992.

Chapter 12. Spiritual Warrior Training

His Holiness the Dalai Lama. *Illuminating the Path to Enlightenment*, 2002.

Shantideva. *A Guide to the Bodhisattva's Way of Life*.

Daniel Goleman and Richard J. Davidson. *Altered Traits: Science Reveals How Meditation Changes Your Mind, Brain, and Body*, 2017.

Ruby Wax. *Sane New World: Taming the Mind*, 2013.

Through the Wormhole (documentary series). 'Is There Life After Death?', 2011.

Bruce Greyson. *After: A Doctor Explores What Near Death Experiences Reveal about Life and Beyond*, 2021.

Attributed to the Dalai Lama, *Never Give Up*.

Recommended Reading and Useful Resources

o o o

These books and resources inspired me in my research and were valuable references during the writing of this book, so this selection is very much from *my* limited knowledge and experience. There is so much more out there, but I can recommend these as worthy and authentic resources. They range from mindfulness and Buddhism to psychology and self-help, so will satisfy a range of interests.

Books

Mindfulness

B.H. Guneratana. *Mindfulness in Plain English*, 2002.

B.H. Guneratana. *The Four Foundations of Mindfulness in Plain English*, 2012.

Mark Williams and Danny Penman. *Mindfulness: A Practical Guide to Finding Peace in a Frantic World*, 2011.

Ruby Wax. *Sane New World: Taming the Mind*, 2013.

Joey Weber. *Why Mindfulness Is Not Enough: Unlocking Compassion with Equanimity*, 2020.

Buddhism

Ian Baker. *The Heart of the World: A Journey to Tibet's Lost Paradise*, 2004.

Jack Kornfield. *After the Ecstasy, the Laundry: How the Heart Grows Wise on the Spiritual Path*, 2000.

Kathleen McDonald. *How to Meditate: A Practical Guide*, 1984.

Radmila Moacanin. *The Essence of Jung's Psychology and Tibetan Buddhism: Western and Eastern Paths to the Heart*, 2003.

Yangsi Rinpoche. *Practising the Path: A Commentary on the Lamrim Chenmo*, 2003.

Karin Valham. *Extended Lam-Rim Outlines: Beginner's Meditation Guide*, 1971.

B. Alan Wallace. *Genuine Happiness: Meditation as the Path to Fulfillment*, 2005.

B. Alan Wallace. *The Attention Revolution: Unlocking the Power of the Focused Mind*, 2006.

Lama Thubten Yeshe. *Introduction to Tantra: The Transformation of Desire*, 1987.

Ethics

Ruth Chadwick and Doris Schroeder (eds.). *Applied Ethics: Critical Concepts in Philosophy, Volume V: Business and Economics*, 2002.

His Holiness the Dalai Lama. *Beyond Religion: Ethics for a Whole World*, 2012.

The mind

Hannah Arendt. *The Life of the Mind*, 1977.

Daniel Goleman and Richard J. Davidson. *Altered Traits: Science Reveals How Meditation Changes Your Mind, Brain and Body*, 2017.

Roger Penrose. *Shadows of the Mind: A Search for the Missing Science of Consciousness*, 1994.

Jeffrey M. Schwartz and Sharon Begley. *The Mind and the Brain: Neuroplasticity and the Power of Mental Force*, 2002.

Popular psychology/self-help

Madelyn Burley-Allen. *Listening: The Forgotten Skill – A Self-Teaching Guide*, 1982.

Viktor E. Frankl. *Man's Search for Meaning: The Classic Tribute to Hope from the Holocaust*, 1946.

Howard Gardner. *Changing Minds: The Art and Science of Changing Our Own and Other People's Minds*, 2004.

Daniel Goleman and His Holiness the Dalai Lama. *Destructive Emotions: How Can We Overcome Them?*, 2003.

Martin Seligman. *Learned Optimism: How to Change Your Mind and Your Life*, 1990.

Symbolism

Joseph Campbell (with Bill Moyers). *The Power of Myth*, 1988.

Life after death

Bruce Greyson. *After: A Doctor Explores What Near Death Experiences Reveal about Life and Beyond*, 2021.

Raymond A. Moody. *Life after Life*, 1975.

Ian Stevenson. *Twenty Cases Suggestive of Reincarnation*, 1966.

Ian Stevenson. *Where Reincarnation and Biology Intersect*, 1997.

Websites

Headspace – Meditations for everyday life to enhance and support mental and emotional health (free trial followed by paid subscription).

www.charterforcompassion.org – Website promoting compassionate action in every aspect of life.

www.fpmt.org – Lama Zopa Rinpoche's website for the Foundation for the Preservation of the Mahayana Tradition.

www.lamayeshe.com – The website for the teachings of Lama Yeshe and Lama Zopa Rinpoche.

www.tushita.info – The website for the Tushita Meditation Centre in Dharamsala.

Acknowledgements

○ ○ ○

I would like to thank my Russian students, who asked me to write this book and who gave me confidence in my maverick teaching style with their typical enthusiasm and good humour. I would especially like to thank Michael Lobsang Tenpa, who plans to translate this book into Russian. Ven. Thubten Tenzin further encouraged me by promising he would 'eat up' the book when it is published. I hope it doesn't cause him indigestion.

I have many good friends who have supported and encouraged my work, and would like to thank them all for their positive reinforcement, mentioning in particular Helen Lawler, Brenda Fishwick and Caroline Winsor. Teresa Brady kindly did an early edit for me and ensured I gave full respect to science. Venerable Robina Courtin put me straight on certain points in Chapter 2 ('How to Meditate') and Nick Ribush and Venerable Sangye Khadro (Kathleen McDonald) gave me guidance with some references pertaining to Lama Yeshe.

My children have been a constant source of encouragement and support: Joey Weber, who has preceded me in writing and publishing a book on mindfulness (Why Mindfulness is not Enough: Unlocking Compassion with Equanimity), and Liza Weber, who is an exacting editor and writer herself. If you can please her then you know you've got something right!

My editors Kerry Laundon and Rachael Chilvers put me through the wringer and squeezed out the very best of my writing with their intensely focused editing. The book would have wandered all over the place without them. Also Megan Hindley for the stunning illustrations and Mie Hansson for her Book Design. I am so grateful to find such women to work with me who clearly love their work and take so much pride in their trade.

I have had some wonderful Tibetan Buddhist Lamas teaching me in my life, but special mention goes to those who have regularly guided me to this point in my understanding and practice of Buddhism and mindfulness. They have been supremely kind in their support of a stubborn and hard to pin down student. Lama Yeshe – my spiritual father – put the seed of this book into my heart and loved me so completely that the thought of him still brings tears to my eyes. Lama Zopa has guided Yeshe Buddhist Group through its many incarnations over the years, and has helped to steer my Buddhist journey since Lama Yeshe passed away. Thanks to Geshe Tashi Tsering, my precious teacher who became a friend and guide for my family, and Professor B. Alan Wallace, who was my first teacher of the four applications of mindfulness and guided me on some transcendental experiences, instilling in me that the goal is achievable.

I would like to thank the many students who have come my way, especially those of Yeshe Buddhist Group, who gave me all the endless opportunities to teach and therefore learn.

And, finally, for providing me with a legacy that enabled me to fund the time to write and publish the book without financial pressure, I would like to thank my mum.

Milton Keynes UK
Ingram Content Group UK Ltd.
UKHW020632051223
433788UK00010B/135